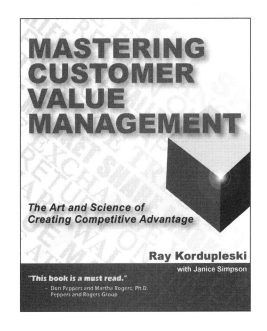

RAY KORDUPLESKI
Customer Value Management, Inc.
(US) 1 973-366-5206
www.cvminc.com
E-mail: ray@cvminc.com

PINN·FLEX

Pinnaflex Educational Resources, Inc.
www.pinnaflex.com

Development and Copyediting: Jody Robinson, Accentuate! LLC, Covington, KY
Cover and Interior Design/Graphics: Michael McCall, Cincinnati, OH

This book was printed and bound by Malloy Lithographing, Inc., Ann Arbor, MI.

ISBN: 1-893673-07-3

about the authors

Ray Kordupleski is president of CVM, Inc. and has 17 years experience in helping companies understand and implement customer value management programs. He was one of the pioneers in determining the value of CVM and how it can dramatically improve a company's performance.

Over the years, Ray's insights, unique consulting style and hands-on approach have helped hundreds of companies around the world and in many industries boost sustainable competitive advantages and increase performance and profitability.

Prior to forming CVM, Inc. in 1996 Ray had over twenty-nine years experience in the telecommunications industry, including customer-related positions with Illinois Bell, New Jersey Bell, Bell Atlantic, and AT&T. At AT&T he was the customer satisfaction director for the corporation, where the use of customer value management had its genesis in the early 80s and resulted in remarkable results prior to the breakup of AT&T.

Ray's work in quality, customer satisfaction and customer value management is well recognized. He has consulted globally with firms in Australia, Brazil, Canada, Chile, England, Finland, France, Hong Kong, India, Mexico, New Zealand, Norway, Sweden and the United States. His consulting, speaking and seminar activities have spanned a variety of industries: energy, telecommunications, financial services, entertainment, insurance, pharmaceuticals, high tech manufacturing, chemical, and consumer goods.

This wide range of activities and experiences has resulted in Ray being considered one of the true leaders in the CVM movement and someone eminently qualified to help your company.

Ray is the author of *Mastering Customer Value Management: The Art and Science of Creating Competitive Advantage* and co-author of *The CVA 2000 Collection*.

Ray has published articles in major journals, including "Why Improving Quality Doesn't Improve Quality" *California Management Review*, "Building and Deploying Profitable Growth Strategies Based on the Waterfall of Customer Value Added" *European Management Journal*, and "Marketing and Total Quality Management" Oxford University Press.

As a member of the American Marketing Association, Ray was the chairperson for its Second and Tenth Congresses on Customer Satisfaction and has regularly addressed its annual conferences. He is a member of the Editorial Review Board of the Journal of Service Research, sponsored by the Robert H. Smith School of Business, University of Maryland.

Janice Simpson is an independent consultant and writer who specializes in organizational effectiveness and using the process of communication to drive change. She spent ten years with Nortel Networks, where she helped shape strategic thinking in the areas of business ethics, social and environmental responsibility, employee engagement, and new models of leadership for a knowledge economy. She was part of the Nortel team that produced ground-breaking work on the statistical linkages among employee satisfaction, customer loyalty and shareholder value.

Prior to joining Nortel, Janice had a global consulting practice focused on human resource development, leadership development, community consultation and change processes, and cross-cultural communication. She has worked in Africa, Asia, Europe and North America with large and small companies, educational and research institutions, governments, and not-for-profit organizations.

Janice holds a Ph.D. in English Literature from the University of Toronto and has taught at that institution and at the University of Western Ontario. She is co-author of *Leadership for Change in the Education of Health Professionals* and author of numerous reports, studies, presentations and articles on a broad range of topics.

what readers are saying

CVM methodology, based on my experience, has proven to be a very effective tool in helping companies build up sustainable competitive advantage in the market. Ray Kordupleski's expertise and assistance is a guarantee of success in implementing it.

    – Sandro Cimatti, Sales Director, Schering-Plough Brazil

Mastering Customer Value Management provides excellent step-by-step advice with practical tools on how to successfully implement customer value management. Many of our European clients, operating in an increasingly competitive and customer-focused market, have seen massive improvements in their businesses through the utilisation of CVM.

    – Colin Bates, President of Customer Champions, UK

Successful business strategy requires more than creating competitive advantages. They must be sustainable. With great clarity, Ray Kordupleski illustrates that managing customer value is the key to achieving sustainable competitive advantage, the ultimate prize every firm seeks.

This book is a "must read" for practitioners and academics alike. For the practitioner, the book offers a detailed ten-step implementation plan, including case studies. For the academic, it serves as an excellent supplementary marketing strategy text that helps explain how to operationalize the key concepts underlying customer value management.

    – P.M. Rao, Professor of Marketing and Chair, Department of Marketing, College of Management, Long Island University

Well, it's finally happened! Some of our field's best-kept secrets are now available to anyone who is wise (or lucky) enough to buy this book. Having followed and applied Ray Kordupleski's work for more than a decade in small businesses and global enterprises alike, I can personally attest to the power of the techniques that Ray shares in *Mastering Customer Value Management*.

– Steve Jacobs, Senior Partner, Continuous Learning Group (CLG)

Ray's framework creates a discipline and alignment around the customer's view of the world—it connects your people to customer needs and serves as a vehicle for communicating strategic and operational priorities. The book is rich with examples of firms who implemented the framework and improved financial value by first focusing on customer value.

– Joe Urbany, Professor of Marketing and Associate Dean, Mendoza College of Business, University of Notre Dame

---

Ray Kordupleski has demonstrated conclusively how important customer data is when it comes to increasing customer value and improving the customer experience.

– Don Peppers and Martha Rogers, Ph.D., Peppers and Rogers Group

---

Ray's guidance to get to know our customers, to ask about and listen to their needs, to meet their needs in a profitable way, and to include our employees in the process enabled us to lead the company into a position of sustainable profitable performance.

With Ray's methodology, we gathered the wisdom of our loyal employees, thoughtfully sifted through the customer base and immediately applied what we had learned. The results were immediate and measurable. The success continues today.

– Cyndi Heller, J. Heller and Sons Hardware

To Donna, who always makes me feel I am worthy of her love;
and to Lauren and Ryan, who are worth everything to us.

acknowledgements

To my writer, Dr. Janice Simpson, for her unwavering dedication as well as her hard and brilliant work. It is clear to me that, without Jan, this book would not have the quality and clarity it does. In fact, it might not exist at all!

Jan is expert in crafting written communication that helps drive change and a professional in organizational effectiveness. She has an uncanny ability to present a person's ideas with exact content, context and passion. Over the course of a year, involving endless discussions with me and interviews of colleagues from around the world, she captured our voices, personalities and messages flawlessly. She took my 17 years of experience and expressed them in writing exactly as I wanted. The result is, I believe, a friendly, easy-to-read, practical book that will help you lead change in your organization.

To my publisher, Jim Sitlington, for his patience, perseverance, and gentle persuasion. Jim recognized the value of my work, the importance of writing this book and never lost faith. His guidance and support kept my desire burning.

Jim's knowledge of the publishing world and what it takes to actually publish a book were invaluable. Without this the book might never have reached the printing press, let alone the readers' hands.

To the senior business leaders who first recognized the true business value of customer value management and spurred my early work. A number of corporate officers at AT&T were instrumental in my developing a passion for customer value. Without their belief in me and the customer value tools and techniques I was championing, it's doubtful I would have continued the quest, proved the concepts, and developed the practical tools.

Robert Allen, Ken Bertaccini, Frank Blount, Dan Carroll, Bob Kavner, Pete Milano, John Mitcham, N. Pete Rhienhart, Jr., Jerre Stead, Phil Scanlon, Jim Walker, Paul Wondrasch

To the experts in marketing, management, customer research and statistics who unselfishly shared their knowledge with me, so we could develop an accurate and complete picture of how these areas meshed together, and helped hone the customer value tools.

Bill Adams, Colin Bates, Rich DeNicola, Paul Dernier, William Feuss, Dr. Nick Fisher, Dr. Bradley Gale, Dr. Khalid Hafiz, Robert Hughes, Philippe Jakimowicz, Jane Maloney, John McKean, John Nemish, Jim Nixon, Patricia O'Brien, Davis Steward, West Vogel, Dr. Frenck Waage

To the academics whose interest in and support of my work gave me confidence in its credibility and importance as a significant contribution to the sciences of marketing and management.

Dr. Jukka Laitamaki (Fordham University), Dr. P.M. Rao (Long Island University), Dr. Roland Rust (University of Maryland), Dr. Joe Urbany (Notre Dame University)

To those who willingly contributed their stories, anecdotes and insights that add a definite touch of reality to the book.

John Acherman (We Energies), Marcelo Chanis (CVM Latin America), Rich DeNicola (Customer Value Analysis), Peter Donovan (eCustomerValue), Dr. Nick Fisher (Valuemetrics), Rolando Pinto Flor (Multibrás Brazil), Rodger Gallagher (CVM New Zealand), Chris Green (Vodafone New Zealand), Scott and Cyndi Heller, Shawn Henry (Vodafone New Zealand), Deborah Hill (Unconventional Wisdom), Adrian Horwood (Celestica, Inc.), Shawne Howell, Steve Jones (Suncorp Australia), Graham Maher (Vodafone New Zealand), Susan Moore (Market Insight), Wally Nugent (Mead Corporation), Dr. John Pelligrino (Mead Corporation), Luis Fernando Reyes (Multibrás Brazil), Timothy Samler (eCustomerValue), David Shieff (David Shieff & Assoc. Ltd), Dr. Janice Simpson, Davis Steward (Customer Opinion Research), Ilmar Taimre (Suncorp Australia), Adrienne Taylor (Roche Diagnostic), Paul Wondrasch (AT&T)

To those who helped edit the technical content of the book for accuracy.

Dr. Nick Fisher, Bill Fuess, Dr. Gerd Haberskern, Ilmar Taimre

To Jody Robinson of Accentuate!, for her structural guidance and copyediting skills; and to Michael McCall, for his graphic skills *par excellence* in designing the cover and interior of the book. Both performed flawlessly and have been a pleasure to work with.

Finally, to my family, Donna, Lauren and Ryan, for their moral support and understanding.

Ray Kordupleski
February 2003

table of contents

Losing Sleep Over Customer Data

introduction

The purpose of my work is to make business leaders lose sleep over customer data – and start using it to create competitive advantage the next morning. Most of you who have opened this book know how it feels to wake up in the middle of the night worried about your company's stock price or revenue forecasts or escalating costs. I'll bet you've also stayed awake late feeling the adrenaline rush from really great financial results. How often have you woken up thinking about the results of the most recent customer survey?

If the answer is "not often" or "never," I hope this book – with its stories of successful companies around the world that have put customer value at the heart of their business – will change that. If the answer is "all the time," this book will give you proven tools and techniques to deepen your understanding of what customers value and help you deliver greater value than your competitors. **Delivering superior customer value will lead to competitive advantage, better business results and shareholder value.**

Customer Value Management: An Emerging Art and Science

The field of customer value management is still in its infancy. A hundred years of accounting history have instilled some science, rigor and discipline into the practice of capturing, reporting and analyzing financial data. Recent high profile instances of companies issuing misleading or fraudulent financial statements – companies such as Enron, WorldCom and Global Crossing – have underscored how much shareholders count on this data being accurate and clear.

Business leaders have been trained to read a one-page summary of key financial metrics and make informed decisions. They trust finance people to follow generally accepted accounting principles in doing the detailed work that lies behind the high-level summary. It's not cut-and-dried and there's certainly art mixed with the science, but a balance sheet is a balance sheet and has meaning to the trained eye.

When it comes to customer data, there isn't yet the same level of professionalism. Company vision and mission statements are full of aspirational language about creating value for customers, but some of the most metrics-driven companies would be hard pressed to explain how they are measuring and managing customer value. An executive moving from one company to another (or even from one business unit to another) is likely to find that the basic terms used to talk about the customer experience – customer satisfaction, customer value, customer delight, customer loyalty – are defined and measured differently. In the absence of any generally accepted way of summarizing and analyzing key metrics, I've seen business leaders wade through pages of raw customer data trying to make sense of it all, or stare at a single "customer satisfaction" number wondering what it means and how to make it move up.

But there is an emerging art and science of customer value management that is proving its worth in increased market share and shareholder value for the companies that practice it. Companies that capture and use customer data with the same kind of discipline, passion and understanding they give to operational and financial data are learning that this business practice is well worth the time and money invested. **The basic concepts of customer value management and the practical tools that have been developed to support them are the subject of this book.**

Purpose of this Book: Sharing Practical Experience

An early book on the topic, Bradley Gale's 1994 *Managing Customer Value,* drew on work that my colleagues at American Telephone & Telegraph (AT&T) and I were doing at the time, as well as experience from Johnson & Johnson, Parke-Davis, Milliken & Company, Gillette, United Van Lines and others. Since then, I've had the privilege of helping companies around the world successfully adapt and apply these principles to their businesses.

I've worked with companies in Australia, Brazil, Canada, Chile, England, Fiji, Finland, France, Hong Kong, India, Mexico, New Zealand, Norway, Sweden and the United States. I've seen the concepts applied in many sectors: energy, telecommunications, financial services, entertainment, insurance, pharmaceuticals, high-tech manufacturing, chemical, and consumer goods. The tools have worked for global corporations with revenue in the billions and for small, family-run stores.

While the way customer value management is implemented (how data is collected, for example) will differ somewhat according to the nature and customer base of each business, there's a remarkable consistency of experience across all these companies as to what works and what doesn't work. The only company where I haven't seen customer value management work was a business that delivered propane to rural customers. All that mattered for that set of customers was that Charlie had delivered their propane as long as they could remember, and Charlie's son would continue to deliver it when he died. No competitor was going to win their business away.

My purpose in this book and the consulting practice that shaped it is to share my experience. My professional satisfaction comes from helping people just beginning the customer value management journey fast-track the process and avoid costly mistakes by learning from others who have taken the path before them. My clients look on me as a kind of older brother who has learned from his mistakes and can help keep them out of trouble – just as my older brother helped me navigate the treacherous waters of primary school. I never did believe he was smarter than me, but I couldn't deny he had been through third grade and I hadn't!

The AT&T Experience:
What Got Me Thinking About Customer Value

My interest in this area was sparked by a puzzling contradiction that surfaced in the late 80s at AT&T, where I was director of quality and customer satisfaction in the General Business Systems division. GBS, as it was generally known, was a customer-focused organization committed to quality and process improvement.

At the time, AT&T was doing 60,000 surveys a month to measure the satisfaction of customers across all market segments, products and services. Overall, we were running at 95% satisfaction. We were confident that we knew what our customers thought and we felt pretty good about it, particularly as our success in achieving such a high score was reflected in our bonuses.

Unfortunately, in spite of all our quality efforts and high satisfaction scores, that year we lost six points of market share. Six points! At the time one point of market share was worth $600 million for AT&T. For the first time in our hundred-year history, we had to do a massive layoff of 25,000 employees. But 95% of our customers were saying they were satisfied. How could this be?

We'll explore the AT&T case study in more detail later in the book, but I want to set the stage here by highlighting three of the many lessons we learned as we investigated this strange set of circumstances. These are basic principles of customer value management that we'll return to throughout the book.

Lesson #1 – Good is Bad

At the time, our surveys asked our customers to respond to the question, "Overall, how satisfied are you?" using a 4-point scale: poor, fair, good, excellent. We counted customers who rated us good or excellent as satisfied – because good is good, right?

Wrong. When we looked at how customers responded to the question, "How willing are you to repurchase from the company?", we discovered that good isn't good enough – in fact, it's pretty bad. Ninety-five percent of the customers who rated us excellent also said they were very willing to repurchase from the company. Only 60% of the customers who rated us good were very willing to repurchase. At fair it dropped to 4% very willing to repurchase and at poor it was down to zero.

Good Isn't Good Enough

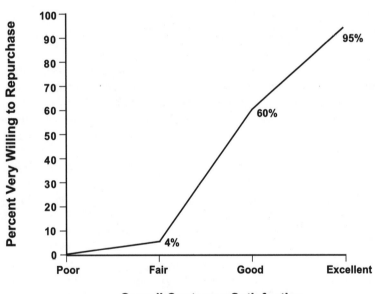

Overall Customer Satisfaction

We had been focusing on figuring out what to do to move the fair and poor scores higher, when we really should have been trying to move the good scores to excellent. This simple correlation was telling us that 40% of the so-called satisfied customers who gave us a good rating were out shopping with our competitors and highly likely to jump ship. Only those customers who thought we were excellent could be considered loyal AT&T customers.

I've run this correlation many times since in my consulting practice, using data from different companies in different countries. Every time, we've produced this same slippery slope – so I've now officially named it the Slippery Slope™ tool. The actual numbers, the height and the exact slope of the curve vary, but the basic shape is the same. It doesn't matter whether it's a 4-point scale, a 5-point scale, a 7-point scale or a 10-point scale (I've even seen an 11-point scale), the slope indicating willingness to repurchase from the company drops off dramatically once you get out of the range of the highest scores. Good is not good enough. Good is bad.

Lesson #2 – Focus on Value, Not Satisfaction with Quality

The second mistake we were making was focusing solely on quality in our surveying. The actual question we used to measure overall satisfaction was, "Overall, how satisfied are you with our products and services?" We did have a question relating to price in each survey, but we considered that a sub-attribute, not a driver of overall satisfaction. Since our products and services were the best, we assumed people would be willing to pay premium prices for them.

We learned from further research that in fact customers were evaluating what they were getting for what they paid: the actual <u>value</u> they received, not just the <u>quality</u> of the product or service. The responses we were getting to the price question were running at around 75% satisfied (counting both good and excellent as satisfied), versus the 95% satisfaction with quality. Not surprisingly, when in subsequent surveys we started asking people whether what they got was worth what they paid for it, the responses to that question ran at about 85% satisfied.

We realized that "worth what paid for" (I sometimes shorten this to WWPF) was where we needed to focus.

Lesson #3 – It's Not About Beating Yourself

Another puzzling situation taught us our third critical lesson. The Allegheny Mountains region was consistently getting customer satisfaction scores in the 98% range. The New York City region was always in the mid-70% range on satisfaction. But while Allegheny was beating out all the other regions and winning our internal customer satisfaction awards, New York was taking home all the sales awards. In fact, we eventually moved out the Allegheny management because the business results weren't meeting the mark.

Here was more evidence for the skeptics who believed there was no connection between customer satisfaction and business results. But the real problem was that while we were busily measuring ourselves against ourselves and vying for the top score in the company, customers were measuring us against our competitors. We thought we were doing well because our scores were moving up each year – we were consistently beating our previous year's record. What we hadn't considered was that maybe our competitors' scores were moving up faster and that's how they were taking market share from us.

The Allegheny/New York anomaly made perfect sense when we started measuring ourselves relative to the competition. While the scores in the Allegheny region were high, they weren't any higher than the scores given to the competition. With the competitors at parity, it was really a tossup as to where customers would take their business. The New York City scores were low because apparently New Yorkers just don't give high ratings. We were in fact leading the competition in that region, and our market share in New York was significantly higher than the market share we had in Allegheny.

What Counts is "Relative to Competition"

Clearly the way we had been defining and measuring customer satisfaction had been lulling us into a false sense of security and we were suffering as a result. The critical metric, we learned, is the Customer Value Added (CVA) ratio:

CVA = The average perceived worth of your company's products and services
divided by
The average perceived worth of competitive offers

To get this data, a company must sample the market and have respondents rate the vendor who provides the products and services they actually use. "Perceived worth" is measured by asking customers, "Considering everything, are the products and services worth what you paid for them?" **This question and the relative-to-competition CVA ratio are at the heart of customer value management.**

Understanding what we needed to measure was just the first step. We had confidence that if we could measure CVA we could find a way to manage it, but we needed a new set of tools to help us. More importantly, we needed to make a 180° shift in our business thinking and look at everything we were doing from our customers' perspective.

Did our surveys truly reflect the drivers of value for customers or were they geared more to our internal measures of quality? Do value drivers vary by type of business and market segment? Did we understand how our customers experienced each of our business processes (billing, for example) and what mattered to them at each stage? How could we use the data to figure out which improvements would be most likely to raise the perceived worth of our offer relative to our competitors? What internal metrics would most likely be leading indicators of changes in customer perception?

These were the questions that began our customer value management journey. The correlations we did between customer value metrics and key financial metrics quickly caught senior management's attention. We started developing tools and methods to present our data in a clear, simple, actionable format. We learned how to teach others to interpret and use the data to pick the few key priorities that would drive greater value for our customers and our business.

The concepts and tools have evolved in my consulting practice since I left AT&T. They've been tested by companies of all sizes around the world and across many industries. Where they've been rigorously and consistently applied to a business, they've been shown to work, creating increases in customer value and shareholder value.

Customer value management is simple – and it's hard. It's simple because most people can "get" the tools intuitively with a little bit of explanation and the concepts seem obvious once you've worked with them a bit. On the other hand, actually implementing customer value management can be difficult because it takes discipline and rigor – just as much discipline and rigor as companies put into the collection, reporting and use of financial data. It often requires people to shed long-held assumptions and habits, and it forces people to learn to communicate internally and with customers in a straightforward and fact-driven way. It asks business leaders to take a long-term view and make a long-term commitment. Too often I've seen companies with short attention spans achieve initial success with customer value management, then become complacent, turn their attention elsewhere, and quickly lose all the competitive advantage gains they had made.

I believe companies that invest in understanding how to use customer data to create superior customer value can improve business results and achieve sustained profitable growth. This book outlines what I've learned in working with others and helping them do this. Along the way you'll hear the voices and stories of a global network of clients and colleagues who are true masters of customer value management. They have taught me and at times learned with me. We'd now like to share what we know about the art and science of customer value management in this book, in the hope that it will help others create competitive advantage for their businesses.

Quick Guide to this Book

If you're looking for a high-level overview of customer value management – what it is, what it has done for others, what it can do for your organization, and what it takes to start and sustain the effort – you'll be most interested in:

- Part I, which lays out the principles and briefly introduces the tools
- Part III, which puts customer value management into context, exploring how it differs from and works together with related concepts such as customer loyalty, customer relationship management and process improvement methods such as Six Sigma
- The case studies at the end of each Part, which show the principles in practice and the results that large and small companies in different parts of the world have achieved through customer value management.

I'd also suggest you read through Steps 9 and 10 of Part II, which are about aligning reward systems and sustaining a customer value focus.

If you're looking for practical, hands-on details, be sure to read Part II – *Ten Steps to Mastery*. With its "how-to" focus, Part II will be especially helpful for customer value management practitioners – people leading company-wide change efforts or team members charged with implementing customer value management in a business unit or department.

Part I:
The Fundamentals

Winning in Three Markets

chapter one

To be successful, businesses must win in three markets:

- The **financial market** – attracting and retaining shareholders and other sources of funding
- The **employment market** – attracting and retaining talented people capable of delivering value to customers
- The **customer market** – attracting and retaining profitable customers.

I used to think that winning in the financial market should be a company's main focus – that businesses exist to create value for shareholders. Over the years, I've come to realize I was looking at things in the wrong way. **I now believe businesses have a greater chance of thriving over the long term if they think of shareholder value as the reward, not the purpose.**

Businesses that sustain success over many years tend to define their purpose in terms related to "improving the quality of life." They're focused on finding customers' needs and providing solutions for them better than any competitor can.

If they have a reputation for winning in the customer market, their chances of getting and keeping the best people – winning in the employment market – are pretty high. Their reward for creating value for their customers and the proof that they've accomplished their purpose is shareholder value. They win in the financial market as well.

Improving the Quality of Life for Customers

Some years ago, I read a biography of Woodrow Wilson, former president of the United States. I was struck by a comment he made in 1906, when he was president of Princeton University, in a speech to a group of business people. He said, "We are not here merely to earn a living and to create value for our shareholders. We are here to enrich the world and to make it a finer place to live. We will impoverish ourselves if we fail to do so."

I think when President Wilson talked about impoverishment he was referring both to the businesses led by the executives in his audience and to the country as a whole. If a business isn't improving the quality of life for its customers, eventually it will be impoverished as a business. In my experience, businesses that start from the principle that their purpose is to create valuable products and services for their customers stand a better than average chance of sustaining success.

Think of examples of businesses that you admire, that have been around for a long time and that continue to win in the market, and then think about what it is they do for you as their customer.

As I communicate daily with business colleagues from around the world via e-mail, I think about Microsoft, a company that I can thank for improving the quality of my business and personal life. I am using the computer as if I were a professional at it, which I am not. My colleagues and I are working from common, compatible and easy-to-use platforms. This was not the case before Microsoft – a company that has weathered some severe storms but continues to achieve solid business success.

The idea that business success comes from focusing on customers is not new. In small, privately-owned businesses, where every employee interacts directly with customers, the link between customer value and business success is reinforced daily. My father was the owner of a corner bakery. He knew that his purpose in business was to make it easier for customers to feed their families by providing the best bread and baked goods they could buy. I spent my youth working with him to care for the people in our community, most of whom were our very good and loyal customers. We created that loyalty by knowing what customers wanted and making sure we delivered it.

Most large publicly traded companies stress in their literature and their leaders' speeches that customers are central to their business. But when you look at what many companies measure, how they use this data to manage the business, and what their people get rewarded for, customers often get lost in the shuffle.

We've seen recent examples of a focus on pushing up the stock price distracting companies from their real purpose. The "dot-com" boom and bust of the late 1990s was an extreme example of how stock prices can be manipulated in the short term – often long enough to make those executives and shareholders who are lucky enough to get in and out at the right time very wealthy.

As I write, we're being bombarded with scandals involving major global corporations. The executives in question – you might call them the "robber barons" of the 21st century – were focused on shareholder value all right, in that they were determined to increase the value of their stock options and personal wealth. This narrow, short-term and self-interested view has dealt devastating losses to the vast majority of shareholders. By losing sight of the long-term purpose of the business – to create value for customers – these business leaders have betrayed employees, customers and shareholders.

Making the Numbers

Every quarter, senior officers of publicly traded companies stake their personal reputations on their ability to predict and control the future. They formally commit to the board of directors to bring in x amount of revenue at y amount of profitability. If they make the numbers, they, the shareholders and the employees all win. If they don't, investor confidence is eroded, the share price falls, bonuses are reduced or not paid at all, and everybody loses. If the results are especially good or significantly poor they are written up and talked about in the *Wall Street Journal* or *Fortune* or *The Economist*. It's no wonder that management puts so much focus on making the financial targets they've committed to.

When I first started recognizing the importance of customer value data to business, I got a lot of push back from leaders who were afraid that I would distract them from meeting their financial commitments – or worse, make it more difficult for them to meet these important numbers. I hear similar concerns from people in almost every business I've worked with, usually expressed as one of the following questions:

- **Will a focus on customer value negatively impact profitability?**
  Some people worry that I'm advocating giving away features or lowering prices to boost the value of the company's offering in the eyes of customers. Doing so would erode profit margins and jeopardize important earnings per share commitments. But in fact the concepts and tools of customer value management offer a way to target investments for improvement – investments that companies are already making – to areas that have the highest payoff for the company and the customer. Companies can actually raise their profits by raising the value of their offering.

- **How does what I do influence the customer value numbers?**
  People don't want to be measured on a number they can't influence, and
  rightly so. Almost every company has some sort of customer satisfaction
  survey and many have customer satisfaction objectives hard-wired into
  their bonus or incentive programs. Fewer have a really solid
  understanding of what is causing their numbers to go up or down. If
  people are going to be rewarded for getting their numbers up and
  penalized if they go down, they want to know what makes the numbers
  move and how that connects to the work they do. They want actionable
  data that allows them to control, or at least influence, the number. Again,
  my experience has been that customer value management can do this.

Customer Value Drives Business Results

But do we really know that focusing on customer value will deliver business
results and shareholder value? Let's go back to AT&T in the late 1980s and look
at the business case that gradually emerged as we shifted our thinking. Instead
of concluding that our customers were satisfied because they were rating our
offerings as good, we started focusing on how customers perceived the value
we provided relative to competitors.

Once we understood what to look for, the AT&T data showed direct links
between customer value and:

- Market share (winning customers)
- Share of wallet (keeping customers and increasing the amount of
  business they do with you)
- Return on invested capital (satisfying shareholders).

In all cases the metric we used was the Customer Value Added ratio – the CVA
ratio for short. We'd learned this ratio accurately reflected the market's
perception of the relative value provided to customers. Remember that the
CVA ratio represents the perceived value (what I call "worth what paid for") of
our offering in the eyes of our customers, divided by the perceived value of the
competition's offering. Later chapters will detail the best processes for
capturing data to calculate the CVA ratio for your business. Here we'll focus on
what the ratio means and how it correlates to business results.

ABOUT THE CVA RATIO

We named our metric the Customer Value Added or CVA ratio because the critical financial metric for AT&T was Economic Value Added or EVA (a Stern, Stewart & Co. trademark). We did this to signal that CVA was just as important to the company as EVA – in fact was a driver of EVA. Others have called it the Relative Customer Value ratio or the Market-Perceived Value ratio. Here's how it works:

It starts with market surveys of customers in your target markets. Customers are asked from whom they buy, and then asked to rate the company they do business with on the question, "Considering everything, are the products and services delivered worth what you paid for them?" Say the responses from customers who buy from you average an 8 on a 10-point scale on this question. If customers who buy from your competitors give your competitors an 8 average rating, then the CVA ratio would be 1.0 – parity.

A CVA below 1.0 means that customers in the market perceive your offering to be of lesser value than your competitors' offering. If your average score is 7.5 and your competitors' average is 8, then your CVA slips to 0.94. You are at a disadvantage.

A CVA above 1.0 means that, on average, customers perceive your value to be superior. If the average rating for you is 9 and the rating for your competitors is 8.5, then your CVA is 1.05 and you have an advantage.

For some companies it works best to multiply everything by 100 to get rid of the decimal because people who normally deal in big financial numbers don't tend to pay that much attention to decimals. I prefer to use the decimal version of the ratio when I can. I find that people think 100 is a good score because it sounds like 100%. In fact, 100 or 1.0 is not great. It means that you have no advantage over your competitor. As far as the market is concerned you are the same, and a flip of a coin can determine which company they'll choose when they next go to purchase. A slight slip-up on your part or a slight improvement by your competitors and you're at risk of losing a lot of business.

Market Share

We looked at and measured market share in three ways: across customer segments in a business, over time in the same customer segment, and as a percentage of purchases from individual customers.

First we simply plotted the CVAs of 12 of our long distance market segments on a scatter diagram to see whether there was any correlation between CVA and market share. The results showed that higher CVA generally equated to higher market share (calculated as the percentage of total revenue).

Revenue Share to Relative Value
12 Different Long Distance Market Segments

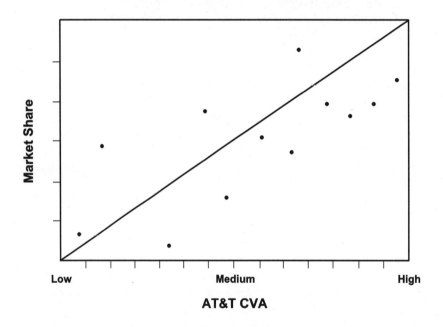

Next we took the CVA data from a different business segment, the General Business Systems division, and plotted changes in CVA and market share over three years. We didn't see the correlation until we shifted the CVA line ahead by four months. Once we did that, we could clearly see market share tracking to what our customers were saying about the value we were delivering. Four months after a shift in perception of our value, our market share shifted accordingly. The statisticians confirmed that the assumption was solid, and CVA was in fact a leading indicator of market share.

Business Telephone Equipment Market Share (Percent Installs) Versus CVA

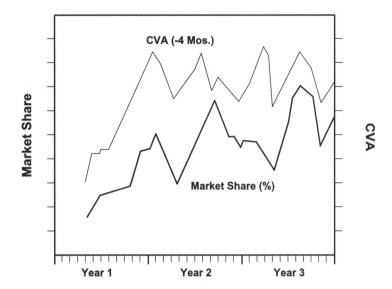

The four-month lag made sense because the typical buying cycle at that time in that industry was three to four months between hot lead and contract. This chart got a lot of attention from AT&T management when we shared it with other business segments, and has since been widely used outside the company to illustrate the importance of understanding where you're trending on customer value. It was published in Bradley Gale's seminal work *Managing Customer Value*[1], which draws on the AT&T experience.

PREDICTING MARKET SHARE AT FEDERAL EXPRESS

I've seen this experiment repeated using data from many different companies, and while the end result is usually the same – CVA is a leading indicator of market share – the lag time varies according to the nature of the business. When I was benchmarking the courier service Federal Express back in the mid-90s, for example, a vice president there told me that the lag time for them was only 48 hours. This makes sense, because it doesn't take a customer very long to decide which courier service to use to send a package – and the cost of switching quickly to another is minimal or nil. Using

[1] B. Gale and R. Wood, *Managing Customer Value: Creating Quality and Service That Customers Can See* (Free Press, 1994), p. 82

customer value management techniques, Federal Express had established which internal metrics were key drivers of customer satisfaction that predict CVA: damage, loss, on-time delivery and so on. They were seeing changes in market share 48 hours after a change in performance based on their internal metrics.

Share of Wallet

Next we looked at the buying patterns of credit card users, because we were interested in seeing how AT&T's Universal Card stacked up against the competition. The consumer credit card business is particularly volatile because customers typically carry more than one card and it's easy to switch from one to another.

Wallet Share Versus CVA

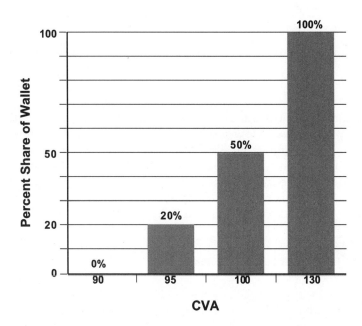

Share of wallet is important because it's an indicator of customer loyalty – of the customer's intention to stay with you and buy more from you over time.

We asked survey respondents which cards they owned (typically they owned three to five) and then which cards they used most (typically they used one or two). We asked them to rate the two or three cards they used most from a value perspective, and asked how often they used each. We then calculated the CVA for each card they used. Customers' ratings of the card they used most produced a CVA of 1.3 (significantly better than the competition). Their response on use for cards getting the 1.3 rating was typically, "I use it all the time – I don't even know why I carry the others." For customers who rated their two most-used cards at parity – a CVA of 1.0 – it was a flip of the coin. Half of the time they used one card; half of the time they used the other.

The really interesting thing about this study was what it said about cards that are below parity. Cards given a CVA of 0.95 based on responses from people who carried them – just 5% below parity – were used only 20% of the time. About cards that rated a CVA of 0.90, people said, "I never use them."

> **NOTE:** *In this study, we asked survey respondents to rate each of the cards they carried with them. So while we were calculating CVA ratios of 1.3 based on how people rated their own favorite cards, no one credit card company had an average CVA of 1.3 across the market. In my experience across many industries, when you look at market averages, most of the time CVA ratios range from 0.90 to 1.10. Only about 10% of companies achieve CVA ratios greater than 1.10. These world-class companies have significantly better financial results than the companies clustered around the middle.*

Return on Invested Capital

AT&T's CFO at the time, Alex Mandl, was convinced by the charts that linked CVA to market share and revenue, but like many others he was worried about what would happen to profits if we set out to raise the CVA scores. I mentioned earlier that the focus in the company at that time was on quality, and the assumption was that people would expect to pay a premium price for superior products. The executives were fine with being measured on how customers perceived the quality of our products and services relative to the competition, because they had control over that. But some of them saw pricing as beyond their control. Given the level of quality expected by our customers and the need to meet commitments on profit, it was generally assumed that the price had to be set at a certain level.

Alex's focus was on Economic Value Added or EVA. We knew from earlier studies that there was a strong link between EVA (return on invested capital multiplied by the amount of capital invested) and share price. So we set out to prove the link between CVA and return on invested capital.

The proof came from research we did in collaboration with analysts from the Strategic Planning Institute in Massachusetts. Working with their Profit Impact of Market Strategy (PIMS) database, we looked for companies which had perceived relative value data similar to our CVA ratio. This chart captures what we found.

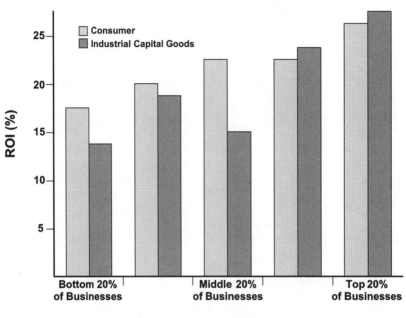

ROI Versus Relative Value

For the approximately 1800 business units and divisions of companies in the consumer and industrial capital goods markets for which we had relative value (CVA-type) data, there was a clear correlation between value and return on invested capital. The top 20% of businesses on the relative value scale had a return on investment (ROI) of almost twice that of the bottom 20%. We also found in the top 20% a mix of premium-priced brands, middle-of-the-road brands and economy-priced brands. That suggested it didn't matter whether a company's strategy was to compete on price or to compete on quality. What mattered was that customers felt they received better value for the money paid than they could get from the competition.

In my consulting practice I've done similar analyses and correlations for scores of businesses around the world and they've always demonstrated a strong relationship between customer value and whatever business measures were most critical for that company. Customer value management is not an end in itself. It's about creating competitive advantage and driving business success.

Applying the Learning

What we were coming to realize from the early AT&T work was that it was possible to predict with some accuracy what kind of CVA scores we'd need in order to make the financial targets. That was a really different concept for us at the time. We considered our customer-related targets to be an internal metric – not in the same category as the public commitments we made to the investment community. While we intuitively knew that customer satisfaction had some impact on business results, the process of establishing customer satisfaction targets was not linked to the financial target-setting process.

We learned the hard way that this was a mistake. The president of the $4 billion General Business Systems (GBS) business unit was a firm believer in focusing on customers, and one of the first leaders to embrace what the statistics were telling us about looking at relative customer value in addition to absolute customer satisfaction with products and services. He was a strong champion of the customer value work.

But this same champion made one decision that year that illustrates how foreign it was to our thinking that you could drive business results by focusing on customer value – a decision to set customer targets lower than our calculations told us they needed to be to meet financial targets.

The Customer Value/Financial Success Link

As part of the regular fall business planning cycle, financial targets for GBS were set by the senior officers of the company. Sometime later, our customer value group was asked for input into what CVA score should be set as our objective for the year.

At the time, the GBS business unit was facing a significant slippage in market share, and this new president had been brought in to reverse the trend. We had good data that showed how CVA tracked to market share and how market share tracked to the financials. Our econometrician, Rich DeNicola, could actually calculate what CVA score we would need to have any hope of reaching our financial targets. It was significantly higher than our current score and would not be easy to reach in a year.

When we told the president what the numbers were telling us, he was concerned. He knew that the financial targets were going to be very difficult to reach and that many branch managers wouldn't be able to make them. The financial targets were a public commitment over which he had no control. But he could control the CVA objective, and he wanted to provide some positive reinforcement for the hard work people would need to do to turn things around. He sent us back to the drawing board to come up with some "stretch but realistic" customer value goals.

That put us in a dilemma. We understood the president's desire to give people something to feel good about. We understood that he had signed up to the financial numbers that the company needed from his business unit to meet their public commitments, and couldn't change those. But we also knew what kind of CVA improvement it would take to make the financial numbers. How could we recommend anything less as a target?

In the end, the president set his own "stretch but realistic" customer value targets and many managers received the portion of their bonuses that was tied to that number that year. But many managers did not make their financial commitments and they were let go. So was the president.

I'm not saying that if only he had set the right CVA target, the required financial success would automatically follow. The situation was more complicated than that. But I believe that in not being up front with managers as to what truly would be required to meet our goals, he missed an opportunity to motivate employees and focus them on the real challenge. To him the financial numbers were real: customer value numbers were survey results and not in the same league. He'd seen and intellectually accepted the charts showing that customer value drives financial success, but clearly didn't believe in his heart that significant improvements in customer value were a prerequisite to meeting our financial targets.

The point of this story is not to reflect badly on the individual faced with this difficult decision (whom I consider a pioneer in customer value management) but to emphasize how difficult it can be to change our own ingrained assumptions. His successor, Paul Wondrasch, learned from this experience, set what looked like impossible CVA targets and got people focused on creating value for customers. Paul succeeded in turning the market share loss around and significantly improved the financials. We'll talk more in Chapter Three about the challenges of driving the shift in a company to a customer value mindset and culture, and we'll hear Paul's account of the turnaround.

The People Factor

We began this chapter with the premise that the purpose of a business is to find a customer need and fill it better than the competition – to create value and improve the quality of life for customers. I've outlined evidence from my experience that if you do that well, you create shareholder value and win in the financial market. And that brings us to the third market in which companies must win to be successful: the employment market.

A business, to my mind, is a collection of people who come together to deliver something of value to customers that they could not deliver as individuals. The people factor in customer value management is a topic requiring a book of its own, so we'll just touch on a few critical points here.

Have you ever heard employee satisfaction initiatives justified on the basis that "Happy employees make happy customers"? I have, often, and I usually cringe when I do. While it's true that customers don't enjoy dealing with openly disgruntled employees, I don't believe that investment in trying to make employees "happy" will necessarily pay off in increased customer and shareholder value. What makes a person happy is very personal and mostly dependent on factors outside the company's control.

Value Exchange

In the context of the business, one thing that's important to employees is that there is a fair value exchange with the company: that the rewards for working for the company are in line with what the company asks of them. By rewards I mean the total package of rewards, not just compensation and benefits. While decent financial compensation is important, recruiters tell me the best people are also drawn to a company by the challenge of the work, opportunities to learn and grow, a chance to work with experts in their field and so on.

One of my colleagues, Davis Steward, runs a research and consulting firm called Customer Opinion Research. He and John Acherman of what was then Wisconsin Electric hit upon the idea of correlating employee responses to the statement, "I am treated as a valued employee of the company" with the same population's responses to the statement, "I perform to my best in my work." The result (see the chart on the next page) looks very much like the Slippery Slope we talked about in the Introduction – the slope produced when we correlated overall customer ratings with their willingness to repurchase from the company. The number of people who say they're performing up to their full potential drops off dramatically once you get past the excellent ratings for "treated as a valued employee."

Only 50% of people who reported a 7 out of 10 on feeling treated as a valued employee feel they're performing to their best. Ninety percent of employees who gave the company a 9 say they're performing to their best. The message is that employees who perceive high value in what they're getting from the company are ready to give their best back to the company, making for a fair value exchange. The same correlation done with data from other companies has produced similar results.

People Performance Curve

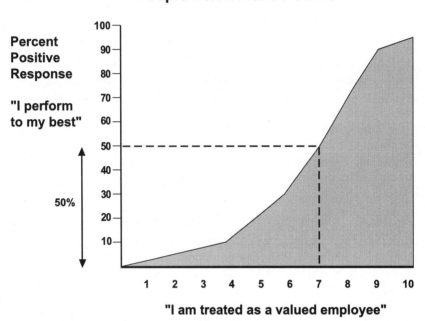

Performing to their best is as important to most employees as it is to the customers and companies they work for. Research done in the mid-90s by Nortel, a Canadian-based global telecommunications company (which became Nortel Networks after the acquisition of Bay Networks in 1998), found that employees were most satisfied when they felt they were being productive and delivering value to customers. Not surprisingly, this is what customers were looking for as well. When Nortel correlated the employee survey data for teams devoted to a specific customer with the customer survey data for that customer, they could show that when employee satisfaction was higher, customer satisfaction tended to be higher as well – and vice versa.

Nortel was focused on traditional customer satisfaction and loyalty at the time, not specifically customer value – but the principle of the employee/customer link is what's important here. Over time, Nortel statistically demonstrated from its employee, customer and financial data that employee satisfaction drives customer satisfaction, which in turn drives shareholder results. What's more, they found that according to responses in the customer survey, 81% of the variance in overall customer satisfaction could be explained by satisfaction with personnel.

Overall Satisfaction Versus Satisfaction with Employees

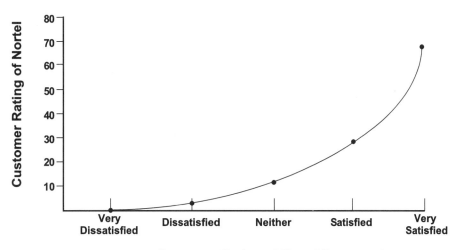

Customer Rating of Nortel Personnel

Sixty-eight percent of the customers who reported being "very satisfied" with Nortel personnel also said they were "very satisfied" with the company overall, while only 29% of the customers who were "satisfied" with Nortel personnel gave the company an overall "very satisfied" rating. More sophisticated regression analysis of the customer and employee survey data at Nortel allowed them to demonstrate statistically that over 52% of customer satisfaction is driven by employee factors.

One important learning from this analysis was that it would be impossible for the company to reach world-class customer satisfaction without ensuring that their customers were very satisfied with their employees. Put that finding together with the Wisconsin Electric data on the strong links between employee performance and their feeling valued by the company, and you'll see how important the "people value" factor really is for a business.

The people factor is also very closely related to the process factor, since people's performance depends greatly on how well their work processes are designed and what level of resources are committed to them. While this book will focus on gathering and using data on what customers value to improve market share and return on invested capital, we can't lose sight of the fact that customers' experience of the company is shaped by people and the processes through which they work.

A BUSINESS TRUTH

No one person can totally satisfy a customer...
But any one person can totally dissatisfy a customer!

Getting the Focus Right

Winning in the customer market requires a simultaneous focus on capturing new customers, keeping the customers you have and winning more of their business. If I'm a business owner, to do this well I need to know what customers consider when assessing the value of what I'm offering and what matters to them in their experience of my company.

Clearly, the thing to do is to ask customers and find out directly, in their own words, what is important to them. The challenge is to do it in a way that produces reliable, meaningful and – most critical – actionable data. I worry that some companies fall into the trap of looking at the gathering of customer satisfaction data as an end in itself rather than a means to an end. They make it much more complicated than it needs to be. They measure everything they can think of and analyze the data up, down and sideways. They compile it into huge reports with nifty graphics. The reports look great on the shelf.

In my view, the purpose of compiling customer data is to figure out what you're going to do to create more value for customers and make them more likely to stay with you than to go to your competitor. More importantly, it's about figuring out what you're not going to do. In every company today, money and time to invest in improvements are scarce. I've learned the hard way that if we try to work on 20 things all at once, most likely we're not giving enough attention and resources to any one of them to really make a difference. The key to success is to determine what few things will have the greatest leverage, and to focus those scarce resources on these critical actions.

Institutionalizing a Customer Value Management Approach

The remaining chapters of this book look at the practicalities of institutionalizing a customer value management approach in a business. You'll hear from:

- **Senior executives** who have used the tools and concepts to shape business strategy, make strategic investment decisions and get employees focused on high priority actions.

- **Change agents** who have learned to present data in a way that gets attention both from decision makers and the people who work the processes every day. They'll also talk about the challenges of creating a sustaining infrastructure and really embedding customer value management into the corporate culture.

- **Technical experts** who have improved data collection and analysis processes to ensure that they have meaningful, relevant, reliable, statistically accurate and actionable information.

I'll share my experience of what has made people successful in driving these changes in their business, and what we've found hasn't worked.

Customer value management is part art and part science. It's partly about understanding techniques of surveying and data analysis, and it's partly about changing mindset and organizational culture. We'll look at all these aspects in the chapters that follow.

The Tools of Customer Value Management

chapter two

At its core, customer value management is really very simple. It's about:

- **Choosing value:** Deciding what value proposition you are taking to market
- **Delivering value:** Making sure your business processes are aligned with your value proposition and working together to deliver it effectively
- **Communicating value:** Educating the market on your value proposition.

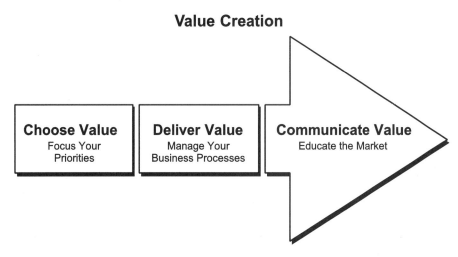

Value Creation

Choose Value
Focus Your
Priorities

Deliver Value
Manage Your
Business Processes

Communicate Value
Educate the Market

This simple three-fold image reflects the collective thinking of those of us who were pioneering customer value management in the late 80s. To my knowledge, the first time it appeared in a published document was in a 1988 McKinsey Staff paper written by Michael Lanning and Edward Michaels (June 1988, No. 41) entitled "A Business is a Value Delivery System." In the document the authors contrast a traditional product-oriented system (create the product, make the product, sell the product) with a value delivery system (choose the value, provide the value, communicate the value).

In this chapter I'll briefly introduce some of the tools of customer value management that business leaders in a variety of industries and countries have helped me develop. The tools have had proven success in helping leaders choose, deliver and communicate value. In Part II of this book, you'll see how these tools support a ten-step process for mastering customer value management that addresses both the hard issues of data collection and analysis and the softer issues of company culture and change leadership.

If it's So Simple, Why Is it So Hard?

Most people can intuitively accept that it makes good sense for a business to find out what customers value, figure out how to deliver value better than the competition, and make sure customers recognize the value they're getting. Sounds pretty simple? So why do so many companies find this so difficult?

I think it's primarily because in most companies, the real focus is on shareholders. People always think first about what's good for the company's balance sheet; customers come second.

Thinking Like a Customer

Ask yourself, for example, "What is the purpose of the billing process?" From the company's point of view it's usually to get the money quickly and keep the cash position positive. The key metric, therefore, is 30-60-90-day accounts receivable. But now think about the purpose of the billing process for the customer. When we've asked customers this question, the answers they give are usually:

- "No surprises: I want the bill to reflect what I was told it was going to cost."
- "Easy to understand: Your product codes don't mean a lot to me. I want to be able to compare my list of what I bought to yours and make sure the bill is right."
- "Easy to correct: If I do find an error, I want to be able to resolve it in one call."

The billing center is usually focused on three measures:

- Time to collection
- Calls handled per person per day
- Talk time per call.

These are good measures from the perspective of the shareholder, but there are no measures on what matters to customers:

- Number of errors on bills
- Number of calls it took to correct errors
- Number of customers calling because they don't understand the bill.

A New Mental Model

So one of the reasons why customer value management is difficult to do well is that it requires a mental model that says the purpose of the business is to create value for the customer. If all of your systems – planning, metrics, rewards, delivery processes – have been designed around different paradigms, then instituting customer value management requires a significant shift in mindset and company culture.

In the next chapter and in the various case studies you'll read throughout the book, we'll be hearing leading executives in a variety of firms tell the story of how they did this. There's a consistent message in all their stories: Shifting to this new customer-focused mental model and embedding it into the culture is the really hard stuff, and companies ignore it at their peril. It's easy to dismiss anything that has to do with company culture as something soft that can't really be managed systematically. The successful leaders whom I've known have tackled this issue head on in a very focused and practical way.

Actionable, Meaningful Customer Data

Another reason that companies sometimes find customer value management difficult is that they don't put enough thought and planning into making sure they're capturing the right data and presenting it in a way that it can actually be <u>used</u> to set priorities. Sometimes they make this much more complicated than it really needs to be. Some key lessons:

- **Getting the survey design right at the outset is critical.** It really matters what questions you ask customers, whom you ask, how you ask and what response options you provide.
- **There are effective ways of getting customer value data in front of business decision makers and there are not-so-effective ways.** If the links to business results are not made clear, the data won't be used. If the data is never actually used to run the business, there's no point collecting it.
- **Customer value data is most useful when it can be linked to underlying business processes that can be quantified and improved.** Only then is the data truly actionable.

- **There are good customer value analysis tools available.** While they're not nearly as well known and understood as the tools of financial analysis, they do exist and they do work.

The Slippery Slope™

You've been introduced to the Slippery Slope tool already. The purpose of this tool is to give meaning to the overall ratings you're getting from customers by showing how they relate to predicted customer behavior.   It's a simple correlation between overall value ratings and responses to behavior questions such as, "How likely are you to recommend the company?" or, "How likely are you to purchase from the company again?" Whenever I've seen this correlation done, it produces a line that drops off quickly as you move from the highest ratings to mid-range ratings and goes totally flat at the low-end range.   That's why I call it the Slippery Slope.

The Slippery Slope

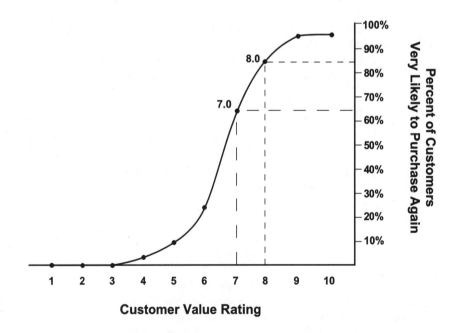

Creating a Slippery Slope from your own data gives you insight into what is going on in your customers' minds. When they rate you a 7, do they think this is a really good score or an average score? Well, if only two-thirds of the customers who give you this score say they're very likely to purchase from you again (as is the case in this example) it's not all that good. There's plenty of room for a competitor to come in with a better value offer and take customers away from you.

If the company in this example could raise their score to an 8, they would cut in half the number of customers who were thinking of taking their business elsewhere, and they would achieve an impressive 83% loyalty rate. Conversely, if they allowed their scores to slip to 6 or even 6.5, it looks like they'd be in serious trouble. This high-level view helps calibrate the numbers and gives you a sense of the challenge you're facing. Companies that have done the necessary econometric modeling (we'll talk about this in Step 6 – *Analyze the Data*) can actually calculate the potential market share gain represented by an improvement from 65% to 83% customer loyalty, and translate this into revenue dollars. This gets the attention of business leaders!

Value Maps

The Value Map is a more sophisticated tool for understanding your competitive position in the overall market (as opposed to just with your own customers) and plotting your competitive strategy.

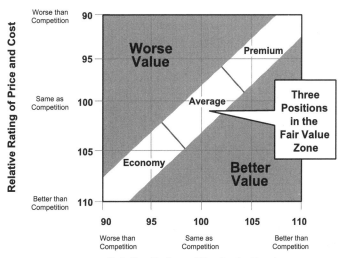

Strategic Zones on a Value Map

Whenever I look at a Value Map I think about the time I visited Winston Churchill's cabinet war room, which has been preserved as an historic site. The walls are papered with maps of the North Atlantic, Europe and Africa. Colored pins on each track the position, strength and direction of movement of the Allied forces and the projected movements of the Axis forces. It was in that room, using those maps, that Churchill's team analyzed the strengths and weaknesses of the Allied and Axis forces and determined military strategy.

A Value Map shows you your position in the market relative to that of your competitors, tracks movement over time, and helps you plan your business strategy.

Later (in Step 7 – *Pick Priorities*) we'll go into the mechanics of drawing Value Maps and using them to play out "what if?" scenarios to shape your competitive strategy. But let's start with a simple example of the insights they can provide.

When I first started using Value Maps, the classic thinking was that companies would tend to cluster in the "fair value zone" within a few degrees either side of the fair value line. We also tended in those days to think that anyone in the fair value zone was well positioned to maintain market share. It didn't really matter if you had staked your claim as an economy brand, a middle-of-the-road brand, or a premium brand. What mattered was that customers felt that what they got was worth what they paid – they were receiving fair value.

But what if a competitor comes along and stakes out the "better value zone"? Think about what Wal-Mart did starting in the late 80s. In the US at the time, the major players in the department store market were companies like K-Mart (an economy brand), Sears (an average brand) and Macy's (a premium brand), all offering fair value to their target markets.

Along came Sam Walton with the strategy of offering the same products at better prices, with better service and stores strategically located closer to their target customers. Where was he positioning Wal-Mart? Squarely in the better value zone. Close attention to supply chain management and other processes kept their costs down and made it possible for Wal-Mart to offer the best prices but still maintain excellent profits. Their in-store data and market research kept them focused on what mattered most to customers and kept their quality high.

With this strategy, he quickly began to take market share from his competition clustered around the fair value line. From 1990 to 2000, Sears' revenue grew from about $25 billion to $40.9 billion. Wal-Mart was a bit ahead at $25.8 billion in 1990 (already up 25% from the previous year), but by 2000 it had grown to

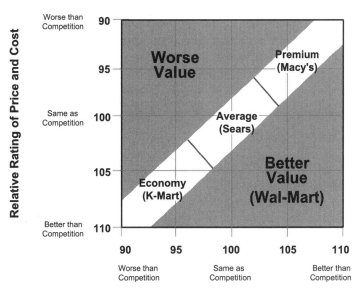

**Relative Rating of Products, Services
and Relationship or Image**

$166.8 billion. By 2002, Wal-Mart topped the list of global companies in revenue and shareholder value, and the late Sam Walton's children figured prominently in lists of the world's wealthiest people. Meanwhile, K-mart declared Chapter 11 bankruptcy protection, Macy's started closing stores and Sears shut down parts of its business. It's an extreme example, but a very clear business case for understanding where you're placed on the Value Map in the eyes of your target market, and planning what you will do if competitors appear and grab better value positions.

That's not the end of the story, of course. At the time of writing, Wal-Mart's competitors are in varying stages of planning and executing a competitive response. It's important to remember that a Value Map is a snapshot of a company's competitive position at a given moment. Given how dynamic most markets are, the fact that you're in the better value zone now doesn't guarantee you long-term success.

Many factors can drive changes in market perception of the value you offer relative to your competitors. Sometimes the playing field changes suddenly because of an aggressive move by your competitors (price cuts, new offerings, advertising), a serious slip-up on your part, or a social trend that changes what the market values. But more often than not, the changes happen more gradually, a result of sustained day-to-day efforts to continuously improve priority processes or change customer perception of value on a key attribute. Companies that sustain success over the long term know that understanding the market is not a one-time effort, and are constantly watching for and responding to these changes.

A Note on Value Maps

Bradley Gale introduced the concept of a Value Map in 1987's *The PIMS Principles: Linking Strategy to Performance*. People familiar with Brad's version of the map will see that the one I use is slightly different. His *y* axis represented actual price paid, with high prices at the top and low prices at the bottom.

The Value Map drawn here has as its *y* axis <u>customers' satisfaction with cost</u>, with low satisfaction at the top and high satisfaction at the bottom. This is an important change, since it's become clear in my work with Value Maps that customer <u>perceptions of the overall cost</u> of the product or service are more important than the <u>actual</u> price charged, just as their perceptions of whether your costs are higher or lower than your competitors matter more than where you know you really stand.

Attribute Trees™

To choose the right value proposition, you need to know what factors customers in your target market consider in deciding where to take their business, and how much weight they put on each factor. The Value Maps looked at two high-level factors: what customers get and what they pay. Now we're going to start drilling down to find out what's important to them at the next level. So we start to build an Attribute Tree™ that looks like this:

The next question is, "What factors impact how people feel about what they're paying?" The answer will vary depending on what type of business you're in and the characteristics of your market. If your product is laser printers, for example, the ongoing cost of cartridges is likely to be as important to customers as the initial purchase price. So the next branch of the Attribute Tree might look like this:

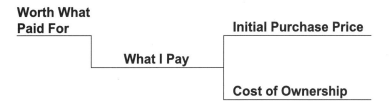

The goal is to keep breaking down each branch of the tree into its component branches, to get a full understanding of what drives value for your target market. On the other branch of our initial tree, you might see:

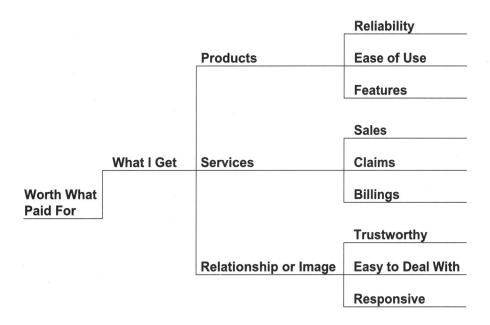

If you can attach impact weights to each of these branches, you have an even clearer picture. If customers in your target market give 70% weight to "what I get" and 30% weight to "what I pay" when they're assessing the value of your offering, you probably want to focus on the "what I get" branch of the tree. You then want to know what weight they put on the product itself versus the services or your brand image, what weight they put on reliability versus ease of use or features, and so on. Later on we'll be looking at methods of determining the weighting from the data you're collecting.

Value Propositions: Two Views

I hear the term "value proposition" all the time, but I wonder whether we all mean the same thing by this phrase. To my mind, you can think about a company's value proposition in two ways:

*1. **Through the eyes of customers:** The value proposition consists of the items on the Attribute Tree – the drivers of value from the customers' perspective.*

*2. **Through the eyes of the company:** The value proposition is the result of decisions you've made as to what you plan to take to market – where you're going to lead the market, where you're happy to be at par, and so on.*

When you do strategic planning, you can use the tools of customer value management to decide on the value proposition that best reflects your market strategy. When you do customer value research, you find out how customers' perception of the value proposition compares to your intended value proposition.

- Dr. Nick Fisher, Value Metrics Australia

Choosing the value that you intend to take to market is only the first step. The Attribute Trees are also useful for determining what actions you can take to <u>deliver</u> the value you've chosen – that second part of the three-part arrow with which the chapter began. To do this, you need to keep breaking down attributes until you've connected the value drivers with an identifiable business process. If you take the billing branch to the next level, for example, you might get:

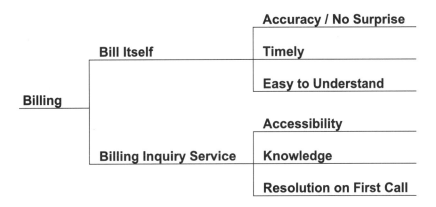

Now you've got some actionable data. You can immediately tie accuracy or resolution on first call to a concrete business process that can be measured and improved.

Every company's Attribute Tree will be unique. It will also change over time. I find, for example, that the relative weighting of products, services and relationship starts changing after a customer has been buying from a company for some years. Generally the products factor starts declining in importance, while services and relationship gain.

> ### What I Get: Relationship or Brand Image?
>
> You'll see that I've attached two alternate labels to the third branch of the Attribute Tree: relationship or image. Depending on the nature of your business, one may be more applicable than the other.
>
> If you're a major manufacturer of food products, then brand image is more likely to be key. But if you're a small local store, relationships may be more important. Most of us can think of favorite stores where the service may be noticeably less efficient than that of the big chains, and where identical products cost a little more than they would elsewhere. But we would not think of shopping anywhere else for some of our requirements, because the owners know our names and ask about our family – the *relationship* is key.

> Relationship is often more important than brand image to businesses that deal primarily with other businesses. Because there are normally only a few players in each business-to-business market, advertising has little role to play in business development.

Competitive Profiles

The Attribute Trees give you essential information on the value drivers and the business processes that impact them, but they alone can't shape a value proposition or prioritize areas for improvement. Just because customers give a high weighting to a factor doesn't mean that's where you should focus. If you're already rated high in that area and are doing it significantly better than your competitors, you're not going to win market share or more customer loyalty by squeezing your ratings up by a small fraction. It's much harder to move from a 9 to a 10 than from a 7 to an 8.

So how do you decide which lever to pull? Of all the improvements that you might make, which ones will have the highest payoff by increasing customers' perception of the value you provide versus your competition? There is no strict mathematical formula that will give you the right answer on this every time. There's a judgment call to be made.

To help them decide where to focus efforts, many of my clients put their data into a spreadsheet or a software program, and work up "what if?" scenarios.[1] Some people prefer to work with simple Competitive Profile tables done on sheets of paper, showing the impact weight of each attribute side by side with customers' ratings of your company, their ratings of your competition and the resulting CVA ratio (your average score divided by the competition's average score).

Competitive Quality Profile

Key Purchase Criteria	Importance Weight %	Your Company	Competition	Ratio
Product:				
Understandable	18	7.4	7.2	1.03
Features	12	9.0	8.6	1.05
	30			
Service:				
Sales	30	8.5	8.1	1.05
Application	8	8.5	8.5	1.00
Claims	22	7.8	8.1	0.96
Billing	10	7.0	8.0	0.88
	70			

---

[1] *A software package specifically designed to create all the customer value management tools described here has been developed by my colleagues West and Heather Vogel. See* **www.twovogels.com** *for details.*

For the insurance company whose data is reproduced in this Competitive Profile, the surprise learning from their Attribute Tree was that how customers felt about the sales process and the salesperson they dealt with carried as much weight as the product. To that point, they had been putting their focus on advertising the superiority of their product's features. They hadn't paid too much attention to the sales side of things. But the good news in the Competitive Profile was that they were outperforming the competition on the sales-related attributes anyway.

From the Attribute Tree they had also learned that billing was almost as important as features in the minds of their customers. The bad news in the Competitive Profile was that they were significantly underperforming the competition in the area of billing, with a competitive ratio of 0.88. Because their score on billing stood at 7.0 (and it's easier to move from a 7 to an 8 or 9 than from a 9 to a 10) this was clearly a high priority area for improvement.[2] The area of claims was next on the priority list, since it had a high impact weighting of 22% combined with a slightly below parity competitive ratio of 0.96.

Once first-level priorities are chosen, the next step is to look at the Competitive Profiles for factors on the next branching of the Attribute Tree and zero in on which business processes would be key levers in making improvements. For the insurance company whose data we looked at above, it was clear that "no surprises" was the place to focus.

Competitive Billing Profile

Key Purchase Criteria	Importance Weight %	Your Company	Competition	Ratio
Bill Itself:				
Accurate / No Surprise	40	6.8	7.8	0.87
Timely	5	7.7	7.7	1.00
Easy to Understand	10	7.3	7.0	1.04
	55			
Inquiry Service:				
Accessible	5	8.0	8.3	0.96
Knowledgable	10	8.1	8.1	1.00
Resolve	30	7.5	8.0	0.94
	45			

While the other tools described here will be used frequently at the start of your customer value initiative and returned to occasionally later on, the Competitive Profiles will be continually updated and put in front of decision makers as part of the *Picking Priorities* process (discussed in Step 7 of the *Ten Steps to Mastery*).

---

[2] *In addition, "understandable bills" also showed up in their "overall satisfaction with cost of doing business" Attribute Tree with a weighting of 20%, so focusing on that area would have an impact on both satisfaction with quality and satisfaction with price.*

Waterfall of Needs™

The Waterfall of Needs™ is another way of looking at the business processes that together make up customers' experience of your company. The Waterfall establishes the sequencing and interconnection of your key business processes and summarizes for each the three or four things that are most important to your customers.

I like depicting this interconnection as a waterfall, because it emphasizes that what happens in an upstream process impacts the downstream processes. Let me give an example. Here is a Waterfall of Needs we created for that same insurance company.

The Customer Waterfall of Needs

Sales
- Accessible
- Responsive
- Knowledgeable
- Follow-up

Products
- Reliable
- Features
- Easy to Understand
- Performance Record

Application
- Time Required
- Easy to Apply
- No Problems
- Get Right Coverage

Billing
- No Surprises
- Easy to Understand
- Timely
- Easy to Resolve Problems

Claims
- Progress Report
- Fast Resolution
- No Troubles
- Follow-up

When we started to discuss what this told us about where improvements should be made, we realized that it would be a mistake to think of any of these as stand-alone processes for which one person was accountable. Whose responsibility is it to make sure that there are no surprises on the bill, for example? Clearly part of the accountability sits with the billing department. But if the salesperson has communicated bad information or failed to communicate the full story in the sales process, that can lead to a surprise for the customer on a bill, even if the billing department is doing everything right.

If the product manager has created an extremely complex offering that is difficult for customers to understand, then he or she may bear some responsibility if the customer is surprised by the bill. Or if a clerk working on the application ticks the wrong box, perhaps it's really the clerk's fault? Fixing downstream processes often demands a close look at what upstream processes feed into them, and fixing problems that start there.

I use the Waterfall of Needs for two primary purposes:

- **As a brainstorming tool** when a company is first starting to think about customer value management. It's a good way of shifting people's mindset to think about business processes from a customer perspective.
- **As a way of presenting what we've learned** about how our processes impact customers' perception of value back to decision makers. This format forces them to think about the downstream impact of upstream processes.

Close the Loop by Communicating Value

We all have the tendency to fall into the trap of thinking that if we've done something really spectacular, people will notice. We've worked hard to choose the right value for customers and deliver better value than competitors. Why aren't our results getting any better?

Sometimes it's because we've forgotten to tell customers what we've done. Companies that are really serious about getting a return on their customer value investment make sure they use the Attribute Tree and Competitive Profile information to shape their marketing and advertising strategies and communicate the value explicitly.

One of the hard lessons of customer value management is that customers' perceptions are reality. And we all know that perception gaps can be created by clever marketing strategies. While I was still with AT&T, one of our competitors was stressing in their advertising that their prices were 20% less than AT&T's. The small print read: "Based on the first minute of the long distance call."

Their claim was accurate: As a regulated body at the time, we were still required to charge this higher rate for the first minute of a call. This was because the actual cost of setting up the calling connection was much higher than the cost of keeping the connection. The competition was not subject to this regulatory rule, and could average their costs over the average length of a call.

The reality, however, is that the average long distance call is longer than five minutes, and if you compared the <u>actual</u> overall cost of an AT&T subscriber's long distance bill versus the competitors' charges for the same amount of time, we were only about 2% to 3% higher.

But the competitors' advertising worked, and when we asked customers to compare AT&T prices against the competitor's prices, we found that most people said we were 20% higher. Not only did the market have the wrong perception, even our employees believed we were 20% higher! I've found since that this kind of advertising-induced misperception is not uncommon, and that's why I use customers' ratings of cost rather than the actual price on the Value Map. But it's also why I urge clients to close the loop and communicate value. It's not enough to listen to customers and deliver what they value. You also need to tell them directly that you've done so.

Simple, Yet Hard

That's a quick overview of the customer value management concepts and tools. They've been developed over the years in conjunction with my colleagues and clients as practical responses to real needs we were facing in the business. It takes some effort to learn how to use them and to institute a disciplined and rigorous data collection process that gets you the information you need to populate the tools. The steps for doing so are outlined in Part II of this book in the *Ten Steps to Mastery*.

Once you've done that, though, the process of getting meaningful and actionable customer value data to the decision makers is relatively straightforward. You can free up time to deal with the harder issues of how to create and sustain a customer value focus in your organization – and reap the rewards of profitability and shareholder value.

The Champion and the Change Agent – Setting the Stage for Success

So far, we've had a quick overview of the basic principles, concepts and tools of customer value management. Before we get into the tactical details of instituting a customer value management focus (Part II), I want to explore a bit further this issue of company or organizational culture and change leadership. I said earlier that these so-called "soft" factors can often be the hardest to deal with. Paying some up-front attention to how you're going to think through and address these is an important part of setting the stage for success. You can follow all the tactical steps and become expert in the technical use of the tools – but if the organizational will to make it work isn't there, it won't stick in the long run and you won't get the results you seek.

The Critical Partnership

In my experience, creating organizational will demands a strong partnership between a champion and a change agent:

- The **champion** is a senior business leader who has the credibility and decision-making authority to shape people's goals and create a sense of urgency around the need to change how things are done.
- The **change agent** may be an expert in quality, marketing, customer satisfaction, operational processes or leading complex change initiatives. His or her technical expertise is less important than possession of the right personal qualities to effect change in the organization.

No matter how expert and talented the change agent is, I believe that he or she cannot be successful without the right business leader as supporter and champion. If you think of the change agent as the show's director, the champion is more like the executive producer – the person who provides the venue and gets the resources in place.

It doesn't matter whether the champion is the initiator of the work or is convinced by the team that this is the approach to take. Sometimes it's the champion who sees the "burning platform" (loss in market share, sudden shift in market dynamics), shakes people out of their complacency, and launches customer value management as a response. Sometimes the situation is reversed. The spadework is done at the grassroots level and the business case for taking action is brought to a potential business leader champion.

The important thing is that at some point the business leader champion – holder of the purse strings and maker of strategy decisions – really seizes hold of these concepts and tools, and personally drives them throughout the organization. And the next most important thing is that the champion has the right person to take on full-time leadership of the customer value management initiative – someone who understands that the work is as much about changing culture, beliefs and attitudes as it is about implementing tools and techniques. A full and trusting partnership between these two players is, I believe, the first key to success.

These two people can't do it alone. In this chapter and the case study that follows it we'll look at the challenges of getting all the right players on board and creating the conditions for success from the macro, strategic view of two business leader champions. The first is Paul Wondrasch, with whom I had the pleasure of working in the early 90s at AT&T. The second is Steve Jones, formerly the managing director of Suncorp in Australia. The Suncorp story illustrates a very productive working relationship between Steve and his change agent Ilmar Taimre, and shows the concepts and tools at work. My intention in these stories is to start to build a picture of where you can take customer value management and what it can achieve, to ground the discussion of how exactly you get there.

The Champion's Perspective

I'm going to start by going back in history to draw on the thinking of Paul Wondrasch – both from my personal experience working as his change agent in AT&T, and in his own words as delivered in a speech to the American Marketing Association (AMA) in 1992.

I introduced Paul in Chapter One as successor to the GBS president whom we'd not been able to convince to set the customer value targets we knew we needed in order to make the financial targets. I said then that we'd look at how

Paul succeeded in turning around that business at a very critical point in its history.

Frank Blount: A Customer Value Champion

Paul himself had a strong champion in his boss, group officer Frank Blount, who later was instrumental in giving me the opportunity to take what we'd learned in the GBS division and apply it in different business units and countries. At the time of my first direct interaction with Frank, he was one of the top five officers at AT&T. He was a firm believer in quality, and was struggling with the fact that our top-notch quality efforts didn't seem to be producing improved revenues.

I'd been invited to present what I was learning about customer value at his management team meeting, but they were dealing with some really big issues in that session, and my 9 a.m. time slot kept getting pushed back. Finally at 1 p.m., I was called into the room and asked to do my one-hour presentation in 15 minutes over lunch. Well, I'd had all morning to prepare for this likelihood, so I did my best to deliver my message as concisely and directly as possible. It sure felt like a make-or-break moment in my career!

I focused on the main message: All the data said we were at parity with our competitors on perceived value. It was really a flip of the coin as to where customers would choose to take their business. Because we were the market leader, there was nowhere for us to go but down – and that's where we were heading.

Frank was intrigued. A few days later, he called me into his office and asked me to go over all my data, conclusions and recommendations with him. A week later he called me in again, but this time he'd asked the vice chairman to join him. To make a long story short, Frank soon became a strong champion of customer value management, taking the message and the tools out to other divisions in AT&T, and eventually to some of our customers. It was through Frank that I got my first opportunity to work in New Zealand, which has become a second personal and professional home base for me over the years.

Frank himself went to Australia Telecom, which later became Telstra. In his book on that experience, *Managing in Australia*, co-written with Bob Joss, you can see the strong influence of customer value management concepts in Frank's approach to turning around a business.

From the perspective of a business leader like Paul, the key contributions of the customer value management champion are to:

- Handle fear with facts
- Get the focus right
- Learn from the best; cascade to the rest
- Create alignment
- Fight the real competition
- Provide the score
- Celebrate wins.

We'll explore each of these points in turn in this chapter, to get a high-level view of how a business leader thinks about customer value management.

Handle Fear with Facts

When Paul told his story to the AMA, an audience member got up and spoke about how hard it can be to convince top management to make the fundamental shift that puts the creation of customer value at the center of the business. He wanted to know what really made Paul buy into all this stuff. Paul's answer: "Fear does amazing things. Living through a recession really focuses the mind. And Ray kept bringing me data I couldn't ignore."

John Kotter, an expert on leading change, makes the point that the greatest enemy of change is complacency, and the most difficult challenge facing a leader of change can be creating a sense of urgency.[1] Paul talks often about how easy it is to be complacent when you're the market leader, even in the face of pretty clear signals that you're already in trouble and it's about to get worse.

Let's hear Paul's assessment of the situation we were facing in the early 90s in his own words:

> *The small business market [GBS's target market] is extremely dynamic. It's among the first to feel the effects of an economic downturn, and among the last to recover. Ninety-eight percent of all US businesses are in the small business market – some 20*

---

[1] John Kotter, *Leading Change* (Boston: Harvard Business School Press, 1996), Chapter 3

million in total. Small businesses are this nation's largest employer, generating more than $1 trillion in revenue each year.

A few years ago, our role in that market changed radically. First, AT&T faced deregulation of its communications equipment business. Then divestiture spun off the Local Bell Operating Companies which were AT&T's primary interface with its customers.

The forces unleashed by these two steps generated changes of cataclysmic proportions. Imagine, if you will, what it's like having and then losing a monopoly on your industry. Prior to divestiture, AT&T was the largest corporation in the world, employing one million people. Then, one day, all that changed. Not only were we reduced significantly in size, but we were thrust into a market that was up for grabs. The effect was profound.

In a way it was like owning a store for years, then one day you walk in and find out that you don't own the store any longer; you're just another store clerk. The experience can be paralyzing. It can keep you from facing up to weaknesses and capitalizing on the opportunities.

The immediate impact we felt was a significant drop in market share and revenues, but we held firmly to a staunch belief that the downtrend would level off quickly. The blow of deregulation should have opened our eyes once and for all.

But we were still feeling its effects, and revenue continued to drop for some time until we were forced to look very carefully at our approach to the marketplace.

- Paul Wondrasch, former President, General Business Systems,
   AT&T

Paul credits the customer value data we had been gathering for a few years with finally getting us over this complacency and paralysis. Part of the problem initially was that everything I was showing him was counterintuitive. We'd become very used to working on the basis of our own perception of what the customer should want. It was hard to internalize and act on the fact that when we actually asked customers, they told us something different.

At that time, the accepted wisdom was that pricing was the main lever we had to pull. Our business model was based on the assumption that we could command a premium price because we were offering significantly superior quality. The data was telling us that what customers were seeing was a large price premium with only a modest quality advantage relative to the competition – and increasingly, that slight advantage wasn't worth the price they were paying.

One of our problems was that we couldn't just keep lowering prices to improve market share. As the market leader, we didn't want to keep and grow our share at the cost of gutting margins for the industry as a whole and creating an environment in which nobody could make a profit.

The quality side of the equation was less understood. AT&T had always stood for quality, but Paul and others were starting to understand that we tended to define quality as conformance to internal product and service standards – quality as defined by our best technical minds. A breakthrough for us was recognizing that customers were the ultimate judges of quality – since they'd vote with their dollars if they didn't like what they saw – so we really needed to understand how they defined quality.

It was typical of our complacency that for a while we were comforted by the chart we produced from our customer data, showing customers' perception of our overall quality rising steadily over time. We finally forced ourselves to look at what they were saying about the quality of our competitors. The picture changed dramatically when we realized that we were just keeping up with their rising curve, not widening the gap at all. No wonder we weren't increasing market share!

The data showed us that overall our customers weighted quality at 60% and price at 40% when they made their purchase decisions. That alone should have been enough to make us sit up and take more notice of the quality side of the equation. But even more telling was the fact that when we dug under the averages to look at the picture for specific segments of our market, we found that for some slices of our customer base, the quality weighting was much higher than 60%.

To Paul the message was clear: He had made some significant revenue and market share commitments to shareholders, and fears were growing that these would be impossible to meet. The data was telling him that customer perception of value was a leading indicator of market share and customer loyalty. The data was also telling him that quality improvements were the way to create value for customers. Using the tools of customer value management – Attribute Trees, Competitive Profiles and Waterfalls of Needs – we could zero in on exactly what quality improvements would have the most impact, and we could predict their impact on value perception and market share. We were speaking his language, tying customer data directly to the financial and market share commitments he'd made.

He decided to "fight fear with facts." To Paul this meant setting aside some long-held but unsubstantiated assumptions, trusting the data, owning up to weaknesses, and switching his focus from worrying about the financials to creating customer value through quality improvements. Let's hear in his words what he saw happening:

> *I think for us, when we saw limited change in market share and recognized that we needed a change in our share position to deal with a commitment that I had made to our chairman – for our shareholders – it forced us to sit back and think about what we had to do very differently.*
>
> *We were very fortunate that Ray had been collecting data for years. The data was absolutely compelling. When one looks at a chart and sees the correlation between quality and market share over two to three years, it is the most powerful argument in the world.*
>
> *A lot of us had intuition that said, "No, no – it's a lot of other issues." But Ray kept bringing the data back to the table and saying, "One more time...let me show you how this works. See what happened when we did this in 1988." And we actually put events on that chart, so we could see what changed the customer perception of quality.*
>
> *I don't think in the absence of that data we would have reacted the way we did. I mean, this is compelling. You can see the correlation and it says if we don't deal with this one, we'll never be successful. It doesn't matter how good the product is or how wonderful the marketing promotions are, you have to deal with quality.*
>
> - Paul Wondrasch

Get the Focus Right

There are two parts to getting the focus right:

- First, shifting from focusing on financials and shareholder value to focusing on customer value
- Second, narrowing the focus to the few critical items that customers are telling you have the highest impact.

While the data convinced Paul of the need to do the first, he still found it hard to let go of long-ingrained habits. "It's easy to accept at an intellectual level," he would say, "that if you focus on customer value, shareholder value will take care of itself. But it's much harder on the emotional level to really change behavior."

This is where the champion's personal commitment becomes a make-or-break factor. We found that making some symbolic changes helped. We changed the name of Paul's leadership team from the "Cabinet" to the "Quality Council." We made it a rule that monthly meetings started with a review of customer value data, and the financials would follow – the reverse of our previous procedure. And we took the time we needed to really grapple with the customer data, even if it meant that we never got to the financials.

Paul made a personal rule that whenever he visited a manager in his business division his first request would be, "Show me your customer data," not, "How are the financials?" He stuck to it, and gradually the message started spreading that the boss really believed in this data, and was convinced that focusing on the customer was the path to shareholder value.

But we also needed to decide where we were going to focus our efforts, so we didn't fall into what I call the "our-problem-is-we-have-too-many-problems" syndrome. The customer value tools helped us understand which attributes we needed to focus on, and then we made a concerted effort to hunt down best-in-class practices.

This point is so important I'll repeat it in different words. Many companies and departments make the mistake of trying to implement an annual business plan containing dozens, or even hundreds, of separate initiatives – all claiming to support one or more of the corporate goals. At the end of the year, many of the items on the list haven't even been touched. Others have been deployed in a half-baked way with little impact.

It is much more powerful to tackle a smaller number of critical projects and execute these superbly well. The customer value data can reveal where this focused effort should be directed. Benchmarking can show what it means to perform "superbly well."

Learn from the Best; Cascade to the Rest

One of the things we learned early on in deciding whom to benchmark was that we were wasting our time trying to find the one perfect company on which we could model ourselves and cure all ills. We realized that we needed to be very precise about what we wanted to learn from which company. Each company did one or two things much better than anyone else and that's where we needed to shine the spotlight. We learned about developing quality leadership from Xerox and Milliken, about policy deployment from Florida Power & Light, and about setting objectives from Federal Express.

Paul understood from the beginning that being the champion didn't mean trying to do it all alone. He knew he needed the entire senior team to believe in this as much as he did and be active in taking it forward. As a first step, he insisted that the whole senior team participate in all of the benchmarking visits. It wasn't fair, he said, to make one or two people do the learning, come back as zealots, and then have to convince everyone else of the merits of what they'd experienced. We all needed "to see the movie at the same time," so that we could collectively analyze what we were seeing in the other companies and agree on which aspects would be transferable to our business. We needed the shared experience and a shared language. Again, the investment of so much of the senior team's time spoke for itself in reinforcing how important we thought customer value management was.

But we couldn't involve all 14,000 employees in the benchmarking, and we knew that somehow we needed to educate everybody on new thinking and techniques. As I said earlier, there was a skill void in the company in the fundamentals of quality, and our customer value data had shown us that quality was key.

Paul was the first to admit that the skill void started with him. His solution was to set up an education program for his senior team, looking at everything from process management to statistical methods of measuring quality. He then had the senior team deliver the same program to their direct reports, then this next layer of leaders delivered to their reports, and so on through the reporting structure. Paul's reasoning was that if you expect 14,000 people to buy in to something new and essentially go back to school to learn it, the senior team needs to lead by example, with the entire management team actively engaged.

Having the business leaders actually deliver the program rather than turning it over to the training organization or outside consultants had a two-fold purpose. First, it focused the minds of the leaders and made them really concentrate on understanding the material. Anyone who's been a teacher knows that there's nothing like the prospect of having to teach something the next week to make you really pay attention to your own teacher!

In fact, once they'd gone through the first course in the curriculum – a course that had looked fine at the first cursory examination – the senior team realized that it needed to be re-vectored to be relevant to the organization. All agreed that if they hadn't taken it themselves with the view to teaching the material, they probably wouldn't have recognized that it wasn't really aligned with the company's needs.

Second, it again reinforced the message that this was critical to the business, worth time and attention at the most senior levels. Paul started seeing the impact:

> *The change in the organization once we'd all been through this was amazing. We were all starting to use the same language. You know how when you walk into a room where there's a debate going on, what you usually find is that one person gets quiet, one person leaves, another person dominates and finally someone pulls rank and makes a unilateral decision. Well, for the first time in my life I was seeing people agreeing to use things like decision matrices and multi-voting – all the techniques that we were being taught and teaching were actually being put to use.*

- Paul Wondrasch

So that we didn't lose too much in this cascade process – after all, most of the "teachers" were only half a step ahead of the "students" in their learning – we had an expert facilitator sit in on the sessions to make sure technical details were properly communicated and to answer any questions that the manager leading the course couldn't answer. Whatever depth of technical insight might have been lost in having management lead these sessions was more than compensated for by the strong signal to employees that management was committed.

Create Alignment

Developing baseline skills and getting people talking the same language was a first step in creating alignment in the organization. We next needed to ensure we were all aligned around a common vision and goals.

As painful as it was for the week or two we worked on it, actually writing the vision statement turned out to be the easy part. We had laid the groundwork through our data analysis and our benchmarking, and had gradually developed a common view (reproduced on the following page) of who we were, where we were focused, how we would give back to shareholders, and what role employees played in realizing the vision.

> ### GBS Direction
>
> By consistently exceeding customers' expectations for quality and value, we keep customers for life and achieve global market share growth.
>
> We are globally recognized as the premier provider of premises-based communications solutions for small business environments.
>
> Our people view the GBS business as their own and work together to delight our customers. Decisions are made as close to the customer as possible.
>
> By exceeding our financial commitments, we provide increasing value to our shareholders.

The much more difficult part was bringing these statements to life. How would we actually know what progress we were making toward achieving this vision? What measurable and objective targets should we set for ourselves? What kind of data would capture how we were doing on such soft items as "our people view the GBS business as their own"?

Two things we learned in the process of establishing objectives:

1. **Focus on best in class:** It's far more powerful to measure yourself against best in class in the specific processes you've chosen as your focus (sales, installation, etc.) than to set general relative-to-the-competition goals. This doesn't mean that you should set yourself up against a mythical super company that doesn't exist and try to compete with that on every aspect of your business. All my subsequent work in doing correlations between CVA and market share have shown that it's important to keep CVA focused on your overall scores divided by the average of your competitors' overall scores – not on how you compare to best in class on one attribute. But when it comes to setting goals for your priority areas, you want to look at how you compare to best in class. We decided on the parameters that were critical to our business, determined what best in class looked like for each of these, and set our goals accordingly. In communicating these goals, we kept reinforcing the underlying message: "Excellence is the goal, and the only excellence that counts is our customers' perception of excellence."

2. **Use the goal-setting process to gain buy-in:** Macro goals are only the beginning. Once those were communicated, each team worked out what targets they needed to set to line up with the overall direction of the business.

   It's tempting to try to speed up this process by dictating these goals from on high. But we knew that for the organization to be truly aligned, people needed to own these as personal goals. We took the time to have the right conversations and gather the right data.

   Each branch office, for example, had profit-and-loss accountability and was essentially running its own business. We asked the leaders to use the customer value management tools to determine what was critical to their customers' perception of quality and to look at best in class amongst the competition in their region in each of these areas. Then they worked with individual process owners to set the right performance targets and timetables.

Our goal was to get everyone from the executive offices to the factory floor saying, "I understand the role I play in delivering customer value, and how my team's success is going to be measured." People had a vested interest in taking the time to make sure that the right performance targets were set, because we tied some of their pay to achieving these goals.

As the process unfolded, the role of the senior team at headquarters gradually changed from telling the local managers what to do, to asking what support they needed to reach their objectives. In most cases the people closest to the customer had the best insight into what the customer valued, and the people who owned the processes had the best ideas about how they should be fixed. For example, our earlier intuitive approach had failed to surface the fact that functions such as billing, which we considered to be "back office," really mattered to customers. In fact, billing carried almost the same weight as sales and marketing functions.

Paul asked the billing clerk in one of our locations why we were lagging the competition. The clerk's response: "I'll tell you why – it's because we're run by this" – pointing to a huge binder of procedures and rules – "and the process stinks." Given the authority to make the necessary changes, the employees came up with a simple and streamlined process that made more sense from an internal productivity perspective and better met customers' needs. This was the kind of initiative we wanted to encourage and support.

Fight the Competition

In the Introduction I set out as a first principle of customer value management that "it's not about beating yourself." Paul was convinced that ranking territories against one another is meaningless and counterproductive. It pits one "good guy" against another, siphoning off resources that could be used to win the real battle in the external marketplace.

But this internal focus, this habit of pitting one team against another and handing out awards for the "top branch" or "best in the region," was deeply ingrained in the culture and hard to eliminate. We needed the champion to set the tone by keeping the focus on how Dallas does against the competition in Dallas, not how Dallas does against New York. We also needed alternate ways of recognizing achievement. We switched, for example, from handing out awards for "top branch" to rewarding operations that improved their value equation relative to the competition quarter over quarter.

Provide the Score

To ensure the time invested in setting objectives and meaningful performance targets would pay off, we also found we needed a sustained effort to communicate how we were doing against these targets. The trick is to get the right type and level of information out to the right people. For process owners, for example, the ideal is daily process performance metrics that are proven to be predictive of customers' overall perceptions of value. Senior decision makers probably want a one-page quarterly summary of the key metrics, they want to get it at the same time they get the financial reports, and they want any anomalies or trends explained clearly and concisely.

In later chapters, we'll look at ways of organizing and presenting data to different audiences. The point here is that customer value management will take hold in people's minds only if business leaders commit to keeping the score prominent and visible all the time, not hidden on the back page of some report that few people see. This demands a willingness on the part of the business leader to open the books and make the data widely available, to highlight gains or issues in all his or her personal communication and to encourage teams to find their own creative ways of keeping the group informed and motivated.

Celebrate Wins

We all know how important it is to acknowledge effort and celebrate victories, and we all know how easy it is to neglect this in the general rush of getting things done. The story of the AT&T GBS division president in Chapter One illustrated the danger of setting customer value goals too low to achieve critical financial targets, with the well-meaning intention of keeping employees motivated through success. At the same time, there's also a danger of creating unrealistic expectations of huge gains in the short term, instead of recognizing that making significant improvements in customer value is usually a multi-year proposition. It's easy to get demotivated if you don't see yourself getting anywhere close to your goals.

It's the business leader's role to assess business realities, listen to the advice of customer value experts and make a judgment call as to what customer value goals are required. If these are clearly stretch goals, it's probably wise to acknowledge them as such, and put some creative thought into where quick wins might be realized and celebrated as small victories along a longer path.

Creating Customer Value and Winning Market Share

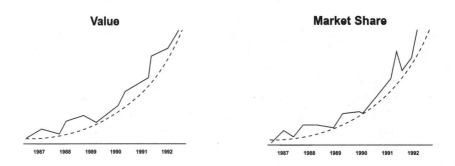

In the case of Paul Wondrasch's effort in the early 1990s, progress was swift and clear. The perceived quality gap started widening, with AT&T's line rising quickly as the competition's line leveled off a bit. The gap also narrowed on price satisfaction. Together, these two factors made customer-perceived value take off dramatically, and with every point in increased value that we achieved, our market share went up one point. One point of market share equated to 8,000 new business customers. The dotted "best-fit" line on the charts above indicates that despite small ups and downs the overall trend was substantial improvement. If you lay the two best-fit lines on top of each other, you'll also see that they're almost identical, allowing for a small lag between improved perceptions of value and greater market share.

A Historical Note

At various points throughout the book you'll find me telling stories of successes achieved within companies or units of companies that are no longer on anybody's "stellar performer" list – such as AT&T. I hope that this subsequent history doesn't obscure the value of successes and lessons learned at a particular point in a company's history. The reasons why success was not sustained over the long term are as varied as the companies in question. Sometimes it's the classic case of new leadership coming in and throwing out the "old" in their desire to put their personal mark on the company. Sometimes people got distracted by the latest management trend and the effort previously devoted to customer value management was diffused.

Other companies have been impacted by significant market discontinuities such as the quick shift from boom to bust in the telecommunications industry that shrunk the market dramatically almost overnight and severely impacted all players.

In the case of AT&T, there are a number of factors at play. Since 1996, when AT&T as I knew it was split up into three businesses (AT&T, Lucent and NCR), each of those businesses has been split and reconfigured and led by a succession of leaders with different visions for the company. In *Big Brand, Big Trouble: Lessons Learned the Hard Way*,[2] Jack Trout provides his analysis of how AT&T went "From Monopoly to Mess." A few of the points he makes are particularly relevant to this study of customer value management:

1. **AT&T made what Trout calls the "everything-for-everybody" mistake.**

AT&T tried to go head-to-head with the so-called "Baby Bells" in cable; with AOL and Yahoo in Internet access; with DEC and IBM in minicomputers; and with IBM, Compaq and Apple in PCs. They started basing strategy on "What do we want to do?" rather than on where they could realistically compete in their target markets.

[2] Jack Trout, *Big Brand, Big Trouble: Lessons Learned the Hard Way.* (John Wiley & Sons, 2001).

2. AT&T started ignoring its own customer data.

Trout points out that AT&T had over 60% market share in long distance but only a 10% lead in overall quality ratings. When you looked at the critical "worth-what-paid-for" score, they were tied with Sprint (which at the time had only 9% market share). Sprint actually passed AT&T on some attributes such as billing quality. Says Trout: "In looking at all these numbers, it was hard to miss the observation that AT&T had allowed its competition to get very close to them in perceptions." (p. 63) My observation is that parity with the competition is always bad news for the market leader, because there's little doubt that the competition will start gaining market share.

3. AT&T wasn't communicating the value.

Trout concluded from the customer value data they had been collecting that the strategic attribute for AT&T's value proposition was reliability. Sprint and MCI, with a fraction of the larger company's expertise, facilities and experience, weren't far behind in customer perception on this critical attribute. And yet in talking to AT&T's technical people, Trout found that in essence the company had a "self-restoring network" that he called "about as dramatic a demonstration of AT&T's reliability that you could ever cook up." (p. 65) But nobody knew about it and the story was never effectively told to the market.

Characteristics of a Champion

By now, you'll be getting a sense of my bias as to what characteristics make a good champion of customer value management. It needs to be someone who:

- Knows how to articulate a vision and motivate people
- Is willing to take risks and go outside the comfort zone
- Is ready to trust the team and the data once the principles and the processes have been explained and accepted
- Is capable of sustained effort, recognizing that making significant improvements in customer value is usually at least a two-year effort
- Has personal credibility with peers, superiors and employees
- Understands that this is a fundamental shift touching every facet of the business, including strategy, processes, and reward systems

- Is willing to devote personal time and energy and be an active proponent of change.

Characteristics of a Change Agent

And what of his or her partner – the change agent? The change agent – the show's director, to revert to the earlier metaphor – shares many of the champion's (producer's) characteristics. This individual is the bridge between the strategic decision makers and the implementers who really make things work on the front lines. With only a handful of direct reports in very large corporations, or all alone in smaller ones, he or she takes on the challenge of leading and managing an extremely complex change effort that touches almost every aspect of the business. To be effective, therefore, I believe the change agent must have the ability to:

- Articulate a clear vision and inspire people to work toward it
- Build coalitions and influence others through the power of personal passion and commitment – without the conferred authority of a large organization and budget
- Understand how things get done in the company – which levers to pull or people to influence to make change happen and make it stick
- Combine strategic thinking skills with a practical process orientation – seeing the big picture, then breaking things down into work flows and manageable tasks
- Earn and keep the respect of the entire organizational community.

The advice I generally give companies is that if you don't have this person, you either need to go out and find a qualified change agent or change your mind about implementing customer value management. This is not the solution to the age-old problem of, "What are we going to do with X – who's a really nice guy and hard worker, but never quite seems to be in the right job?"

In fact, if you're implementing customer value management in a large corporation you probably need several of these people: one change agent for each of the business units involved in the effort, and one to coordinate and lead the charge at the corporate level.

You'll see in the real-life case study from Suncorp (Australia) that follows this chapter an example of a champion and a change agent partnering to institutionalize customer value management in a sizeable financial services organization. The story of J. Heller and Sons, which closes Part I of the book, shows how customer value management techniques were successfully adapted by a family-run hardware business in the United States with just over a dozen employees.

Suncorp
(Australia)

case study

Note on the Case Studies

While I've woven my real-life experiences and stories from colleagues throughout the book, I've anchored each of the three Parts of the book with one or more case studies from different industries in different parts of the world. I hope these stories will help tie together the points I'm making about customer value management, bring the tools and concepts to life, and demonstrate how they work in practice.

The first study looks at a financial services company in Australia. It shows how Suncorp used the tools and concepts of customer value management to choose, deliver and communicate value – and gain competitive advantage.

Some of the most gratifying experiences in my career have come from watching business leaders take the tools and concepts of customer value management with them when their careers move from one company to another. This tells me they see customer value management not as an optional program that may or may not apply to an industry or a company, but as fundamental to their way of doing business.

Formerly head of ANZ Banking in New Zealand and lead champion of the customer value management initiative we instituted there, Steve Jones was managing director and CEO of Suncorp in Australia in the late 1990s. He retired late in 2002, and the program that began under him is continuing under the new leadership. Here's what Steve had to say when I asked him why he chose to champion the customer value management approach when he took on the Suncorp role:

The best way to answer that is to think about what's important to a business. The obvious reason to take this approach is the connection between business success in financial terms and high levels of customer satisfaction and customer perception of value. These links have now been academically proven – but way before that, common sense told us that high perception of customer value was going to translate into revenue growth, customer loyalty, word of mouth referral and so on. To me it's pretty obvious that there's a direct financial benefit for the company.

The second reason is I've never been in a company where the staff didn't want to believe that the company's main purpose was to do a good job for its customers. If customers are happy with the company's products and services, then the staff can feel proud of the place and know that their work is worthwhile. I think there's a real connection between high levels of staff satisfaction and achievement of high levels of customer satisfaction.

Most people don't get up and go to work every day to help the company make more profits. They go for other, more important reasons: doing a good job; doing the right thing for the customer. There's a certain altruism I see in many people. They want a relationship with customers that everyone feels good about.

The first reason is reason enough, but the second reason is a really powerful one. If it were accepted and understood by more executives, it might make the drive for customer satisfaction really take hold in more companies.

So why wouldn't I take these ideas with me into new companies? Being a CEO is a lot like being a head coach. When successful head coaches go to a new team, they take with them the fundamentals that made them successful. So it's not surprising that people who believe customer value is very important take this belief with them when they move companies. Your beliefs about what's important in business don't change.

- Steve Jones, formerly Managing Director and CEO of Suncorp

Steve goes on to say that the customer value management approach was a particularly good fit for the challenge he was facing at Suncorp when he first took over the reins. The company was formed late in 1996 through the merger of three Australian financial institutions: Suncorp, Metway Bank and Queensland Industry Development Corporation. The new organization offers a full range of banking and insurance products.

From 1996, when Suncorp Metway (currently Suncorp) was formed, to 2002, the market capitalization of the company increased from approximately $2.2 billion to more than $6 billion. For Steve, focusing on customer value management was in part a way of keeping people focused on a common purpose and the guiding principles that had made them successful in the past:

> *These were three fairly small financial institutions relative to their national competitors, and they came together in a merger to create a significant medium-sized institution. They had successfully competed against much larger companies in part because they delivered a different style and tone of service: friendlier, more approachable, perceived as being simpler and easier to deal with. Their image was that of the classic community bank, as opposed to a multinational institution.*
>
> *When they came together to form a bigger organisation, it would have been easy to lose that sense of customer orientation. We were going through significant downsizing. Greater efficiency had been a goal of the merger. The three small institutions realized that on their own they didn't have enough economies of scale to compete, and would eventually have been squeezed out of the industry. In that kind of atmosphere it would have been easy to get internally focused and forget their guiding principle of delivering value to customers.*
>
> *So I made a point of talking about customer value add right from the beginning and putting measures in place and working it into peoples' performance objectives. We started doing small things to cumulatively drive customer satisfaction, as well as big things that we could advertise both inside and outside the company. This was all aimed at preserving and fostering the customer orientation that the three small companies had had before the merger.*
>
> - Steve Jones

Steve brought in Ilmar Taimre to be his director of customer satisfaction and lead change agent on this project. I should note here that while to many of my colleagues customer satisfaction and customer value are very distinct concepts, within Suncorp the terms are sometimes used interchangeably to refer to their overall program of customer value management. For the purposes of this story, it's important to know that Suncorp is actually using the customer value concepts and tools described in this book – which they sometimes call CVA or customer value add and sometimes customer satisfaction.

Ilmar had worked for Steve in ANZ New Zealand, and subsequently had the opportunity to apply customer value management in his role as head of personal banking for ANZ Grindlays Bank in India. Under his leadership, Suncorp's customer value management program followed a rigorous process of choosing, delivering and communicating value.

With customer value data and tools such as Value Maps telling them that no competitor had yet staked out the "superior service" high ground, the company decided to build on their history of strength in that area, making the delivery of world-class services their strategic goal. The illustrations that follow are taken directly from internal Suncorp presentations:

Having chosen their value proposition, they used their CVA data to decide where to focus:

To Achieve World-Class Service

Add "Positives"	Remove "Negatives"
• "Blue Ribbon Service Initiatives" • "Best Practice" standards in key service encounters • Other product & service quality improvements	• Reduce number of defects • Fix remaining problems superbly well

---

The "Blue Ribbon Service Initiatives" mentioned here are a best practice in:

- identifying business processes linked to the drivers of value for customers
- setting internal performance measures to focus the improvement efforts (delivering value)
- communicating the results to customers.

Steve Jones feels strongly that rhetoric about customer value must be backed with quantifiable service guarantees that are made explicit to customers:

> *Your good intentions are worth nothing. What it all gets down to is, "What have you actually done that can be measured and verified? What is it that you're doing to make your intentions real?"*
>
> *I'm really keen on standards of service. For example, we learned one thing that matters to customers is getting their car repaired quickly if they've been in an accident. So we instituted a service standard that says if customers can drive their car into one of our assessment centres, 95% of the time we'll have the car repaired and back to them within seven days. In the few instances where it takes longer, we'll provide a free courtesy car.*
>
> *That's our internal standard. We can hope that customers notice on their own that we have this standard and are meeting it, or we can make sure that they notice it by turning it into a guarantee. A guarantee is just a way to make the standard more newsworthy, something we can communicate to current customers and advertise to potential customers. When you communicate it, you have to make sure it's not just an empty guarantee, but something that's backed up with particulars on how you're delivering what you've promised.*
>
> - Steve Jones

The team first turned to the Waterfall of Needs to get them thinking about how customers experience the company.

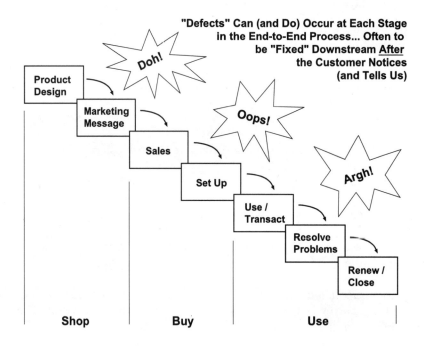

They then delved deeper into the customer value data to determine where to focus:

"Blue Ribbon Service Initiatives"

Implement & deliver "world-class" performance on one critical aspect of service:

- which we know customers value highly
- which no other competitor - including us today - is able to deliver.

Clearly publicise (e.g. with a service promise) what we can consistently deliver, in a way which:

- touches a "hot button" in the market
  - positively with customers
  - negatively with our competitors
- may even be newsworthy.

Most of their Blue Ribbon Service commitments have a strong enough impact in the marketplace to justify separate newspaper and sometimes television advertisements. All of the commitments are published together in a straightforward brochure that makes explicit the link between what the company learns in its customer research, and what it's doing in response. The cover reads simply: "Remember service? We do."

Sample Content – Suncorp Brochure

The Customer Asked:

- **"Buying a home can be stressful enough, do we really need to wait to find out how much we can borrow?"**

- **I've spent time and energy house hunting, and I don't want to go through the same hassle finding a home loan."**

- **"When I find the car I want to buy, I want to find out quickly if I'm able to afford it."**

- **"I want a fast Internet banking service that's there when I want it."**

- **"If I do have a problem, I want it resolved quickly without being given the runaround."**

Customer Service Commitments:

- We're committed to confirming how much you can borrow, with one 15-minute phone call to xxx-xxxx.

- We're committed to having our Mobile Lenders come to you at the agreed time or we'll rebate the Loan Establishment Fee.

- We're committed to advising personal loan customers how much you can borrow with one 5-minute phone call to xxx-xxxx.

- We're committed to being available 99% of the time. And our Internet banking site has been rated Australia's fastest on average.

- We're committed to acknowledging your complaint within 24 hours. At this time we'll assign a person to look after your problem.

Ilmar picks up the story here and talks about what these public commitments mean inside the company:

> *The key is to become very serious about picking important customer-focused internal process measures that you can track daily. First we used the CVA methodology to survey customers to find out what's most important to them, and where we and our competitors were falling short. Then, we assigned senior business leaders and teams to do the hard work of making significant process improvements in areas where we already knew from the CVA data analysis we would achieve the greatest impact quickly. But if you don't start locking these improvements down by making them part of the day-to-day operational management focus, it's too easy to drift back into a "near-enough-is-good-enough" approach.*
>
> *That's why we decided to publish our commitments to our customers, and why we've made them so specific. It's easy to advertise that "we have the fastest turnaround time in the industry in dealing with business loan applications." But if you quantify it – commit to a five-day turnaround standard when the industry average is more like 12 days (it sometimes stretches out to many weeks) – then we're able to continually measure how we're doing against our performance standards. And we are in a position to take action as soon as something starts to slip. When you make a very specific public promise, especially when it's backed by a tangible guarantee, it really crystallises everyone's thinking.*
>
> - Ilmar Taimre, Director of Customer Satisfaction, Suncorp

The company put a lot of effort into choosing the right commitments and making sure that the promises could be met before their advertising campaigns and brochures were launched. For example, one simple service standard which most of us can relate to stems directly from the customer value research. It's a promise about time spent in queues during branch visits. The customer survey data showed that "time spent waiting" was a high leverage area for improvement, because the mean rating was low and the impact weight was relatively high.

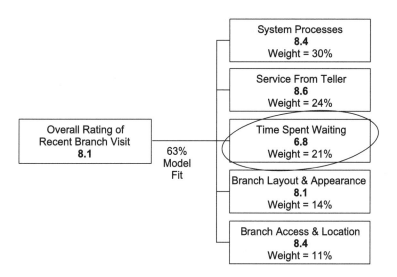

The survey data also showed that customers expect to be served within five minutes. The number of people who find anything more than a five-minute wait to be acceptable is very low, as indicated by the steep cliff in the graph below.

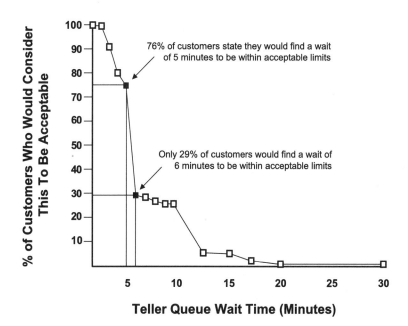

When they first saw this data, Suncorp wasn't measuring actual wait times, but knew from the survey data that 36% of customers perceived they were waiting longer than five minutes to be served. An internal process standard of "95% in five minutes" was adopted and in February of 2001 a Six Sigma project was launched to deliver this standard. By May of 2001 the company was consistently meeting the standard.

Branch Queue Wait Time Standard

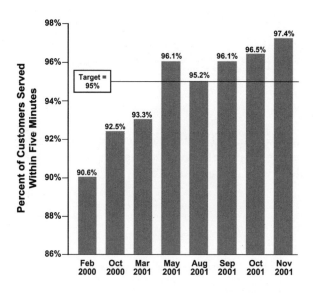

In October of that year, they published this customer promise and backed it with a focused newspaper and television advertising campaign:

> *Suncorp dislikes teller queues as much as you. Which is why we schedule more staff to keep the busier periods flowing. Nine times out of ten you'll wait less than five minutes. And when you're in a hurry, every minute counts.*

Notice how the promise is worded. It makes a clear link to what matters to customers. It gives a quantifiable service guarantee that is actually being met. And, to Steve's point earlier, it not only tells customers what the company guarantees, but how the company plans to make good on this promise – by scheduling more staff in busier periods. The initiative has paid off in higher ratings on customers' experience of branch visits, as measured by Suncorp's surveys of branch customers.

Customer Satisfaction - Branch Service

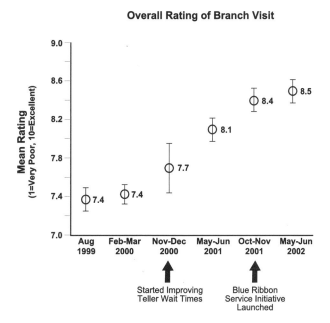

Overall Rating of Branch Visit

Suncorp is achieving similar results for all their Blue Ribbon Service Initiatives.

One important lesson Suncorp learned is that a significant process improvement, if it really matters to customers, will quickly translate into a significant increase in applicable "recent experience" customer surveys. However, depending on the frequency with which customers experience a particular service, it can take a little longer for these improvements to be reflected in the value survey results for the market as a whole. The intensity of advertising/communication campaigns is a key factor as well.

In Part II, Step 2, we'll talk in detail about the difference between "recent experience" or transaction surveys and overall market value surveys, and their respective roles in customer value management. For the purposes of this case, it's sufficient to know that transaction surveys measure customer satisfaction with a specific interaction they've had with the company (getting a loan, making a claim), whereas value surveys measure how the market as a whole perceives the value of your offering relative to your competition.

For Suncorp, the customer value data clearly showed that the time taken to repair their car was a key driver of value for motor insurance customers. So when Suncorp started delivering to their seven-day car repair promise, the satisfaction ratings of customers who had recently experienced this level of service increased dramatically and quickly. However, it took a little longer for the total customer base to recognize that the company was delivering a significant service quality improvement, simply because in any one year most motor insurance customers do not have a claim. That's why communicating value is so important. You want those of your customers and competitors' customers who may not experience this value in the short-term to understand that it will be there when they need it.

The following charts show trends for Suncorp's recent experience survey results and the overall market value survey results for their motor insurance customers in Queensland. Notice that the customers who actually experienced the motor insurance claim process increased their rating of this service encounter very quickly after the Blue Ribbon Service Initiative was publicly launched and delivering on its promises.

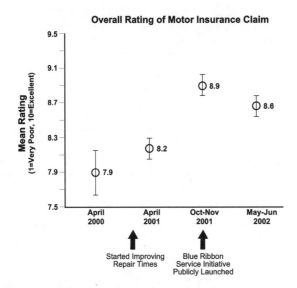

However, it took another six months or so of advertising – helped out by word-of-mouth communication from satisfied customers to their friends – before the relative product and service quality ratio in this market started to break out of the flat trend of previous years.

Product and Service Quality

Mean Rating (1=Very Poor, 10=Excellent)

Sep-Nov 1999: 7.7
Feb-Mar 2000: 7.7
Oct-Nov 2000: 7.8
May-Jun 2001: 7.7
Oct-Nov 2001: 8.0
May-Jun 2002: 8.2

Car Repair Blue Ribbon
Service Initiative Publicly Launched

For this and the other Blue Ribbon Service Initiatives Suncorp has been launching, customers are even taking the time to write Steve congratulatory letters. Comments like the following indicate the focus on world-class services is being noticed and valued by customers:

> *I must say I was totally impressed with your people to whom I spoke on the telephone and also at the Assessment Centre at Aspley. They could not have been more courteous and the service they provided was such that I could not help but be impressed. Their service exceeded my expectation.*
>
> - Darryl Somerville, Office Managing Partner
>   PriceWaterhouseCoopers, Brisbane (14 March 2001)

The obvious next questions are, "How much is it costing Suncorp to meet all these great customer promises, and are they seeing a payoff in business results?" I asked Ilmar about costs.

> *Steve Jones' overall challenge to the management team was to meet all these commitments without adding to the cost of the process. That's big. In some instances Steve might authorize a small increase to headcount in the short term, in order to make rapid progress on*

delivering an important customer service standard. But our complementary goal has to be to quickly figure out how to deliver the new service standard without eroding the productivity gains we have worked so hard to achieve. In fact, in addition to our customer satisfaction goal of being number one in all lines of business, we also have a company-wide goal of improving productivity faster than inflation, year over year. We are firmly of the view that it is possible to achieve both goals at the same time.

What we've consistently found is that the work required to make things faster or simpler from the customers' perspective involves reducing complexity, inefficiency and errors – and hence cost – in our internal systems and processes. That's one reason why, in addition to my original change agent role for customer satisfaction in the company, I now have a similar role for Six Sigma and "Workouts": the two cornerstones of the company-wide process improvement toolbox we have adopted in Suncorp. Sometimes it's simply a question of reviewing what we do through the lens of its real purpose. For example, one of our challenges was to reduce the amount of time customers spend on hold when they call in with an inquiry, without adding a lot of call centre staff. We used a version of the GE "Workout" concept, which is essentially a one-day workshop to focus a cross-functional team on solving a specific problem, to trim down the call centre scripts. We got all the key stakeholders in the room (people from legal, from marketing, front-line staff) and we went through every statement asking, "Why is it here?" At the end of the day we made it a few sentences shorter. That doesn't sound like a big thing, but our call centres handle many thousands of calls every day. If you trim each call just a little, you can save a lot of time and money.

In some cases it was a matter of making our processes more explicit, both to ourselves and to our customers. There were a few cases where we actually added sentences to call centre scripts because we realized we weren't giving customers "closure". We had fully handled the customer's claim over the phone and would be sending them the cheque – but we hadn't told them that, so they didn't know it was all done until the money actually arrived. Because they weren't sure where things stood, too many customers were calling us back a second time, which added to call centre workloads. By adding a few extra words in the scripts to make things clearer to customers, we reduced those customer callbacks.

There was a similar issue in our handling of business loan applications. When we started trying to figure out how to meet a service standard of five-day turnaround (which is what our survey data indicated customers considered a fair and reasonable time) we found that we hadn't clearly defined either for ourselves or for our customers when the process began and ended. We realised we had to be very explicit as to when we had everything we needed from the customer and the clock was starting on the five days. Otherwise, they were never sure whether we were going to call back tomorrow and ask for more information.

We also never formally and consistently told them exactly when the loan was approved. Sometimes we'd phone them, sometimes we'd let them know when they came into the bank for something else, sometimes they just found out when the final paperwork arrived. This is clearly unacceptable to a business customer whose ability to capitalise on an opportunity can depend on how quickly he or she knows for certain that the loan is approved.

- Ilmar Taimre

By making the process faster and simpler from the customer perspective, Suncorp is also stripping out inefficiency from the business perspective. They're both saving the company money and increasing the value delivered to customers. The fact that process improvement can reduce cost while driving value for customers (and by extension revenue for the company) is clearly recognized within Suncorp. That's not to say that investments aren't sometimes needed. But Suncorp does not accept customer satisfaction as a soft excuse for tolerating increasing costs or poor productivity gains relative to industry best practice.

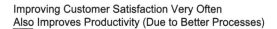

Improving Customer Satisfaction Very Often
<u>Also</u> Improves Productivity (Due to Better Processes)

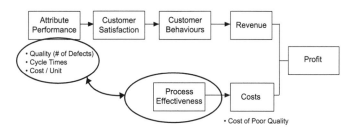

On the revenue side of the equation, Ilmar and his team recently analyzed the relationship between how customers in key markets answer the "worth-what-paid-for" question and the average number of products they hold with Suncorp.   Here's a representative chart showing the results:

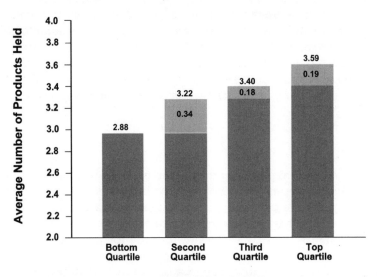

"Worth What Paid For (WWPF)"
Is Linked to Product Holdings...

Average Product Holdings Per WWPF Quartile
Example - Transaction Banking Market, Queensland 2000-2002

The results are similar for other segments of the Queensland market. The top 25% of customers in terms of their "worth-what-paid-for" ratings of Suncorp hold on average 0.6 to 0.7 more products with the company than those in the bottom quartile. That may not sound like much, but Suncorp calculates that each 0.1 gain the company makes in the number of products sold to Queensland-based customers is worth approximately $15 million in pre-tax profit.   An increase of 0.6 across their total Queensland customer base represents a pre-tax profit difference of $90 million. Last year, Suncorp more than doubled the size of its customer base across Australia by acquiring GIO, one of the largest general insurers in the country. This acquisition makes the potential profit impact of increased "worth-what-paid-for" scores even higher.

One key to Suncorp's success in mastering and reaping the benefits of customer value management is that they've been very clear about what's expected of employees and how performance will be measured. Critical process improvement measures are reflected in the performance assessment system as "key performance indicators." At the top of the organization, Steve Jones had overall customer satisfaction commitments to the board as well as specific performance goals on initiatives that he was championing, such as the Blue Ribbon Service Initiatives and the Six Sigma quality improvement projects that help them meet their service guarantees. Steve stresses the importance of assigning the right targets and objectives at all levels of the organization:

> *Don't just give people the outcome measures (CVA score) that you want them to aspire to. Require the steps and the actions and the initiatives that will create that score. In financial terms, it's the difference between giving someone just the bottom line objectives and helping them see what's required to get there: e.g. grow revenue x% while growing cost no more than y% while keeping asset utilization at z factor. Give people specific objectives on things that you know will drive the score. That's the lesson we learned.*
>
> - Steve Jones

He also has this to say to CEOs considering starting the journey:

> *If you need to be convinced that it's worthwhile, don't start. If you are convinced and are about to start it, be prepared for a three- to five-year horizon for it to become part of the culture and of the value that the marketplace associates with the company. Because <u>doing</u> real things takes a lot more time than <u>saying</u> you're going to do things.*
>
> - Steve Jones

Steve has always been determined to put his money where his mouth is when it comes to delivering on promises made to customers. He also puts money in people's pockets for doing the right things for customers by tying the performance and reward structures to meeting service guarantees.

But most importantly, he understands that the employee satisfaction/customer satisfaction link is not about making employees happy so they'll feel like making customers happy. He sees that most employees care a lot about delivering good value to customers and feeling proud of what they're doing. And that's what so many executives miss when they put together vision and mission statements that are all about being number one in the market and making a lot of money. These are good goals to have, but by themselves they aren't going to tap into the power and passion you get when people care about what they're doing.

J. Heller and Sons (United States)

case study

Applying Customer Value Management in Small Businesses:
J. Heller and Sons Hardware

Much of my work has been with large companies. That hasn't been a conscious decision on my part. It's simply a fact that most of the requests for help I've received have come from people in large companies who have heard about my work from their counterparts in other large companies. Many of the stories in this book are from companies with hundreds or thousands of employees, although in most cases the work has begun in one or two smaller business units and then gradually spread to other parts of the company.

But the principles of customer value management apply equally well in small businesses. Some of the greatest satisfaction in my career has come from helping such businesses adapt the work to their reality and budgets. And so to even out the picture, I'd like to tell the story of how Scott and Cyndi Heller used customer value management to turn around a 14-person, family-owned hardware business.

Scott is the fourth generation of the Heller family to take over the reins of J. Heller and Sons, Inc. The company was founded at the turn of the last century as a wholesale distributor of maintenance, repair and operation (MRO) industrial hardware supplies. For its first eighty years, J. Heller supplied the thriving manufacturing market in New Jersey, meeting an expanding need in the business-to-business arena. The company was an established, recognized and valued member of the community.

Scott and Cyndi were asked to run the business when Scott's father fell suddenly ill and was forced to retire. For both, this was an unexpected turn in their career plans:

> *I really had no intention of going into the family business. I'd dabbled in it a bit from time to time, but my interests lay elsewhere. All of that changed when my father became ill and the business just fell into our laps.*
>
> - Scott Heller

> *To tell the truth, at first it felt like a bit of an albatross around our necks. It was a mature business in a difficult market; it had stopped growing, and it was struggling. We saw that it really needed a boost to make it vital.*
>
> - Cyndi Heller

Albatross though it might be, there was no question of just letting the business go under, so Scott and Cyndi stepped up to the challenge of restoring it to profitability. They set out to create a five-year plan, and contacted the Small Business Administration (SBA) office in Newark, New Jersey for advice and counseling. By a circuitous route involving a summer intern from Vanderbilt University who was working with me at the time and boarding with the Hellers, I was introduced to Cyndi and her SBA counselor in the early 90s, and the three of us discussed my approach to customer value management. We all thought it was worth seeing what customer value management could do for them, and so I found myself some weeks later in what we call the "Iron Bound" section of Newark after store closing, making a presentation to Scott, Cyndi and their 14 employees.

Scott describes the market situation they were facing:

> *At the time we were just trying to keep our heads above water. The trend in the industry was toward consolidation, with bigger hardware stores competing on price and gradually taking over the market. At the same time, the consultants we'd talked to were telling us that to become profitable we had to raise our prices and make better friends with our customers.*
>
> *We were suffering from the transition from the old days, in which customers were happy to wait until we got in stock what they needed. For our customer base, it was now critical that they got the material quickly. For us, that meant we could no longer shop*

around for the best price. We paid the price we had to in order to satisfy our customers' needs at the right time. But that made it impossible to compete with the bigger outlets on price, and so we had a problem. Some of our customers were actually costing us money. If we raised prices, how were we going to stay friends with our customers, much less become "better friends" as our consultants were advising? How could we make customers see the value of the service we were providing?

- Scott Heller

Cyndi picks up the story to talk about the situation inside the company:

We had a sense of hope and really believed the business could improve, and somehow we needed to communicate that to the employees. The employees had been there a long time, and they had a lot of great knowledge about the business and about our customers. Our problem was that we didn't know how to get this knowledge out of them and put it to work. What Ray helped us to do was to put our collective knowledge together, find common ground, and capitalize on our strengths.

- Cyndi Heller

J. Heller and Sons Hardware wasn't in a financial position to do the kind of extensive market research I recommend to companies making decisions that have millions of revenue dollars riding on them. They weren't going to do the econometric modeling I'll talk about in Step 6 of the *Ten Steps to Mastery* to thoroughly understand what drives value for their customers and their competitors' customers. But because they were small enough that their staff interacted directly with customers every day, they had a fabulous base of customer knowledge. The challenge was to surface this and turn it into actionable data.

In Step 7 of the *Ten Steps* I'll talk about what I call "desktop research." This involves getting the experts in the company together to brainstorm what they know about how customers experience their company and what matters to customers. We then use this information to do a preliminary cut at populating the customer value management tools I introduced in Chapter Two. Normally, we then do the surveying and statistical analysis to validate the Attribute Trees, compare how we <u>think</u> customers rate us relative to the competition with what they actually say, and create Competitive Profiles for business leaders to use in decision making. This is extremely important for large businesses playing in a variety of markets with a large customer base.

But for a small family business like J. Heller and Sons with a relatively small customer base, there was good value simply in doing the desktop research.

> *Ray brought us all together in some workshops to talk about why we existed as a business, what our customers valued and how they rated us in these critical areas. For the first time we had our inside and outside sales people together sharing their insights about customers in a structured way. It was great: By the end of the workshops everybody knew what we were trying to accomplish together. The workshops gave us a sense of unity and purpose. I've still got the flipcharts from that session!*
>
> - Cyndi Heller

> *It was a difficult situation. It was an old business, and we were suddenly introducing new and alien ideas. Also, everybody realized we weren't in the best financial shape, and would need to pare down staff. Eventually we went from 14 employees to 8, mostly through attrition. But in the process, we set a standard of proactive communication, and we ended up with a core staff committed to working together to deliver the best customer value we were capable of.*
>
> - Scott Heller

For me, the satisfying moment in the workshops was when the light bulb went on and people suddenly started to see what we were trying to do. They figuratively rolled up their sleeves, began throwing out ideas and started working with one another's insights. We ended up with a pretty clear picture of J. Heller and Sons' value proposition – the value that they knew they could deliver effectively – and who their most valuable customers were. They followed up this internal session with some external research:

We sent out about 60 letters: 10 to really good customers, 30 to mediocre customers, and 20 to companies we hoped would become customers. This mini-survey was for us an opportunity to learn about the market: who our target customers were doing business with and why, what their experience with us was, how we stacked up, what they thought about how we presented ourselves to them.

\- Scott Heller

The workshops and the surveys helped us keep things focused. We were able to advertise and brag to our customers, saying, "This is what we do really well." We'd stopped trying to be everything to everybody and became much more specific. Our salespeople learned to say, "This is what we do. If that's not what you need, here's a reference for somebody who offers the specific thing that you want."

This also helped us understand better what we needed from our vendors. We went back and renegotiated some of our vendor relationships; others we just ended because they didn't fit what we now understood to be our business model.

\- Cyndi Heller

Scott and Cyndi's five-year plan to make the business profitable was a success. In fact, they started turning a profit after 14 months. As early as four months from the start of the plan, weekly cash flow snapshots indicated they had gained control over expenses and were effectively marshaling their resources. Gradually, the improvements became more consistent and eventually were sustained over consecutive quarters.

At the same time, however, they were finding that the long hours they were putting into the business were incompatible with their plans to start a family, and so they started looking for a buyer. Scott explains:

When we were looking to sell, we consciously decided to sell to someone who understood and would maintain the business focus we had chosen. We looked at a couple of very large companies, but they weren't willing to go that route. We finally sold to a local competitor who was intrigued by the high profit margin we were managing to maintain.

I practically guaranteed him that we would bring him 80% of our business if he bought the company. He said that was impossible. We feel a certain sense of victory that we were proved right.

- Scott Heller

I remember pulling out our stack of surveys and saying, "Here's how we know our customers will stay loyal if you maintain this focus." And the numbers backed us up. One year after the sale, in dollar terms he was getting about 80% of our previous business. I know that's unheard of. We were so confident because the customers we had focused on retaining were "our customers." They valued the service we offered and they were willing to pay for it.

- Cyndi Heller

Scott and Cyndi made the business profitable by using the tools and concepts of customer value management to understand which customers were most valuable to them and what exactly these customers wanted, by delivering this value to them, and then "bragging about" (communicating) the value to these customers. By selling to a buyer who shared their vision that the business existed to provide value to customers, they managed to turn the family business over to someone with the capital and resources to sustain and grow it over the long term. The Hellers could then move on to their next career adventure.

Part II:
Ten Steps to Mastery

Ten Steps:
An Overview

chapter four

If you're part of a change agent team and will actually be responsible for implementing customer value management, by this point you're probably thinking, "Okay, that's all great advice, but how do we get this going? What do we do first? Whom do we need on the team? What's in the work plan?"

In Part II of the book, the emphasis shifts from concepts to practical application. It's focused on what you need to get in place internally to effectively choose, deliver and communicate value to customers. I'll introduce the *Ten Steps to Mastery* in this short overview chapter, and then we'll work through the steps one by one in detail. I'll also talk in this chapter about the makeup of the implementation team — the combination of internal and out-sourced knowledge and skills required to make this process work.

As in Part I, we'll close Part II with real-life case studies of how business leaders in different industries and countries have applied the steps and achieved success.

So far, we've talked about three very high-level steps:

Value Creation

Choose Value	Deliver Value	Communicate Value
Focus Your Priorities	Manage Your Business Processes	Educate the Market

We've laid out a vision of knowing what drives value for customers, and knowing this in enough detail that you can identify key sub-attributes which link to your internal business processes. These processes can in turn be managed, measured and improved. If you put that understanding all together on one chart, it might look like this:

Customer Value Management System

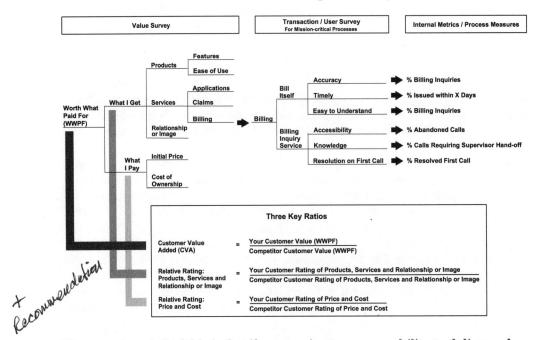

The premise of all of this is that if you can improve your ability to deliver value to customers, it will drive competitive advantage and pay off in increased market share, revenue and shareholder value. The work you do to make your processes more efficient in the name of delivering customer value often has a positive impact on the cost side of the Profit Tree as well.

Profit Tree
Impact of Billing Branch on Revenue and Cost

But what do you need to actually do within the company to make all this happen? I've found it helpful to think of customer value management as a process consisting of ten steps.

Ten Steps to Mastery

Step 1   Get Aligned: *Work Plans that Work*
Step 2   Get Focused: *Survey Strategy and Scope*
Step 3   Get Prepared: *Secrets of Survey Design*
Step 4   Capture the Data: *Effective Survey Processes*
Step 5   Share the Results: *Reports Leaders Will Use*
Step 6   Analyze the Data: *Customer Value Tools*
Step 7   Pick Priorities: *Action Planning and Implementation*
Step 8   Get Going: *Engagement Strategies*
Step 9   Reward Success: *Recognition Practices*
Step 10 Embed the Concepts: *Sustainment Strategies*

 Get Aligned: *Work Plans that Work*

This step is about reaching agreement among the change agent, the champion and other important sponsors on the purpose or mission of the customer value initiative; the objectives, performance measures and targets, scope of the work, operating principles, resources and roles, and support from top level leadership.

 Get Focused: *Survey Strategy and Scope*

Most organizations will not try to collect and use customer value data on all of their customers – the law of diminishing returns kicks in at some point. This step is about deciding how you're going to study the market: what type of surveys you'll do, what markets you'll survey, what individuals you'll survey, and how you'll manage the respondent list.

Get Prepared: *Secrets of Survey Design*

It's important to decide on survey standards and guidelines up front, so that data is collected and reported in a consistent and useable manner. In this step, we'll look at the data collection standards I recommend and why, how to focus the survey on the right value drivers, and what to look for in the survey testing phase.

Capture the Data: *Effective Survey Processes*

I recommend that you outsource to an outside vendor the actual interaction with customers to collect the data. This step walks you through thinking about what you need in an outside market research firm, which vendor to engage, and how to manage/monitor the survey process in partnership with that vendor. To my mind, it's important to find a vendor who is willing to work in partnership with you rather than sell you their proprietary approach.

 Share the Results: *Reports Leaders Will Use*

In this step you'll think about how and when to publish high-level results to the executive leadership for maximum impact. I provide a template for the regular high-level report to officers and key executives, and I discuss who should get the report and how the report comes together. At this point in the process, you're simply answering the question, "What's the score?"

 Analyze the Data: *Customer Value Tools*

This is a "how-to" chapter, focused on the mechanics of using the customer value management tools described in Chapter Two to understand the data, so that important decisions can be made. It covers the Slippery Slope, the Value Map, assigning impact weights to Attribute Trees, Competitive Profiles and the Waterfall of Needs.

 Pick Priorities: *Action Planning and Implementation*

Also a "how-to" chapter, this step first looks at how to design and deliver hands-on workshops that get people rolling up their sleeves and actually working with the data. It suggests a method of picking priorities, ensuring they're aligned with the company's business priorities and with what customers are saying they value. This step is key to ensuring people understand, accept, and are prepared to act on the customer data.

 Get Going: *Engagement Strategies*

Here we turn to strategies that deal with what might be considered "softer" aspects of customer value management: getting the leadership engaged, understanding who in the organization needs to be engaged and how, looking for early wins, and dealing with resistance.

Reward Success: *Recognition Practices*

This is a critical chapter for all senior leaders in the company. The best-designed customer value management program in the world will fail if this piece isn't done right – and it can be tricky to do. This step looks at how to set appropriate individual and team-based performance targets. It covers both monetary and nonmonetary ways of reinforcing customer value management principles and recognizing success.

 Embed the Concepts: *Sustainment Strategies*

We touch on three areas here: keeping the leadership commitment visible, integrating customer value management into business processes such as business strategy planning and advertising, and integrating customer value management into people processes such as training.

One caveat: While these activities are presented as a linear sequence roughly in the order in which they're likely to take place, they're intended to work together as an integrated system. So, for example, while *Reward Success* shows up as Step 9, you really have to start thinking about recognition practices up front as you establish your work plan. It will certainly shape your discussions with business leaders as you present and work with results, and it will be an important element of your education and training program.

Building the Team

Before we launch into Step 1, let's talk about what skills the change agent needs to have on the team. The good news is that you don't need to build a huge new and costly organization. People across the company will be mobilized and involved in making the effort successful, but the core team driving the work can stay quite small. The core team does need to include the following capabilities:

- Market research
- Information system management
- Econometrics/statistics
- Communication/training.

Market Research

While in most cases the actual research is outsourced to a third party, in my experience it's important to have someone with market research expertise on the internal team to make sure you get what you need from your outside vendor, to provide continuity, and to remind people inside the company how important it is to maintain this "customer listening post."

Market research companies tend to have their preferred way of doing things. It's faster, easier and more profitable for them if they can sign you on to their proprietary approach. But be careful: Their approach may not bring you sufficient data and the <u>right</u> data to populate the customer value management tools. The best companies will be willing to work with you to understand what you require (a framework is set out in Step 3 – *Secrets of Survey Design*) and adjust the approach to meet your needs.

So you need a market researcher on the team to work with the chosen vendor. The researcher should be:

- Knowledgeable about survey design/layout
- Trained and skilled in market research techniques
- Able to design and conduct telephone surveys and focus groups
- Up to speed on the basics of sampling techniques, such as assembling a sampling frame.

The market researcher's role is to design, develop and manage the data collection process, and to be the prime interface with the vendor. He or she manages the survey respondent list and coordinates customer activities with other internal stakeholders (such as the account teams and marketing folks). He or she brings knowledge of customers and internal stakeholders to bear on the analysis of data and structuring of reports.

Information System Management

The information system specialist takes the lead on designing and managing the customer value database, maintaining the actual survey and making sure it adheres to agreed standards, creating and supporting inquiry and reporting tools that make the data accessible to others. As a "super user" of the database, he or she performs basic data manipulation and helps others extract the information they need in the appropriate format.

In companies that have developed very sophisticated Web applications, this role may be split between two people: a detail-oriented administrator who handles the database and manages reporting, and an IS specialist who does development work and takes on such tasks as integrating with other databases (e.g. finance, employee satisfaction) to support statistical linkage studies.

However the roles are structured, it's important to have people on the team who cover these skill and knowledge bases:

- Expertise in the design and use of databases, including structuring reports to meet a broad range of user needs
- Expertise in Web-based programming for analyzing and reporting survey data
- "Power user" of spreadsheet, presentation, word-processing and desktop publishing software
- Strong project management skills.

Econometrics/Statistics

To get real value from your data, you need at least one person who knows how to perform sophisticated statistical analysis – regression, multivariate and time series methods, for example – and how to translate the results into layperson's terms. If you decide to contract the actual statistical modeling to an outside source, you still need someone in-house with a deep understanding of how to read and interpret statistical models. I've introduced the term "econometrics" here because a general knowledge of statistics is not sufficient. It's important to get someone who understands the practical application of statistics to economic problems – which is what econometrics is all about. You're likely looking for someone who has:

- A graduate degree in statistics or a relevant field that relies heavily on statistics, such as economics
- Experience in econometrics and data mining
- The ability to bridge the worlds of strategy, analysis and practical implementation
- In-depth knowledge of the business
- Understanding of business process management.

Communication/Training

A significant and sustained communication and training effort is critical to embedding customer value management into the company culture. Many will be involved in this effort: the business leader champions; the change agent or agents; the quality, marketing or customer satisfaction professionals who embrace this work and become "ambassadors" to the rest of the company; internal and external corporate communications teams; human resources and training professionals.

Ideally, over time this becomes an organic process that is not controlled by any central function or master plan. But it's wise in the initial stages to put someone in charge of being a catalyst for these activities and keeping them coordinated. This person's role is to make sure that your messages are clear, consistent and pitched appropriately to different audiences. He or she will lead efforts to get key players outside the direct customer value management team up to speed on what this work means for the company, and to think through how best to use all available channels to get the messages out.

This may be a full-time position or a part-time assignment, depending on the size of the organization, the scope of the communication effort and the extent to which the change agent can play this role him or herself. Characteristics of this player:

- Able to synthesize and present complex concepts in simple terms, without losing accuracy or richness
- Understands how communication and training happen in the organization (channels, key players, important influencers) and is respected by this community
- Understands the different communication needs, styles and preferred vehicles of the various audience segments targeted for communication and training
- Able to create comprehensive communication and training strategies and plans.

Summary of Resource Requirements

Discipline	Internal Team	Could Be Outsourced
Change Management	• Dedicated change agent	• Expert advice on customer value management and change processes (recommended)
Market Research	• Market researcher with sufficient knowledge to guide survey design and process	• Data collection (recommended)
Information System Management	• Person (full or part-time) to manage survey and database • May need IS specialist to handle integration with other databases for sophisticated statistical analysis	
Econometrics/ Statistics	• Person with deep understanding of how to read and interpret statistical models	• Actual statistical modeling (recommended)
Communication/ Training	• Person (full or part-time) to guide design and coordination of communication/training strategy	• Facilitation of experiential workshops (recommended) • Other training design/ delivery tasks • Writing

Many more players from across the organization will join the team as the work progresses. It will be important, for example, to ensure that the right people are working on integrating customer value management with business planning processes and with process or quality management initiatives (such as Six Sigma). You may want to consider bringing in external experts to help the leaders of these initiatives within your organization make the right links.

But with these core resources in place, you're ready to begin the process of gaining **commitment**, doing customer value **research**, planning and implementing the right **response** to what you learn in your research, and getting **reinforcement** strategies in place to sustain your customer value focus.

The *Ten Steps to Mastery* will guide you on your way.

Ten Steps to Mastery

Commitment			Research			Response		Reinforcement	
1	2	3	4	5	6	7	8	9	10
Align	Focus	Prepare	Capture	Share	Analyze	Pick Priorities	Get Going	Reward Success	Embed Concepts

Step 1–Get Aligned: *Work Plans that Work*

chapter five

I said in Chapter Three that the partnership between a champion and a change agent is critical to the success of a customer value management initiative. Key to the success of this partnership is alignment between these players on the:

- **Purpose or mission** of the initiative
- **Objectives**, or how you intend to achieve the mission
- **Performance measures and targets**, or how you will measure success in meeting the objectives
- **Scope of the work**
- **Operating principles** that define the approach
- **Resources** required to deliver the objectives
- **Support and visibility** the work will get from top level leadership.

This chapter introduces the first of the *Ten Steps to Mastery*, which is designed to get this alignment.

Ten Steps to Mastery

Commitment			Research			Response		Reinforcement	
1	2	3	4	5	6	7	8	9	10
Align	Focus	Prepare	Capture	Share	Analyze	Pick Priorities	Get Going	Reward Success	Embed Concepts

Step 1: Get Aligned: *Work Plans that Work*

1. **Articulate Purpose or Mission**
2. **Clarify Objectives**
3. **Establish Performance Measures/Targets**
4. **Define Scope of Work**
5. **Establish Operating Principles**
6. **Determine Resource Requirements**
7. **Decide Leadership Structure**

How these seven items actually get fleshed out and endorsed will vary depending on your company culture – how your company tends to like going about these things. It will also vary according to the path by which the company has reached the decision to do customer value management. Sometimes this comes about through a top-down process in which the champion and his or her peers map out what the company needs, then look for the right change agent to take on the challenge. In other cases, it's a bottom-up process. A group of committed customer satisfaction or quality professionals sketch out their vision for the company and sell it to the leadership.

What's absolutely critical is that the champion and the change agent share an understanding of what the work is about and feel personal ownership of its success. What doesn't work, in my experience, is to hand either party a finished document and have him or her sign off on it. Unless there's been an opportunity for real dialogue in which hard questions get asked, general statements get translated into concrete specifics, contentious issues get debated, you can't be sure that the lead players have reached a deep understanding of what they're signing up to.

Both champion and change agent bear responsibility for making sure this kind of dialogue happens – not just at the outset, but at regular intervals and key milestones along the journey. This is even more important when you have a large organization with change agents at the business unit and corporate levels. It's not enough for the corporate champion and change agent to be aligned if the business unit change agents are galloping off in different directions. It may be that you need to create a formal mechanism like a Council or a Steering Committee to keep all these players agreed on the course and pulling in the same direction. We'll talk more about this when we discuss engagement strategies in Step 8.

1. Articulate Purpose or Mission

I firmly believe that a successful customer value management initiative needs a formal statement of its overall mission. You may prefer to call this set of words your "purpose" or "charter" or "rallying cry" or something else that has special meaning to your team. Whatever it's called, the best ones I've seen share certain characteristics. They're:

- **Concrete:** New members joining the initiative instantly "get" what the team is committed to accomplishing. The mission is written in clear, simple and concrete language, not abstract concepts.

- **Authoritative:** The mission opens doors to key influencers, decision makers and implementers across the company, and makes them want to clear any obstacles out of the path. It has a ring of authority.
- **Relevant:** The mission serves as a touchstone when the team starts to lose sight of the larger purpose in the day-to-day details. It provides practical guidance on both strategic and tactical decisions encountered by the team.

My own professional mission is:

> *To help organizations bring customer data to the leadership table and use it with the same level of understanding, discipline and passion as financial data to achieve business results.*

Naturally I'm gratified when companies incorporate some of these words or ideas into their own mission statements. But what's truly important is that the words you use are:

- Grounded in your business
- Linked to your overall corporate vision
- Understood by your team
- Ratified by the senior executive officer responsible for the business unit, market segment, region or product group that's taking on the mission.

The business leader playing the champion role clearly needs to be on board, but in the case of more broad-based initiatives in large companies you may also need to get the endorsement of higher-level executive sponsors.

The mission sets the framework. It should be short, easy to remember and capture the essence of what you're trying to do. You want to have something that people will sign on to with enthusiasm.

2. Clarify Objectives

The statement of objectives puts some flesh on the bones and gives clear direction as to how the mission is to be achieved. Here is a sample template of objectives – something I've used to get companies thinking about what's most important to them.

Customer Value Management Initiative Objectives

1. Develop competitive market intelligence

- Segment our customer base and understand which product, geographic and market segments are most critical to our business strategy
- Understand our current competitive position in these segments
- Understand our key competitors in these segments and their strategies
- Develop an in-depth understanding of customers' needs in relation to product, service and price (both "hard" and "soft" factors)
- Understand current customer perceptions of the value they get for our products and services given the price paid, and how this compares to the competition
- Identify key internal business process measures that are linked to external customer needs and predictive of customer satisfaction and loyalty.

2. Develop planning process to capitalize on market intelligence

- Institute a process to measure our performance relative to major competitors in targeted markets
- Set up a performance target and goal-setting process grounded in statistical models that predict improvements required to deliver strategic goals
- Establish a priority-setting process to help focus scarce resources on high-leverage opportunities
- Institute a process that calibrates the level of satisfaction required on each of the attributes to increase customer loyalty
- Create a process that determines relative importance of product, service and price attributes (and sub-attributes) to customers' perception of value.

3. Create action plans to improve customer value

- Understand how customer needs link to key business processes and functions
- Identify process metrics that will help front-line staff measure, manage and improve

- Build skills within the company to develop and implement customer-focused process improvements
- Institute a process that facilitates cross-divisional and cross-functional cooperation and action.

4. Create "pull" for customer value data/tools and encourage widespread application

- Understand and institute best practices in communicating the data in a meaningful, actionable format
- Institute an experiential learning approach to help people:
  - manage their function or process using customer value tools and techniques
  - understand, accept and use the data effectively
- Institute strategies to overcome skepticism and resistance to change.

5. Recognize, reinforce and repeat success

- Monitor action plan and track results
- Recognize and celebrate success
- Learn from experience and institutionalize best practices
- Design and implement reward strategies to reinforce desired behavior.

These are generic objectives and as such are likely to be broadly applicable to most companies who have chosen the customer value management path. They need to be debated, tweaked, added to, slimmed down, reworded and otherwise massaged to be relevant to and owned by your team. But this list should give you a good head start.

The third program objective in the list above ("Create action plans") talks about developing specific process improvement objectives. This is a different kind of objective that will emerge from your own analysis of customer value data and links to your business processes. Not surprisingly, these will vary greatly from company to company. We'll look at how you do that in Step 8 – *Pick Priorities*.

3. Establish Performance Measures/Targets

I've just highlighted the difference between the overall objectives of the customer value management program and the specific process performance objectives that get set as part of that program. This is a useful distinction to keep in mind when you're determining performance metrics.

Most successful companies take the time to attach performance metrics to the high-level objectives of their customer value management initiative. These are not the "billing-inquiries-should-be-resolved-in-one-call" type of metric that we'll be discussing later on. These relate more to the success of the core customer value management team in achieving its mission and objectives.

Some examples of this type of metric:

- Full market intelligence is available in standard customer value management format for targeted market segments accounting for 80% of revenues (within six months)
- All account and support teams that service these customers have received two days of training on understanding and using the data (within eight months)
- Customer value management training and workshops are getting average ratings of at least 8 (on a 10-point scale) from participants on the question, "Was the value you got from the training worth the time and effort invested?"
- Board members are regularly receiving customer value management data bundled with financial data the week before quarterly meetings
- Customer value management tools and concepts are in regular use across the top four business units (within 12 months)
- Overall CVA scores in target markets have risen from 0.98 to 1.03 (within 12 months).

Defining Success

I believe it's worth taking the time at the outset to go through each of your program objectives one by one, asking:

- How will we know when we've achieved this objective?
- How quickly do we expect to (or need to) achieve this?
- What are the key milestones along the way that we should be tracking to?
- How will we measure achievement and where will we get the data?

A performance metric and target should be set for each of the objectives you identify. To be useful, the target should be clear, measurable (exactly how will you measure this?) and time-bound (exactly when do you aim to reach this level of performance?). Anyone who has gone through this type of exercise knows it's not always as easy as it sounds. It can be particularly difficult to get useful data on items such as, "Institute strategies to overcome skepticism and resistance to change."

You don't want to get so bogged down in internal sensing that you forget it's all about delivering value to customers. But I believe it's worthwhile investing a small amount of time in quick surveys of internal stakeholders or interviews with sponsors and decision makers. This can help you make ongoing adjustments to the program to better meet the company's objectives, saving time and money over the long run. And it's useful to think up front about the few key metrics that will convince decision makers that your program is adding value. You don't want to be scrambling around at budget time trying to retroactively establish baselines and show quantifiable improvement.

A Common Pitfall: Overpromising

A potential trap for customer value management teams is getting so caught up in their excitement about what's possible that they publicly overpromise and then fail to deliver. If you have the luxury of working quietly in the background until you have confidence in your data and your analysis of where the big improvements will come from, then by all means take the time.

Sometimes you don't have the luxury, because you're down to the last few inches of burning platform and the company or business unit will fail unless drastic improvements come quickly. Sometimes, as I've argued before in the GBS story, business realities force you to set performance targets that are a real stretch. In that case, I suggest you acknowledge them as such, explain to people why they've been set so high, then get down to figuring out how to achieve them.

But if you rashly promise unrealistic improvements for whatever reason of personal pride or ambition, then be aware that you're risking the credibility of the entire approach if you don't deliver. You may not get a second chance.

Getting the Facts: Notes from a Practitioner at We Energies

In my experience, two elements need to come together before customer value management really takes off in a company: a robust measurement system with a history of capturing reliable data, and a leader committed to driving change. Some people seem to believe that if you measure customer satisfaction hard enough, the scores will go up all on their own. It doesn't work that way: Measurement by itself doesn't move scores. On the other hand, if a leader rushes into making decisions and setting goals based on incomplete or inaccurate data, then he or she is risking the credibility of the whole initiative.

Hard as it is to pull off, the best approach is to get the measurement system in place well before customer value management becomes a strategic priority for the company as a whole. I've had six years now to establish a coherent set of data collection guidelines and standards for We Energies, to understand the correlations between customer value and financial indicators, to analyze what customers are telling us about what they value, and to build management confidence in our data. We've been using the data all along but not, in my view, to its full potential. That changed this year, as the company leadership put a stronger focus than ever on delivering customer value. They were ready to set goals and make data-driven decisions, and we were ready with the information they need.

I work for a large utility. When we originally started collecting data, the perceived wisdom was that deregulation was coming at us like a locomotive down the track and we'd better start getting our arms around what it takes to keep customers in a deregulated market.

In my opinion, we weren't ready in the first year or two to set ambitious customer value goals. We had lots of customer data, but we weren't collecting it in a way that made it easy to understand and use. The surveys looked like they had been put together by committee, with lots of different scales and approaches all mixed together: some yes/no questions, some 3-point scales, some 5-point scales, some 7-point scales and so on. We had to start by streamlining this infrastructure and building a database that could really be used for decision making.

While deregulation hasn't happened as quickly as people expected, we have been through a period of intense change. For a long time it looked as though we were going to merge with another company, but that fell through. Then we successfully acquired a third company and were occupied with the integration and restructuring work that entails.

Interestingly, you can see the effects of these and other events in our data. You can also see where we perhaps missed opportunities to communicate better to customers about what was going on and correct some misperceptions. Even in a regulated industry like ours, our data shows a strong correlation between return on assets (a key financial indicator) and customer value – not just for us, but also for other utilities that we have plotted using publicly available information.

As we improved our data collection and analysis practices, individual managers started understanding that we could give them actionable feedback related to processes that shape the customer experience. They feel strongly enough about the value of this data that they pay for it themselves and keep the data collection effort alive.

Over time we have been able to marry transactional surveys (focusing on key events in the customer experience) with our value surveys (focusing on what drives customer perception of value in the marketplace as a whole) to build a more complete and in-depth picture of the business. We're now starting to apply this data to strategy setting for the company. We've turned a corner and the right elements have converged.

Our business context made it possible for us to start small and build our data history before making large-scale commitments based on the data. Even if your timelines are much shorter, my message to change leaders is that before you start making public commitments to goals, seek out and talk to anyone and everyone in your company who has been collecting customer data. Find out what you already have and what you will need to support your efforts. You may be surprised to find that people have been quietly collecting really useful information that has had little visibility to top management.

If you're one of the people who has been struggling to keep customer data collection alive, my message to you is "keep evangelizing." If you're collecting and presenting relevant information in a practical and actionable way, your leadership needs you.

- John Acherman, Manager of Customer Value Management, We Energies

4. Define Scope of Work

With your mission and objectives as a base and the *Ten Steps* as a guide, it should be relatively easy to create a four- to six-page work plan that maps out how you will meet the objectives. This is something you'll revisit and add detail to as you work through each step in the process. The purpose of doing a high-level version up front is to make sure there's agreement among the key players as to what's in or out of scope for the initiative, as well as who's accountable on each item.

While the corporate-level change agent will likely take the lead on drafting this plan, normally he or she will involve the key implementers in fleshing out and finalizing the document. The "key implementer" group would normally include functional leaders outside of the core customer value team and business unit teams who have their own customer value plans. Negotiating to clarity at the beginning can save misunderstanding later on, particularly in those areas where the work crosses onto the "turf" of other teams such as marketing, quality or training.

The actual contents of your work plan will be driven by your objectives and ideally will touch upon each of the *Ten Steps*. I want to highlight here a few areas that companies sometimes miss or struggle with.

Market Segments

You want to select the most relevant and important markets as your focus: markets that account for a significant percentage of your revenue. If washing machines account for 70% of your revenue and microwaves for 5%, then you'll probably want to focus on the market segment that buys washing machines. Unless, that is, you've identified microwaves as a strategic growth area and have ambitious plans for growing that number exponentially.

A major pitfall I've seen companies fall into is not defining markets with sufficient accuracy. If you mush together data on different markets in which you're facing different competitors, you will not be able to get clarity on your value proposition and you will not get actionable data. On the other hand, if you try to slice and dice too finely – breaking markets down into the smallest of segments – you may have difficulty getting enough customers responding to provide a reliable sample.

Note from My Partner at CVM Latin America

It's critical to continually remind ourselves that customer demand segments the market, not the company offering. Some companies *make the mistake of developing complex segmentation models built around predetermined product and marketing strategies. They're based on what the company would <u>like</u> different types of customers to need – not on what customers think they need. Good segmentation models take into account:*

- ***Profitability*** *– how much profit is generated for the company by different types of customers*
- ***The customer life cycle*** *– recognizing customers' needs and value perceptions change over time (e.g. when they purchase, during ownership, when they need to purchase again)*
- ***Habits of use*** *– how different customers use the product*
- ***Purchasing options*** *– the presence of niche competitors targeting specific customer segments*
- ***Both "hard" and "soft" variables*** *– identifying "hard" variables (socio-economic level, age, etc.) before considering "soft" variables (such as lifestyle, emotional needs, attitudes).*

- Marcelo Chanis, Partner, Customer Value Management
  Latin America

The balancing act here is that you know at some point a product manager is going to say, "Give me my numbers," and you want to be able to provide actionable data that will help in making the right decisions for that specific business. One of the things I've seen happen as companies gain a deeper understanding of their markets is that they discover the way they think about their market segments doesn't actually match customers' purchasing habits. A possible outcome is an internal reorganization to more closely align their product groups and account teams with how the market works.

In Step 2 we'll look in more detail at the issue of defining markets and determining whom to survey.

Existing Data and Initiatives

In the excitement of launching something new, it's easy to forget that there's probably lots of good data already available and many useful things are happening that you can build on. I suggest building into your scope of work the mining of existing data. This is likely to give you a good head start on determining which criteria strongly impact customers' determination of value in each market. Sometimes you'll find you can package historical data using customer value management techniques to give people new insights into why the numbers have been behaving the way they have, and suggest how to have better control over them. Many companies, for example, can produce a Slippery Slope from existing data.

It's also useful to look at what's already happening in the organization and think about what you need to do more of, what you need to tweak to be more aligned with the new direction, and what you need to stop.

Communication

In Step 5 – *Share the Results* and Step 6 – *Analyze the Data*, we'll look at ways of packaging and publishing customer value results. In Step 8 – *Pick Priorities*, I'll describe an approach to training people how to read and use the data that has had success in many companies. But the impact of these very focused actions can increase exponentially if they're done in the context of a broad-based and coordinated communication plan. As part of the work plan, I suggest you think about how you engage opinion shapers and any communications professionals who support them in permeating the company with customer value messages.

The balancing act here is between the discipline and control that keeps everyone "on message" (thereby avoiding confusion) and the personal spin and passion that bring the message to life. You want all the key business leaders and as many ambassadors as you can enlist out there evangelizing customer value management concepts and techniques – not as a stand-alone topic, but as an integral part of the business strategy. You want to get them in the habit of asking their teams about things that matter to the customer before they ask how the financials look.

But if the leaders are all defining terms differently and sending different messages, this may actually serve to undermine the integrity of the customer value management initiative. On the other hand, if they're reading from scripts prepared by a third party, the message will fall flat and it will sound like corporate propaganda – the latest flavor-of-the-month message that no doubt will be superseded by something else next month.

In my experience, a little coordination goes a long way. A simple message board, like the kind they put in briefing kits for public figures or the media, can keep all communicators focused on the important points while leaving them the freedom to share their own stories and examples. A short glossary can ensure that everyone is working from a common definition of the most critical terms.

A calendar of high-profile events can make it possible to get the best possible leverage from each communication opportunity. It's obvious, for example, that a customer value workshop or training event scheduled for the week <u>after</u> the CEO cites raising CVA scores as top priority for the next six months will have more impact than an event scheduled for the week <u>before</u> this announcement. But, surprisingly, this kind of opportunity for leverage is often missed, simply because a different group is responsible for each event and nobody has been charged with taking the big picture view. Assigning someone to keep the calendar and link all the parties involved in planning communication helps make sure that the messages build in a logical way and each event has impact.

Reward and Recognition

Now is the time to start the dialogue among your team, business leaders and your compensation experts to set the stage for building the right kind of measures into your reward and recognition program. You will need to decide:

- **Whom to reward:** Some companies make the mistake of thinking that rewards for creating customer value should be confined to customer-facing employees. In my mind, they're failing to recognize that customer value is created when all employees work together toward a common purpose with a common set of measures.
- **What to reward:** When I talk about a common set of measures, I don't mean that everyone should be assessed against the same high-level measure. I'm a firm believer in establishing measures that people can clearly link to the work they do. If they can see the direct impact of their actions in the measure, it will have meaning to them. They also, however, need to see how all the measures work together to impact customers' overall perception of value. We'll discuss this further in Step 9 – *Reward Success*.
- **How to reward:** We'll also discuss both cash and non-cash (performance reviews, promotion practices, visibility in the company) ways of reinforcing customer value management principles and recognizing those who are successfully applying them.

Operational Issues

My advice is to keep operational issues such as complaints handling out of scope when you're launching a customer value management initiative. While over time it may make sense to include them, at the outset these activities will only distract the team from the significant data collection/analysis and change management challenges they face.

5. Establish Operating Principles

In my opinion, there are several critical operating principles that should be debated and agreed upon at the outset. I'll describe those here, recognizing that each team will have others that have specific relevance to them.

Measurement Standards and Guidelines

"Calibrate my mind," Alex Mandl, the CFO of AT&T, used to say to me as I put customer value data in front of him. "Help me read and understand what I'm seeing."

You'll find this task becomes much easier over the long term if you agree on and document a set of measurement standards and guidelines in the early planning stages. Human nature being what it is, each new person coming into the team will bring personal biases and a desire to leave his or her own stamp on the work. If that means changing from a 10-point scale to a 5-point scale, or changing the anchors so that 10 becomes poor rather than excellent, you're in trouble. It's kind of like shifting from Fahrenheit to Celsius: The number 32 suddenly has a whole new meaning!

If you change the meaning of your measures, all the effort you've put into training decision makers to read the numbers goes out the window, along with a good measure of credibility. Business leaders don't expect a new CFO to put his or her own creative stamp on the layout of a balance sheet; why would they expect the meaning of the customer data to shift because one person came up with a bright new idea?

Because the practice of customer value management is still relatively new, there is no one accepted standard. I have my own opinions as to which standards will prove to be most reliable, based on my experiences. I'll share these in the discussion of Step 3 – *Get Prepared*. What I'm highlighting here is that the standards and guidelines you agree on should be formally captured in the list of operating principles that dictate how the work will be approached. I suggest you consider standards relating to:

- Sampling requirements
- Questionnaire design
- Response wording
- Response scales, labels and definition
- Survey methods
- Attribute impact weight method.

Standards will become particularly important when you're negotiating with outside market research companies, who will bring their own biases to the table. If you're a large company and have autonomous teams leading this work in each business unit, it's also critical that all of the teams agree to use common standards. If everyone's measuring things in a different way, nothing can be meaningfully rolled up to the corporate level. This lessens the impact of everybody's work and creates a general sense of confusion and chaos that undermines its value. If a large number of people are involved in capturing data, it may be wise to set up a standards team (making sure it includes a representative from finance) to periodically review the standards and make sure everything's working.

Audit and Review

Alex also used to tell me that I was the "conscience of the company." That sure made me think about how much confidence I had in the data I was putting forward!

I suggest you include in your operating principles some discussion of the audit and review standards you will adhere to and what this means in practice. Reliability of data is all-important in overcoming the skeptics and building credibility.

We decided early on at AT&T to use best practices in financial management as the benchmark we would meet in our management of customer value information. Nothing went into the report to the board without being thoroughly reviewed. You wouldn't put a number in a financial report with a footnote that said, "Danger – small sample size may impact the reliability of this figure." So we decided we wouldn't do that with the customer data either.

We looked at and discussed all the numbers and the key correlations, in an attempt to catch and investigate anomalies before they were made public. If the CVA numbers had gone up but market share was unexpectedly lagging, we wanted first to be sure that our numbers were accurate, and if they were, to be able to explain what other factors were at play.

From time to time we went back after the initial release and did a thorough audit of numbers that had passed the first review to be absolutely sure that the surveys were being done properly and the software was programmed to do the calculations correctly. If we found errors, we corrected them in the next report.

Working Relationships

While a small core team can drive data collection and analysis, implementing the changes that result in improvement involves stakeholders from across the company. As part of your up-front planning, it's useful to think about how you intend to interact with partners across the company and to negotiate the relationship with them. The list of partners could include:

- Customer value teams that report into business units rather than the central corporate group
- Staff groups whose work may overlap with or complement the customer value team's work – like marketing, quality, sales, finance, human resources, training, communication
- Owners of end-to-end processes that have significant impact on the customer's experience of the company.

It may be a matter of gaining initial buy-in, keeping the teams informed and then collaborating with them at an appropriate time later on. You may need to set up a formal structure that brings stakeholders together to set and adjust direction or share learnings and best practices. Or there may be existing forums with related agendas that you can tap into rather then setting up a duplicative structure that just means more time in meetings.

Clarifying expectations early on as to how other groups or forums will be involved and the role they will play in decision making helps avoid a scramble to bring key players up to speed midstream, as well as the worry of smoothing ruffled feathers later on.

Note from a Change Agent: Getting Buy-in

To be effective, a change agent must be personally convinced that customer value management is right for the organisation. Without this inner conviction, we cannot hope to persuade others, or to overcome the setbacks that will surely come.

However, there is a potential "dark side" here. The benefits of customer value management may seem compelling and obvious to us. So much so, that it may be hard to fathom why many of our colleagues don't seem to "get it" the first time they hear about it. Sometimes, when things aren't going so well, we may even fall into the trap of thinking that people have an obligation to agree with us; or, worse still, of concluding that there is something wrong with them *when they don't! That would be a mistake.*

One basic principle of human behaviour is that most people do not lightly modify their long-held views. None of us is predisposed to quickly change our accustomed ways of doing things. People are simply not made like that. If we forget this, then our attempts to convince others may end up being perceived as arrogant or irritatingly dogmatic, no matter how noble our intentions. Just because something strikes us as important and worthwhile does not mean that it will instantly – or even ever – strike others the same way.

We can save ourselves a lot of frustration if we accept the fact that achieving positive and lasting change takes time. The bigger the organisation, the longer it usually takes. This is especially true if there is no major crisis facing the company, or no urgent reason to alter course.

It's not that people in the organisation are against customer value management. It's just that they're not actively for it. Not yet anyway. Initially, most of our colleagues will simply be neutral. They haven't really thought about it much. And, very likely, they won't have the spare time or energy to start thinking about it now, just because you – the change agent – happen to be excited.

If we stop to reflect, it becomes clear that the essential first step to getting "buy in" is listening. Our ability to influence the opinions of key stakeholders and decision-makers is directly dependent on how well we understand their view of the world. The best way to gain that understanding is to actively listen to what they have to say. Only then can we talk, with any relevance, about how the principles and methods of customer value management can help them deal with their immediate problems and concerns. And even then, we will still need plenty of patience and perseverance to move things forward, one small step at a time. But, above all, if we can't establish a clear connection with the top priorities of the people we hope to convince, then we can't reasonably expect them to pay a lot of attention to what we have to say.

- Ilmar Taimre

Continuous Improvement

I also believe it's useful for the core team to discuss at the outset how they intend to track and use the performance measures that relate to their own success in meeting program objectives.   How often will they get this information and in what format? How will the performance data impact team or individual rewards? Who will be responsible for recommending changes in process or approach to improve performance? Who will decide on these recommendations?   How will the team keep up to speed on emerging best practices and benchmarks on customer value management, and ensure that their own program continues to be state of the art?

6. Determine Resource Requirements

"What will this cost me to do well?" is one of the first questions out of the mouths of business leaders deciding whether to launch a customer value management initiative. It's also one of the most difficult questions for a neophyte change agent to answer. Here are some guidelines on what to consider in making this assessment.

Core Team

I described in Chapter Four the small core team that I believe is critical to success. Depending on the complexity of your business, that's likely to come out to salaries and associated costs for four to seven full-time equivalents:

- Change agent – full time
- Market researcher – full time
- Information systems manager – one or two full-time roles
- Econometrician/statistician – may be part-time or outsourced
- Communication/training professional – may be part-time.

External Costs

Your outside vendor costs will vary depending on how you're collecting data (interviews, focus groups, telephone surveys, web surveys) and the number of customers you're surveying. Since you're probably already doing some type of customer surveying, you should be able to get some ballpark estimates here. Also be clear on whether you're talking about redirecting money that is already being spent elsewhere, or asking for additional sums, or a combination of both.

Redirecting Effort

Most companies are already collecting a lot of customer data. Customer value management helps you do this in a more disciplined and focused way. It focuses on identifying very clearly the data that you do need, so you can stop collecting data you don't need.

One of the things that has killed many performance improvement programs over the years – quality programs, for example – is that they're seen as additional to all the things that are already happening. This is not fair: People can only do so much, and if you just heap more work onto them nothing will get done well. Customer value management should guide redirection of effort. You need to decide what you're going to stop or make a lower priority. It's important to ensure that priorities are made clear.

- Dr. Nick Fisher

You may also need to include costs of external consultants to help with the initial setup of the program, and to design and deliver training on the tools and approaches. Other possible cost items: materials for training and workshops, software to manage and report the customer value data, the cost of getting econometric models produced.

As a benchmark, I've found that companies or business units within companies can run an effective customer value management program at a cost of 0.02% or 0.03% of revenues. I've seen companies invest as much as 0.5% of revenues.

If you multiply that out for a large company, it comes out to a big number. But before you start panicking, think about how much it costs to track and use financial data. Count how many people are directly hired to manage finances. Think about the systems investment that is made and the cost of producing reports. How much do you spend on outside auditors? Companies that I've worked with have reached about 6 to 8% of revenues in total devoted to financial management doing this calculation. That's "six percent" – not "zero point six percent" – and it's a long way from two- or three-one-hundredths of a percent.

If you're really serious about using customer data with the same discipline and passion as financial data, then this amount of investment surely seems reasonable. In fact, I find that financial officers who really understand customer value management tend to be the strongest supporters of investing in doing this well. After all, the financial data – while you couldn't run a company without it – is an after-the-fact summary of how you've done. If you think in military terms, what it records is how much impact your missiles have had. With customer data, you're investing in strategic intelligence that will help you laser guide the missiles to the right targets for maximum impact, instead of just lobbing them in the general direction of the enemy.

7. Decide Leadership Structure

I spent a lot of time in Chapter Three on the role of the business leader champion and what he or she can do to create the right environment for getting customer value management off the ground. If you skipped that chapter, and you're a change agent about to close on a set of mutual expectations with your champion, I suggest you go back and read it. I won't repeat myself here.

But I will add one point. Rightly or wrongly, in my experience with organizations, people read a lot into reporting structures. If the change agent has direct-line reporting into the CEO or the head of the business unit, then people will believe that this work is on the radar screen of the senior leaders and treat it with appropriate attention and respect. Launching the initiative as a special project that is being personally overseen by the CEO is a good strategy, although it means that special attention needs to be paid early on to the long-term plan for embedding the work into ongoing business processes and management structures. There's a real danger of the initiative becoming so identified with one or two people that it dies as soon as those people leave or move to a different role.

If the change agent reports a layer or two down, but still has good visibility and regular access to the top decision maker, then that indicates strong support as well. But if he or she is buried down in the organization, or reports into a staff function with only a partial connection to customer value management, then people will not perceive that this work has support from or visibility to the highest levels – no matter what anyone says to the contrary.

It can be equally important that the change agent has dotted-line reporting into – or at least visibly strong relationships with – other key leaders whose support is necessary for the work to take hold. These could be business units or staff groups such as human resources. Perception is what counts in this area as it does with customers. Unless an organization has some really serious leadership issues that are outside the scope of this book, people can be expected to line up and support what their leaders show, not just tell, them is important.

Step 2–Get Focused: *Survey Strategy and Scope*

chapter six

Before launching into designing surveys and hiring vendors, it's important to give some serious thought to how you're going to study the market. There are four key questions to ask:

- What type of surveying are we going to do?
- What markets are we going to survey?
- What individuals are we going to survey?
- How are we going to manage the respondent list on an ongoing basis?

This chapter provides a way of thinking through each of these questions, and some practical survey strategy approaches based on the experience of companies I've worked with.

Ten Steps to Mastery

Commitment			Research			Response		Reinforcement	
1	2	3	4	5	6	7	8	9	10
Align	Focus	Prepare	Capture	Share	Analyze	Pick Priorities	Get Going	Reward Success	Embed Concepts

Step 2: Get Focused: *Survey Strategy and Scope*

1. **Decide Type of Survey**
2. **Identify Market Segments to Survey**
3. **Identify Individuals to Survey**
4. **Manage Respondent List**

1. Decide Type of Survey

I believe that a sound customer value management program should include two types of surveys:

- Value surveys
- Transaction surveys.

Two Types of Surveys: Working Together

If you think about how mining companies operate, you'll find it easy to understand how value and transaction surveys work together. Mining companies are continually running high-level exploration surveys looking for hot spots – places that show good potential for drilling. These are like the value surveys. They identify the areas where it's worth "drilling down" for more information through transaction surveys.

- Dr. Nick Fisher

Value Surveys

What I call value surveys or market perception surveys are designed to find out how well you stack up against the competition on the key elements that drive value in your target market. They're also known as decision-maker surveys or relationship surveys. Their design reflects the Attribute Trees we discussed in Chapter Two. Remember the Attribute Trees consist of those things that most impact customer perception of value.

Value surveying looks at the big picture. You're looking for breadth rather than depth. You take a random sampling of decision makers in a specific market: people who buy from you, people who used to buy from you but have defected to another company, people who have never bought from you. These surveys ask the critical "worth-what-paid-for" question, allowing you to calculate CVA ratios and do correlations with market share. They are essential for competitive analysis.

Transaction Surveys

Once you've used the data from your value surveys to decide where you need to focus, you can use transaction surveys to get a better sense of what exactly you need to do to drive up customer ratings on an attribute. Everyone is familiar with this type of survey. You take your car in to get the brakes fixed, and the next day you get a call from the service department. The person on the phone asks a few questions about your satisfaction with the service provided: how long the work took, whether the problem was fully fixed, the courteousness of the staff, whether the bill was clear and so on.

Also called recent event surveys or incident specific surveys, these surveys are triggered by a specific interaction between a company and one of its customers – what's sometimes referred to as a "moment of truth." Their point is to reveal performance issues and lead to action. Whereas value surveys are going for breadth, with transaction surveys you're looking for depth. They are essential for process improvement.

Value and Transaction Survey Relationship

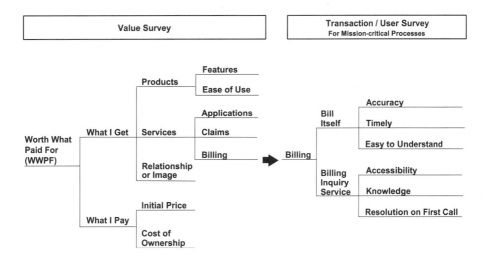

Both Are Important

When I think about the difference between these two types of surveying I get the image in my mind of a big bathtub with one spigot for hot water and one for cold. Doing a transaction survey is like putting your hand under the hot water spigot and testing the temperature of the water coming out. That tells you whether the water heater in the basement is functioning properly.

Doing a value survey is like putting your hand into the middle of the bathtub and testing the overall temperature. That tells you whether the net result is a comfortable bath. Since value surveying is not as well understood as transaction surveying, you'll find that I focus more on the former in this book. But a good customer value management system will include both.

Value Surveys	Transaction Surveys
• Random sampling of all customers in a target market	• Triggered by specific customer interaction
• Surveys the key decision makers	• Surveys the individual who had the experience
• Focused on high-level attributes	• Focused on sub-attributes that link to business processes
• Searches for understanding of market position	• Searches for actionable feedback
• Essential for competitive analysis	• Essential for process management

2. Identify Market Segments to Survey

The more thought you put into defining your markets and deciding where to focus your efforts, the more confident you can be that your research will be relevant and actionable. There are five things to keep in mind:

- How the market is naturally divided from a customer perspective
- What you know from competitive intelligence about who your competitors are in each segment and what their strategies are
- How your company is organized
- Where your revenue comes from now – markets in which you want to create customer loyalty
- Where you think your revenue will come from in the future, given expected shifts in market dynamics and your business strategy.

The Customer View

By now, you will not be surprised that I believe you should begin with the customer view. You need to understand the characteristics of the different customer segments in your markets and how customers perceive your products.

If you're a major computer manufacturer, for example, you might say, "We sell to large businesses, medium-sized businesses, small businesses and individual consumers. Each of these segments has different characteristics and needs."

If your product is white goods, then you might want to segment the rural market from the urban market on the basis that people living miles from the nearest corner store are going to want larger refrigerators and lots of freezer space. The same thinking might suggest that consumers with large families have different needs and buying criteria from single people with no kids. People who entertain a lot might have different needs again.

What you're trying to do is look at who buys your products and what natural divisions fall out when you understand how they assess the value of your offering. When you survey, you want to be sure that you are researching the right target market. If most of your revenues, for example, come from oversized, built-in refrigerators, surveying urban apartment dwellers is not going to be very productive.

You also want to understand how your products are grouped in customers' minds. You may have one division manufacturing both dishwashers and clothes washers because they're based on a common technology platform. But customers probably think of one as a kitchen appliance and the other as a laundry appliance and apply an entirely different set of evaluation criteria to each. If you don't understand these as two distinct markets when you're doing your research, you risk coming back with very confused data.

The Competition

Since the purpose of doing the value surveys is to understand how you're positioned in a specific market relative to the competition, how you define the market should also reflect the nature of the competition.

To continue with the white goods example, if you're up against one set of competitors in the laundry category of your business (washers and dryers) and a different set in the cooking category (cooktops, ovens, rotisseries) then it's clearly a distinct market and should be treated as such in your research. Or you may be playing in three price categories with a premium brand, an average brand and an economy brand, with different competition in each. Again – you'll want to consider these as distinct markets when you design your research.

My colleague Marcelo Chanis once told me that the South American appliance maker he was working with (Multibrás) faced different competitors in the market for one-door refrigerators than they faced in the market for two-door refrigerators. Sometimes you have to describe the market at this level of detail to get really useful data. In other markets, taking it to that level of detail would be a waste of money. You have to do some careful analysis to make this decision.

The Company View

The third thing to consider is that business decision makers within your company can act on the data only if it can be sorted to reflect the company's organizational structure. The product manager responsible for the apartment-sized refrigerator wants to understand the overall market for refrigerators, but he or she also may want data on the specific target market for his or her product. The general manager responsible for the economy washing machine brand will want to be able to break out this data from the data on premium and middle-of-the-road brands.

So when you're building your database of people to survey, you need to make sure that at the end of the day you will be able to sort the data by any factor that is important in your company. Business unit, product category, specific product, brand, geography, customer segment and distribution channel are some possibilities that come to mind.

Note from a Change Agent:
The Right Data for the Right Audience

Each presentation I made was carefully tailored. I had the database structured so that very quickly I could pull out the data that was most important to whoever was asking for it.

We had enough data that we could do statistically valid cuts on all sorts of things. We could examine specific issues associated with a category or a brand. We could analyze new product launches. We could look at what product features were most important to different types of customers. People started getting really excited about the data when they saw how closely it related to their critical business challenges. That's how we started truly integrating customer value management into the business.

- Shawne Howell

Determining Your Focus

Once you have a solid understanding of how the markets you sell into are defined and segmented, you need to decide where you're going to focus your research. Most companies I've worked with set a goal of having customer value data for about 80% of their revenue stream. It would be great to have data on everything, but you'll get the most value for research money spent by focusing on what's most important to your company and your strategy.

Let's continue to follow our fictional white goods company through the process of determining where to focus. For each cut at the market that they've determined is important – region, category, product – they list out everything included in that view and the approximate percent of revenue associated with each.

An example:

Region	Percent of Revenue
Europe	50%
North America	30%
Asia	17%
Africa	3%

At first glance it seems that they should focus their research on understanding the European and North American markets.

Except that their business strategy is to grow the Asian market. They're close to saturating the European market and are unlikely to capture significantly more market share. On the other hand, they see huge untapped potential in Asia and want to understand that market better. As far as they've been able to determine, their chief competition is not well positioned to succeed in Asia. They're definitely going to include Asia. In fact they might even start there.

They go through the same exercise from a product category standpoint, and understand that 60% of their revenue comes from laundry-related products and 30% from cooking-related products. They don't see that mix changing very much, so they decide to focus on these two categories.

Within the laundry product category they start to break down exactly which products are responsible for the greatest proportion of the revenue stream. Then they think about the characteristics of the customers who are most likely to be interested in these products. Step by step, they design their research strategy.

A Common Pitfall: Fixate on Your Organization Structure

Time and again, I've seen companies get into trouble by fixating on their own organization structure rather than the natural divisions of the market. While the structure may in fact reflect the market pretty well, all sorts of factors go into decisions about organization design that have little to do with market segmentation, including the specific skill mix and experience of the leadership team.

What's more, many companies change their structure frequently to reflect changing business conditions. One year they may institute a model that has separate business units reporting to product line general managers in order to promote closer collaboration among the product development, manufacturing and marketing functions. Another year, they may move back to a functional model to find economies of scale in a tough market.

If you've looked at the market from all perspectives at the beginning, you'll likely have designed research and structured a database with sufficient flexibility to accommodate these changes. If you haven't, you risk ending up with numbers that can't be compared year over year, or that aren't acted upon because they can't be attached to a defined unit in the company.

A Common Pitfall:
Confuse Distribution Channels with Market Segments

Another issue I've run across is confusing distribution channels with market segments. Back at AT&T, we made a clear distinction in our minds between business customers and home customers, and we set up separate distribution channels for each. But there's really an overlap between these two segments because some people want three or four phone lines for their home and some businesses likewise need only three or four phone lines. We'd find business customers going into the phone stores – which were really intended for home customers only – to get their services set up.

Our researchers needed to understand that if they based transaction surveys on the population that used phone stores, they were actually getting a mix of business and home customers. What's worse, they were probably getting some disgruntled business customers whom we'd tried to redirect to our business distribution channel after they'd taken the trouble to come to the phone store.

It's also important to remember that if you want to do a value or market perception survey of a specific market segment, you need to sample from all of the distribution channels you use for that market, or you'll be building a bias into the research.

Think about desktop or notebook computer sales, for example. If you want to buy a computer, you have three options:

- Go into a computer store
- Call a toll-free number and place the order by phone
- Place an order via the Internet.

Some companies' strategy is to focus on one or two of these channels, but some offer them all.

Someone capable of putting the right system together on a website likely has different characteristics and value drivers from those of the person who gets into the car and goes to the local electronics shop. If you confine your research to only one of these groups, you will not be getting a full picture of what drives value in the desktop/notebook computer market.

3. Identify Individuals to Survey

Let's assume that by now you've determined you need to do both transaction and value surveys. You've decided how you're going to study the market and you know the demographics/characteristics of the customer segment you're targeting. Now you need the actual names and contact information of people to survey. Where do you start?

For transaction surveys, it's relatively easy as long as your system is set up to capture the right information. These surveys are triggered by an event – a moment of contact between your business and one of your customers. You have records of these transactions: call center records, billing records, repair records. You may have a sophisticated customer relationship management (CRM) database that pulls all this information together in one place. As long as you know the name, address, telephone number or e-mail of the customer and have a generic description of the event (brought something in for repair, called to question a bill, purchased a product), you're in business.

It's more complicated for value surveys. The first issue is that you need to have enough information on your customers to determine who fits the profile of your target market for a specific piece of value research. If you have a good CRM system, you're probably tracking enough information on demographics and buying patterns to be able to segment your customers appropriately. If you don't, you'll have to try to piece this profile together from information such as addresses and purchase records. If you're in a business-to-business market, you will need first to identify which companies you want to survey, and then which individuals within each company.

Finding Your Competitors' Customers

The second issue is that it's critical to include in your sample people who have never bought from you. Some researchers make the mistake of thinking you can get a valid read on market perception by asking your customers how you rate against the competition. But the fact that these people at some point made the decision to spend money with you – even if they also spend money with your competitors or have entirely defected to your competitors – introduces a huge bias into the equation. To get an accurate picture of how you're doing relative to the competition, you must track the opinions of people who purchase exclusively from the competition.

You can open a telephone book and start calling people at random, but it's hit or miss as to whether you're calling people who match the profile of your target market. This approach can work well in broad-based consumer markets, where most of the general population regularly buys a given product or service from at least one competitor. For example, it is not difficult to find consumer banking customers by random dialing.

In other cases, however, you'll find that you have to buy competitor customer contact information from market research organizations which specialize in compiling this type of data. Step 4 walks you through things to consider in vendor selection and management. But clearly one big consideration is the vendor's ability to provide enough names that match the target market criteria you've established to get statistically reliable information.

If you have a decent tracking system, you can supplement vendor lists with your own information. Some companies get quite inventive in coming up with ways of tracking people who considered buying from them but didn't – since if they didn't purchase from you, it's highly likely they purchased from a competitor.

If you have a toll-free number or an e-mail inquiry function, you can keep the names of and contact information for people who called for information. If you're in a business where you do formal quotes or proposals, you can keep records of requests for proposals or quotes on business that you didn't get.

In some countries, consumer privacy laws can limit your ability to use this type of information even if you have it. That's another reason to involve a professional market research vendor to conduct your surveys. Vendors should fully understand the specific legal issues governing customer research in your markets.

Finding the Decision Maker

The third issue is that ideally you're looking for the opinion of the decision maker – not the opinion of just anyone in the company. If you can't get the decision maker, next best is the opinion of someone who strongly influences the actual purchase decision. In direct-to-consumer businesses where the person making the purchase is usually also making or influencing the decision, that's not so difficult. In business-to-business it can be a challenge. Often the people managing the direct interactions with the company – calling for information, questioning a bill, seeking a repair – are not the decision makers. They may be key influencers, but not necessarily.

One approach is to start by contacting the people whose names you do have, explain the purpose of the interview, and ask them whether they are the decision maker. If they're not, ask them who is. Your sales people are also an excellent source of intelligence here. The account teams generally know who's really making the decision even if much of their interaction is with the influencers.

4. Manage Respondent List

I believe it's wise to invest in a good customer database. If you regularly track the names, street addresses and e-mail addresses, telephone numbers and demographic characteristics of your customers, you won't find yourself scrambling every time you want to do a piece of market perception research. If you can sort this database by name, telephone number, geography, type of product bought and important demographic characteristics you'll really be able to hone in on the target market every time you launch a piece of research. You'll be confident that you're getting the best value for the money you spend surveying.

Managing this database can be a big job. Since names come in from a variety of sources, catching duplication is always an issue. Over-surveying – going back to the same people too frequently – is a big problem because it can alienate people to the point that they stop participating in surveys at all. You need to have a way of indicating when a name in your database has been surveyed, and then put a block on that name so the person doesn't get contacted again for at least six months.

It's even more important to track people who are contacted but refuse to take the survey. Did you get them at a bad time? Did they indicate they'd be willing to be surveyed at another time? Or did they ask not to be contacted for this purpose at all? All this information should be captured in the respondent database.

It's also a reality that the information in your database is going to get out of date quickly – particularly if you're in a dynamic business-to-business market where people change jobs frequently. Each survey call is an opportunity to do a quality check on your data: Is the individual still at the same address and phone number? Has his or her job changed? Has the decision maker changed and if so, who is it now?

Protecting Information

The more data you collect and track on your customers, the better you will be able to understand what they value. But this also means you're in possession of sensitive and confidential information that you have an obligation to protect.

If you're a global company, it's particularly important to make sure the vendor you use understands the cultural norms and legal requirements of the countries in which you do business. In some European countries, for example, you can't just send out e-mail surveys to people. You need to phone or send a letter first, asking their permission.

Professional market research companies are bound by laws and ethical standards set up to protect the people they survey. I always make sure I specify in requests for proposals that the successful bidder will take responsibility for compliance with all such rules and guidelines. You can't leave it at that, however, since any breaches of these rules and guidelines will impact your reputation as an ethical company and may lead to penalties or charges. It's important that you understand the specific obligations and requirements in your markets and satisfy yourself that all reasonable steps to achieve compliance have in fact been taken.

The Bottom Line

Deciding how you're going to study the market can be a complex and time-consuming process. You may have to force yourself and others to think about your customers and your products in ways that don't at first seem intuitive or reasonable. Careful management of the respondent list can seem like a big bother. But I strongly believe that time invested in this step pays off in superior quality data that relates directly to your priority business needs.

Step 3—Get Prepared: *Secrets of Survey Design*

chapter seven

I've mentioned before that my mission is:

> ***To help organizations bring customer data to the leadership table and use it with the same level of understanding, discipline and passion as financial data to achieve business results.***

This chapter is concerned with the discipline of survey design. Its purpose is to ensure that the output of your survey is reliable, meaningful customer data. It outlines:

- The data collection standards I recommend and why
- An approach to focusing the survey on the right value drivers
- What to look for in the survey testing phase
- The importance of getting stakeholder buy-in to surveys before they're administered.

The section on standards is somewhat technical in places. If you're responsible for customer value management implementation or for survey design, I'd urge you to read it carefully. **For ease of future reference, I've summarized my recommendations in a box at the end of the chapter.**

When we get to the stage of looking at how to present data to top decision makers you'll see why these decisions are critical. If at the end of the day business leaders don't understand or have confidence in the results, everybody's time will have been wasted. Discipline and rigor in data collection are key to acceptance and use of the results.

Ten Steps to Mastery

Commitment			Research			Response		Reinforcement	
1	2	3	4	5	6	7	8	9	10
Align	Focus	Prepare	Capture	Share	Analyze	Pick Priorities	Get Going	Reward Success	Embed Concepts

Step 3: Get Prepared: *Secrets of Survey Design*

1. **Establish Standards and Guidelines**
2. **Conduct Qualitative Research on Value Drivers**
3. **Design Survey Based on Standards**
4. **Test Survey with Customers**
5. **Finalize and Obtain Stakeholder Approval**

1. Establish Standards and Guidelines

Put two experienced researchers in a room together and before long they'll be in heated debate over some technical aspect of survey design. What are the pros and cons of a 10-point scale versus a 5-point scale? Should each point on the scale be labeled, or is it better just to anchor it with labels on each end? What wording works best for these labels? Should questions be in random order or arranged in logical groupings? What standards of precision and confidence are acceptable?

There are many strong opinions on these and other key questions, all backed up with some measure of theoretical or experiential evidence. I'll outline the most common options in the sections that follow, and identify the approach that I've found works best for customer value data collection and transaction surveys.

Even if you prefer to use a different standard from the one I recommend, I want to stress how important it is that you make a decision on what you're going to do, document it as a standard, and stick with it.

Common standards make it possible to compare data from different business units, to roll data up into an overall corporate view and to track trends over time. They also make the task of training decision makers to read, interpret and use the numbers much easier.

Business leaders don't want to wade through a new explanation of how this particular survey was designed and what scale was used every time they look at customer data. They shouldn't be expected to remember that a score of 4 on this report is pretty good because it uses a 5-point scale, whereas a score of 4 on that report is really bad because it uses a 10-point scale. Once their minds are calibrated to what the numbers mean, they want to be able to apply this same mental framework to all customer value data they look at.

Think about how people look at financial results. You wouldn't expect people used to seeing quarterly results expressed in US dollars to suddenly adjust to seeing results in Canadian dollars because the new CFO is a patriotic Canadian. And yet I have seen companies change their approach from one survey to the next and then wonder why people don't understand what the data means. I've also seen them allow one division to adopt one standard while allowing another division to adopt a different standard, making it impossible for corporate leaders to get a coherent view across the business.

This is not to say you should never make a change to your survey. If it turns out that the approach you initially chose is not working well, then by all means change it. Just make sure you think about how you will manage comparability of data over time, and how you will recalibrate the minds of the business leaders you expect to use the data.

Documenting your standards and guidelines is important for three reasons:

1. **Alignment:** The act of writing decisions down and circulating them to all the players will often reveal differences of opinion on the nuances of what was actually agreed.
2. **Quick reference:** The document serves as a kind of key to the data – a quick reference guide that business leaders can use to help them read and understand the data. Having this captured in writing makes it possible for leaders to find information on their own and reduces the demands on the customer value implementation team.
3. **Future reference:** The standards provide solid guidance to players who join the customer value implementation team later on.

In my experience, if you want to consistently get results that your business leaders know they can rely on, it's important to document your company's standards and guidelines on the following six elements:

i. Sampling requirements (precision intervals and confidence levels)
ii. Questionnaire design (mandatory questions, layout, ordering, length)
iii. Response wording
iv. Response scales, labels and definitions
v. Survey methods
vi. Attribute impact weight (stated or derived).

i. Sampling Requirements

In my experience, most business leaders are looking for a high degree of confidence in any survey results. They typically want to be able to say something like, "We can be 95% confident that the sample mean is within +/- 5% of the true population mean."

Business leaders are not going to make decisions based on data they don't trust. Because different survey samples from the same population of customers can give slightly different results, it's important to be very clear up front what standard of precision and confidence will be acceptable to the ultimate users of the results.

Rigorous mathematical rules determine how big the survey sample must be in order to meet this standard. How large a sample do you need to get a result you can trust? Up to a certain point, the rule is that greater precision comes from larger sample sizes. The bigger the sample size, however, the higher the costs. In order to double a statistic's precision (halve the margin of error), you need to quadruple the sample size. At some point you come up against the law of diminishing returns.

The top decision makers in the company must be involved in making the cost versus precision/confidence trade-off decision. If at the end of the day they're going to dismiss the results because the sample size is too small and the results imprecise, why spend the money at all?

This was drilled into me by Bob Allen when he was chairman of AT&T. Each quarter, he sent the customer value data for each of our 19 businesses to the board of directors along with the financial data. He had to be confident that the customer value numbers had as much integrity as the financial numbers, and that they could be defended and used for important decisions. As chief customer officer, he told me I bore as much responsibility as the CFO for assuring that all published information met the reliability standards we had set and documented. There were to be no asterisks pointing to footnotes like, "Small sample size does not meet confidence standards." If the sample was too small to meet our standards the result simply was not published.

This is not intended to be a statistics textbook and I won't get into the mathematical formulae used to calculate sample sizes to ensure accuracy of results. I said in Chapter Four that you need to have people with expertise in statistics and sampling available to your team to do this kind of work. The point here is that you need to agree on and document up front what standards will be acceptable to decision makers.

You will want to specify both:

- **Precision interval**, which is expressed as a plus or minus range, (you may know this as the "confidence interval" – the terms are interchangeable), and
- **Confidence level**, which is expressed as a percentage.

As I said at the start of this chapter, companies typically decide on precision intervals within plus or minus 5% from the sample mean score and confidence levels of 95% as their standard for customer value data. If a sample has a precision interval which extends from 7.6 to 8.4 (plus or minus 5% of the sample mean 8), and the confidence level is 95%, then you are 95% certain that somewhere in this interval is the true mean rating of the population you are surveying.

Another way of expressing the precision interval is to say that you want to confidently detect any improvement (or deterioration) in an attribute from one survey to the next greater than a specified plus or minus score range. In the example above, you would need to see an improvement or deterioration greater than plus or minus 0.4 of the mean on a second survey to be absolutely confident that the market perception had changed – that the variation wasn't just a result of surveying a different sample of your target population.

Does that mean if you're working with a precision level in this range and your score rises from 7.6 to 8.2 between one survey and the next, you shouldn't be pleased? My answer is that you should be cautiously pleased, and pay a lot of attention to what happens the next time you survey this population. What's important is the trend over time. Look at it this way: If you and I each clock how long it takes us to run 100 yards and your time is one-tenth of one second less than mine, can we conclude that you're a faster runner than I am? Of course not. But if we repeat the experiment 20 times, and every time you are one-tenth of one second faster than I am, then we probably <u>can</u> conclude that you're the faster runner.

If your scores show consistent improvement (or deterioration) over several surveys, then it's probably not just a result of your sample and you should pay attention to what the numbers are telling you. Companies who survey quarterly, using a different sample every quarter, often choose to track trends using rolling four-quarter average scores to lessen the impact that different samples will have on the results.

Once you decide on the precision and confidence levels you want, you can work with your market research sampling expert and/or outside vendor to determine the correct sampling size and procedure to achieve these levels, given the target population for each survey.

ii. Questionnaire Design

Later in this chapter we'll look at methods of developing a working hypothesis on what value drivers are most important to your market, so you know where to focus your survey. While most customer value surveys will touch on similar themes, the choice and wording of questions will vary according to the priority concerns and unique characteristics of the target market for each survey.

There are, however, three items on which I suggest corporate standards be set:

- **Mandatory questions**
  There are five to six key questions that I believe should be asked on every survey in the same way, to allow for corporate roll up of results and trend tracking over time.

- **Layout/order**
  Questions should be arranged in logical groupings rather than random order, with the critical "overall how would you rate" question at the end of each grouping, and the "worth-what-paid-for" question at the end of the survey.

- **Length**
  Transaction surveys should take no more than 8 to 12 minutes of respondents' time; value surveys should be in the 15 to 20 minute range.

Mandatory Questions

Customer value data is most useful if business units and product groups have the flexibility to tailor their surveys to the priority needs and purchase criteria of their target markets. At the same time, decision makers at the corporate level will want to roll some key metrics up into a bigger picture number, and make correlations between customers' perception of value and their buying behavior.

I therefore suggest that you decide on a set of mandatory questions that must be included in every customer survey and across all markets. There are two types of questions I recommend making mandatory:

Value Questions
- Overall how would you rate the price (or cost of ownership)?

- Overall how would you rate the quality of the products, services and relationship (or brand image)?
- Considering everything we have discussed – the products and services received, the relationship (or brand image), the price you paid (or the cost of ownership) – how would you rate the company's offer on being worth what you paid?

Behavior (Loyalty) Questions
- How likely would you be to recommend the company to others?
- How likely would you be to purchase from the company again?
- How likely would you be to increase the amount you spend with the company?

To do basic customer value analysis, you need to consistently ask all the value questions listed above and two of the behavior questions (you probably wouldn't include all three).

Some of my colleagues suggest that "attitude questions" is a more accurate label for the second category of questions, since what you're measuring is people's attitudes about expected future behavior rather than actual behavior. I've stuck to the more common label "behavior questions" in this book, because in the end management's interest is in creating the kind of loyal behavior that leads to business results. This is one of those occasions where the art of framing things so that the business relevance is clear wins out over strict scientific accuracy.

From the behavior category, I suggest that you include the "recommend" question and whichever one of the other two questions is more relevant to your business strategy. In my experience it's harder to get high scores on the "recommend" question than the others, I guess because people are putting their personal reputations at stake with their friends when they recommend a company or a product. But a customer recommendation is the best form of advertising, so you definitely want to know where you stand on this one.

The exact wording of these mandatory questions will vary depending on the nature of your business, but within your company the questions should be worded in the same way in each survey.

In some industries, for example, customers are focused on the initial price of the product. In others, they are more interested in overall cost of ownership. Customers purchasing laser printers will be just as concerned about the cost of ink cartridges and how long they last as they are about the initial purchase price. Companies selling directly to consumers will be looking for a rating on brand image.   Companies that sell business to business may be more interested in a rating on the business relationship.

It's important to tailor the overall "worth-what-paid-for" question to refer very specifically to the questions that have gone before in the survey. For example, a mortgage company might use the following wording for the "worth-what-paid-for" question:

"Now, considering the overall quality of the service you received during the loan application and closing processes, the loan itself, and the overall cost of the loan, how would you rate XYZ Mortgage Co.'s loan on being worth what you pay for it?"

Layout/Order

When it comes to collecting customer data, I recommend a modular approach, in which questions are grouped in logical blocks and the overall rating questions come at the end of each block. The "worth-what-paid-for" question comes at the end of the value modules, just before the behavior questions.

The modules are based on the branches of the Attribute Tree, with each module focusing on the three to five main attributes that drive customer perception of value in that category. In the product quality module, for example, you might have reliability, performance, and ease of use. While the modules should appear in the order in which customers experience them (your Waterfall of Needs will help here), within a module it's a good idea to randomly rotate the order of the sub questions, since ratings tend to be higher for the first questions asked within a block of questions.

So in a value survey, the structure would look something like this:

Sample Value Survey Structure

1. Quality

- Product quality
    - 3 to 5 sub-attribute questions
    - Overall rating of product quality

- Service quality
    - 3 to 5 sub-attribute questions
    - Overall rating of service quality

- Relationship or image
    - 3 to 5 sub-attribute questions
    - Overall rating of relationship or image

- Overall quality rating

2. Price

- Initial price
    - 3 to 5 sub-attribute questions
    - Overall rating of initial price

- Ongoing costs
    - 3 to 5 sub-attribute questions
    - Overall rating of life cycle costs

- Overall price rating

3. Worth What Paid For

4. Behavior Questions (2 of the 3)

- Likely to recommend
- Likely to repurchase
- Likely to purchase more

Transaction surveys are much more focused than value surveys and generally zero in on at most one or two of the key experiences that impact value ratings, taking it down to the level of sub-attributes that are directly linked to business processes. Say, for example, you discover in your value surveying that complaint resolution is important to customers in your target market and your rating on this services attribute is low relative to the competition. You could use a transaction survey to drill down and find out exactly what sub-attributes are responsible for the low score.

In a transaction survey on complaint resolution you can have separate sections on types of complaints, on call centers, on telephone answering systems and on service representatives – each with five to seven subquestions. Now you're getting actionable data tied to specific business processes that can be measured and improved.

An Aside from Ray: Doing it All at Once

Sometimes companies I work with want to do everything with one survey. They want to determine the relative value ratings and get lots of detail on customers' transactional experiences with the company all at once. There are two reasons why I think that's not the best method.

First, it makes the survey so long that you tend to get a high percentage of respondents either tuning out or actually dropping out somewhere in the middle. That compromises the quality of the data.

Second, for relative value ratings, you want to ask the decision makers. In larger companies, these people probably will not have intimate knowledge of all the transactional experiences. They don't pay the bills themselves or worry about getting invoices fixed if they're wrong. They don't have personal experience of the training or installation process and so on. To find out more about what's working and not working in relation to those key processes, you want to get to the people who have actually experienced them shortly after the interaction takes place.

What's common in both types of survey is that they are modular, not random, and the overall question is asked at the end. Many will argue that the overall rating and "worth-what-paid-for" questions should be asked first so that you get a fresh, top-of-mind response. They believe that if you take the respondent through all the other questions first, you're leading the witness and biasing the results.

But I think it's important to remember that what customers think about a company is based on the set of experiences they've had with the company. These experiences generally follow a logical sequence in time, over the duration of a customer's "ownership lifecycle."

Remember that generally you're catching respondents in the course of a busy day during which they may not have thought about your company at all. Especially in value surveys, it may have been quite some time ago that the decision to purchase from you was made.

So when a question about accessibility or responsiveness comes at them out of left field, it doesn't come with enough context to allow them to give a thoughtful response quickly. Customers have to think through, "Now what does responsiveness mean in this context and when might I have wanted the company to be responsive, and can I think of a moment when they were or weren't?" But when the question is presented in a specific and familiar context, like…"How would you rate the company on quickly responding to your repair request?" they can easily recall the experience and do the rating.

In my experience, this approach yields:

Customer-friendly interviews
• It's easier on the customer responding to the survey to think through one topic and then go to the next logical topic, rather than jumping about.

More thoughtful responses
• This approach enables customers to go back through the decision-making process they used before purchasing the product or to relive a specific experience with the company. Whenever the decision to purchase was made, chances are that it wasn't made on the fly without some serious thought. Customers likely thought through what they would be getting, calculated the cost and made an educated guess as to whether the purchase would be worth what they paid for it. Laying out the survey in the way I recommend allows customers to reconnect with this thought process and give more reflective responses.

Actionable results
• It's easier for the survey designer to ensure that questions are tied to business processes and key attributes within each process that drive customer value, and that the questions yield data that can actually be used.

Stronger models
• The relationships among drivers and their correlations with overall ratings are easier to analyze and explain. Asking the questions this way tends to yield a model fit in the 60% to 85% range. Model fit means that variations in how customers rate the sub-attribute questions explain 60% to 85% of the variation in how the overall question is rated. When the overall question is asked before the subquestions, the model fits are much lower. It can be hard to persuade anyone to accept a model with a 25% to 35% fit attached to it.

Length

It's difficult to hold most people's attention past 20 minutes in a telephone or mail survey, although you'll find some people who are willing to take more time. As I said at the beginning of this section, I usually recommend:

- Transaction surveys: in the 8 to 12 minute range
- Value surveys: in the 15 to 20 minute range.

Face-to-face surveys can be a bit longer, because people's attention span is usually longer when they're interacting with someone in person rather than over the phone.

Data Management Tip

It's a good idea to specify in your standards your protocol and rules for numbering questions. It may seem insignificant now, but for future data management purposes it's important that Question 19 on the survey is <u>always</u> the same question. If the question changes, the label should change as well. Otherwise, you'll have data on two different Question 19s showing up in one bucket in your database.

iii. Response Wording

How you word the response options you provide can make a difference in the results you get. The next section will cover the related topic of rating scales and labels.

Responses on Value Questions

In my experience you get the most useful and accurate responses for the purposes of customer value analysis when you stick to asking people:

How would you rate...from poor to excellent?

Here's what I see as the primary disadvantages of other options:

Satisfaction
- How satisfied are you...from very dissatisfied to very satisfied?

The problem with using this scale goes back to the lesson that good isn't good enough. Analysis of years of customer data has shown that customers may be satisfied with what you offer but still be shopping around for better value. When satisfaction rating results are improperly interpreted, you risk lulling management into a dangerous sense of complacency.

Grading
• How would you grade...from F to A?

This scale comes with a lot of personal and cultural bias. A person used to getting all As in school would be devastated by a C. An average student expects to get the occasional C, so thinks of it differently. The grading system has the additional disadvantage that the distance between grading points is not usually equal. At some point in the sequence there is a big psychological chasm that marks the difference between a passing grade and a failing grade. Where this chasm falls differs depending on the school system. In one common system, A represents 80% and above, B 70 to 79%, C 60 to 69%, D 50 to 59%, and E or F represents a failing grade of 49% and below. The non-linearity of this scale makes statistical modeling very difficult.

Likert
• Do you agree...from strongly disagree to strongly agree?

The problem with this scale is that it measures agreement, not performance level, and is likely to lead you into some difficulties with logic. I saw one employee survey that asked the question, "Do you get regular performance appraisals from your manager?" What can you do with a neither disagree nor agree response to such a question? It has no meaning. Similarly, if the statement in the survey contains strong wording such as, "The tech support person was one of the finest people I've ever had the pleasure to work with," a strongly disagree response doesn't really tell you anything. Did they dislike the tech support person? Or are they just taking strong exception to your statement, even though they might have thought that the tech support person did excellent work?

Expectations
• Did we meet your expectations...from did not meet expectations to exceeded expectations?

The difficulty with this formulation is that everything is relative. You have to know what the customer's expectations were in order to interpret the response. My daughter might watch me play a basketball game and respond that I exceeded her expectations. She then might watch Michael Jordan play a basketball game and respond that he met her expectations. Does that mean she thinks I'm a better basketball player than Michael Jordan? Even allowing for a daughter's bias, I doubt it!

There are times when it is appropriate to choose one of these alternate wording choices, rather than the poor to excellent rating I generally recommend. You have to consider the context. If you're asking about performance in a transaction survey, for example, questions about expectations can be very useful. You might ask customers how long it took to repair their car, how long they expected it to take, and how they rated the repair overall. You then start to understand how well you're living up to the performance standards in your customers' minds, and you can use this information to set your own speed-of-repair performance targets.

Responses on Behavior Questions

I recommend that the wording of these questions be, "How likely are you to recommend/to purchase again/to purchase more?" and that the scale be anchored to "not at all likely" and "very likely."

The other option is to ask how "willing" people would be to recommend, purchase again, etc. That can work, but using "likely" gives you more accurate predictive data. Most people I know would be very <u>willing</u> to buy a BMW or a Porsche, but fewer of them would say they are <u>likely</u> to own one.

iv. Response Scales, Labels and Definitions

This decision is clearly related to the decision on response wording, since the different approaches naturally lend themselves to different scales and labels. I recommend a 10-point scale where 1 is poor and 10 is excellent for value questions. For behavior questions, 1 means not at all likely and 10 means very likely. I don't recommend attaching labels to the other numbers on the scale (2 to 9).

My rationale is as follows:

- **Ten-point scales are easy to use.**
  The imperial and other ancient systems of measures notwithstanding, we're largely living in a world in which counting systems are based on 10. Most people learn to count on 10 fingers. Most people have at least some familiarity with the metric system. Most people find it natural to rate

things on a scale of 1 to 10. With 10-point scales you don't normally run into the "central tendency" problem: the risk that people will avoid making tough decisions and gravitate to the mid-point on the scale (see box below).

• **Ten-point scales have useful statistical properties.**
Experience has shown that it is relatively easy to derive importance weights and develop predictive models when people rate their responses using a 10-point scale. Three-point, 4-point or 5-point scales don't usually give you enough granularity to do multiple regression and other advanced statistical analysis. Studies suggest that 7- and 10-point scales are preferable for this work. I have had much success with the 10-point scale and recommend its use. Statistical studies have shown that a 10-point scale is adequate for this work.

• **Using labels as "anchors" at both ends keeps things simple.**
If you try to attach a label to every point on the scale, you're going to confuse or bore the respondent. Can you imagine the interviewer listing all the labels for each of the points on a 10-point scale after each question in a telephone interview? You may also skew the results by introducing an element of personal interpretation that disrupts the linearity of the scale. An individual may perceive the difference between good and excellent to be much bigger than the difference between good and fair, for example.

Survey Design Tip

Beware of introducing confusion by attempting to spread out customer responses across the full 10-point scale. Some surveyors try to do this by asking customers to rate using a scale of 1 to 10, where 5 is average.

My experience is that when you ask the question this way and plot the resulting data on a Slippery Slope, you find a small blip – an anomalous increase in the number of customers demonstrating "loyal" behavior while rating the company at 5 – that you wouldn't get otherwise.

This is because most people think a rating of 7 on a 10-point scale is an average or fair rating, and a 5 is the lowest mark they feel comfortable giving. Unless they have had a seriously bad experience, survey respondents seldom use the lower end of a

10-point scale, because it seems unfair to rate someone so low. So the suggestion that 5 should be considered an average score goes against most people's grain and won't really sink in for most respondents.

Given this tendency, if we ask everybody to use 5 as the average, we find that some follow this instruction but most still go with what seems fair to them. Since we don't know how many respondents have followed instructions and how many have gone by what they think is fair, we end up with distortion in the data.

There are times when it's appropriate to use other scales. If it's important to include a question where the obvious answer is either yes or no (like the "Do you get regular performance appraisals from your manager?" employee survey question I mentioned earlier), then introducing more or different options just confuses the issue.

v. Survey Methods

I've included survey methods in the list of standards to be documented at the outset because the vehicle you choose to use for data collection impacts both the design of the survey and the results. The most common survey options are:

- Telephone
- Mail
- Web-based
- Face-to-face.

It's important to discuss up front what methods you intend to use for what purpose (you might choose one method for transaction surveys and another for value surveys) and stay consistent over time. You might assume that you can do surveys by telephone one quarter and by mail the next quarter and have comparable data, but that's not necessarily the case.

First, mail questionnaires usually have to be shorter than telephone questionnaires, because you can hold people's attention on the phone longer than you can with a written questionnaire. Second, research has shown that mail surveys tend to be completed by people who are either very happy or very unhappy with the service provided, while telephone surveys catch a broader representation of the target population.

If you are going to change techniques, I suggest that you manage this transition carefully. If you run duplicate surveys for a few cycles – that is, administer the same survey at the same time by the new method and the old method and compare results – you can get a good read on what change you can expect to see in the data simply due to the change of data collection method.

Telephone Surveys

For most businesses I recommend telephone surveys as the preferable option. Here's why:

- **Better response**
  Response rates tend to be higher than those for other methods.

- **Less waste**
  It's easy to keep track of response rates and stop surveying when you've got the number of randomly completed samples you need. In mail surveys, you have to guess at how many you'll need to send out to get a sufficient sample of responses.

- **Better control**
  You know who is answering the questions. Mail surveys can be delegated to others without you knowing.

- **Timely response**
  You get timely responses, which is especially important on transaction surveys. Mail surveys can sit at the bottom of people's "to-do" piles for months before they surface.

- **Opportunity for quality control**
  You can listen in to selected calls to monitor the quality of the interviewer's work.

- **More information**
  You can ask more questions in a 15-minute telephone survey. If you put the same number of questions in a mail survey it would look too long and intimidate respondents.

- **Efficient data capture**
  You can take advantage of Computer-Assisted Telephone Interviewing (CATI) tools that make it easy for the interviewer to follow a prepared script and record responses quickly and accurately. "Skip logic" built into the program automatically takes the interviewer to the appropriate next question, based on the response the customer gives to the previous question. As in, "If no, skip to question 7," or "if yes, please respond to questions 4 through 6."

Telephone surveys are normally more expensive than mail and Web-based surveys, but less expensive than face-to-face surveys. A variation on the telephone survey that I've seen successfully employed is the Automatic Voice Response survey. Customers are invited by letter to call a toll-free number and prompted to enter their responses to survey questions on a touch-tone telephone pad.

Mail Surveys

One advantage of mail surveys is that people are free to complete them at a time and place that suits them. Because they can write their verbatim comments directly onto the survey, the possibility of this information getting distorted by the interviewer is eliminated.

There tends, however, to be a large non-response rate for mail surveys and a big time lag before the information is received. You can never be sure whether the person to whom you sent it filled it out or delegated the task to a junior person. And research shows that people who are either very pleased or very disgruntled tend to answer mail surveys more often than people who are more neutral or positive. You need to be aware of this bias.

If you decide to do mail surveys, it's important to be sure that your cover letter clearly explains the purpose and intent of the survey, and that the questionnaire is self-explanatory. With no one to help them through the survey, respondents are likely to give up if they run into a question they don't understand.

Mail surveys are less expensive to administer than telephone surveys. But make sure that when you're estimating cost you have factored in the cost of inputting the data from the paper responses to the database, and of any incentives you're offering to increase response rates.

Web-based Surveys

Increasingly, surveying over the Internet (sending customers an e-mail letter with a link to a Web-based survey) is becoming a good way to collect data, especially for recent event surveying. Pros and cons are similar to those for mail surveying, except that data can be directly extracted to the database without the need for manual input. Also, you can control the skip logic.

Web-based surveying of a customer base with e-mail access is normally cheaper than the telephone option.

Face-to-face Surveys

The most expensive option, face-to-face surveying is often the best method for business-to-business companies with a relatively small customer base. Especially for value surveying, such companies are targeting a small population of senior decision makers, and looking to create or sustain a very close relationship.

Face-to-face surveys should be done by an independent interviewer, not by members of a customer's account team. The interview may be conducted by a member of the senior team who doesn't have a day-to-day relationship with the customer, or by an outside consultant. The important thing is to choose someone who can listen impartially and report the results objectively.

Face-to-face surveys can be slightly longer and cover more topics than the other methods. They're more flexible, in that the interviewer gets visual clues that the respondent is struggling with a question and can introduce visual prompts or additional explanation. For the same reason, they're more subject to interviewer bias. While they generate more in-depth verbatim responses, they're more difficult to record, tabulate and analyze.

There is now a Computer-Assisted Personal Interviewing (CAPI) tool that provides the interviewer with a prepared script and allows him or her to record responses directly into a database. While the use of a CAPI tool lessens the likelihood of bias, the scripted nature of this approach also detracts from the relationship-building potential that face-to-face interviews provide.

vi. Attribute Impact Weight

Impact weights are a measure of how much influence each attribute has on customers' overall ratings. The decision to be made is which method will be your standard for determining impact weights. The options are:

- Stated importance
- Derived impact
- Both.

In the long run, the derived impact approach is more predictive of customer behavior. Until sufficient data is available, though, stated importance is a good interim approach. If you choose stated importance, you need to build a separate section into your survey to handle this.

Stated Importance

In the stated importance method you ask customers in the course of the survey to tell you which factors most influence their value ratings. Ways of doing this include:

- **Interval scaling**
  The respondent rates the importance of each attribute on a scale of 1 to 10. Note that in this method the respondent is not forced to prioritize. If he or she chooses, he or she can rank every attribute as equally important. This is one of the major problems with stated importance ratings.

- **Rank ordering**
  The respondent puts the attributes in order from most important to least important. With this method, you don't get any information about the magnitude of the difference in weighting of the items. An item in the middle of the list can be almost as important as an item at the top of the list, or it can be significantly less important. There's no way of knowing. Accordingly this method is not recommended.

- **Forced allocation**
  Respondents are given 100 points to allocate as they choose across the attributes. This method gives you the clearest sense of the relative impact weight of each attribute. In my experience, however, people have difficulty doing the exercise with more than four or five attributes. Normally I recommend doing this exercise only to understand the relative importance of the key attributes:

  - What they receive versus what they pay
  - Products versus services versus relationship/brand image
  - Initial price versus overall cost of ownership.

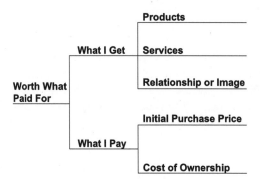

The forced allocation stated importance method is a good place to start. If you're doing face-to-face surveys or have a small sample, it is your best option, since you need about 50 responses per variable to do derived weightings (more on this in Step 4 – *Capture the Data*). But it can double the length of the survey, and the results are less accurate than derived impact as predictors of overall ratings and customer behavior.

Derived Impact

The derived impact method involves using techniques such as multiple regression on either time-series or cross-sectional data to determine the degree to which variation in the rating on an attribute influences variation in the overall rating. While the stated importance method tells you what customers believe is important to them, the derived impact method tells you what weight customers are *implicitly assigning* to a factor when they're assessing its value.

The two types of impact weight – stated and derived – can be very different. In the airline industry, for example, safety is usually cited by customers as an important attribute, but statistical analysis shows that it is not a significant predictor of airline choice. On-time arrival of flights and luggage handling are much better predictors. Safety is an expected minimum requirement and as long as no one airline stands out as having a poor record in this area, people will concentrate on other factors when making their choice.

The derived technique is highly reliable and efficient. You do, however, need an econometrician and enough data to produce good statistical models. The statistics expert on your team will be able to determine how much data you must gather to take this approach.

Both

If your survey is short enough to accommodate the time required to determine stated importance, and you can afford to do the statistical analysis required to get derived impact as well, doing both and comparing the results can provide some useful insight into the market. I know one research firm that does both and then plots the results on a quad chart with stated importance (high to low) on the *y* axis and derived impact (high to low) on the *x* axis. Items that appear in the top right-hand quadrant are both consciously (stated) and subconsciously (derived) very important to respondents, items in the lower right-hand quadrant are subconsciously important (derived) but are not stated as important, and so on.

Importance Quad Chart

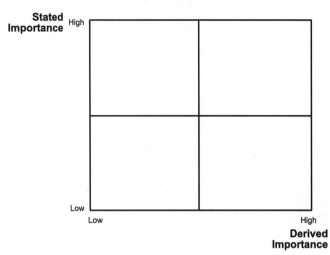

What does this tell you? Well, sometimes when you delve into the details you find out some interesting things about the market which may influence your business strategy. I've known cases where customers said that they place 25% weighting on price and 75% on quality. But when we looked at the derived impact it came out in reverse: 75% weighting on price; 25% on quality. What we found when we looked at the relative quality scores was that the companies in this market were at parity on quality, whereas there was a significant variation in the relative price scores.

What the customers were really saying was, "I'd love to make purchases based on quality. That's what's really important to us. But since there isn't really any differentiation in quality in the market, it just comes down to who has the best price."

It's not essential to do this kind of comparison, but it can be useful if done selectively. It's important that you <u>don't</u> try to do this for every question on the survey. Stick to the one or two key relative value questions.

2. Conduct Qualitative Research on Value Drivers

Up-front work ensuring that the survey questions focus on relevant value drivers is time well spent. You have customers' attention for a very limited time and you want to make the best use of it.

I always recommend that before companies launch into designing surveys, they do some qualitative research to determine what they already know is important to customers. This information can be used to decide which attributes to focus on and how to word the questions. There are at least three good sources of such information:

  • Internal subject matter experts
  • Existing documented research
  • Customer focus groups.

Internal Subject Matter Experts

I suggest beginning this "desktop research" phase by talking to people within the company who have regular interaction with customers. These could be senior officers, account teams, installers or call center staff – anyone who has direct customer contact and who can tell you in the customer's language, not the company jargon, what customers are interested in. You want the survey questions to use words and concepts customers will relate to.

Existing Documented Research

Existing documented research includes everything from previous survey data and verbatim comments to letters or phone calls of commendation or complaint. If customers take the trouble to call or write the company – whether with good news or bad news – then clearly whatever issue they're addressing is important to them. Be sure also to look for and review any specialized research that might have been completed for new product development or branding initiatives.

Customer Focus Groups

You can use the data you've collected from internal sources to guide customer focus groups aimed at determining which attributes are most important to include on your survey. I normally suggest you use a professional facilitator from your market research vendor to lead these sessions, although it's fine to have members of your team observing them (from off to the side or through a one-way mirror). There's a fine line between leading the witness and prompting customers to give a full and thoughtful response. Experienced facilitators stand a better chance of getting the balance right.

You can collate the "desktop research" you've done into a discussion guide that helps the facilitator make sure he or she is appropriately addressing all of the elements of your Attribute Tree. You want to go through in turn each component of what customers get (products, services, relationship or brand image) and of what they pay (initial costs, lifecycle costs).

> ### When a Product Is a Service
>
> I sometimes find that people get confused over the difference between a product and a service – particularly when what the company offers might be thought of as a service (like accounting, or doing outsourced manufacturing of another company's products).
>
> When I talk about "product" in a customer value management context, I mean what the company sells – whether it's a consumer article or a professional service.
>
> When I talk about "service," I mean how the company provides the product: the sales process, delivery, training, billing and so on.

If the customer doesn't mention something that the internal team has identified as important, it's fine to prompt with something like, "We haven't talked about technical support – is there anything you want to say about that?" You have to listen carefully to how the customer responds to this kind of prompt. Obviously, a response like, "Yeah, I guess that's important too" should carry much less weight than, "Oh, I'm glad you brought that up – that's really critical."

Normally you're not asking customers to weight the importance of each attribute here, although if a participant gives you a 20-item list of important price factors you might do some weighting to isolate the most important ones. The sample size is too small to get really useful weighting information.

3. Design Survey Based on Standards

You now have the information you need to take a first stab at survey design. Remember to follow all the design standards you agreed on in the first task and include the mandatory questions.

4. Test Survey with Customers

Before you do widespread surveying, I suggest a phase of testing on actual customers in the target market and refining based on that experience. The process I find works best is this:

- Pull together a small team that includes a couple of interviewers, the person responsible for customer value management implementation, the person responsible for the survey, and a line person who represents the actual users of the data.

- Brief the interviewers thoroughly on the purpose and intended outcomes of the survey. This helps them ask the questions in the right way and answer any questions that respondents may have.
- Do three or four interviews, and listen in on them. Then have the team huddle and compare notes about any problems with the survey they noticed.
- Make the changes on the spot.
- Then do three or four more interviews to test the changes.
- Repeat the process if you're still finding problems with the survey. If you've done your homework properly, you should be able to get to a final survey within two iterations. You're in trouble if you end up using up much of your customer sample in the test phase!

Things to watch for in the survey test:

- **Length**
  Clock the length of time required for each module as well as the overall length. Was the overall time within your documented standards for the type of survey? Was the respondent's attention held for the full time? If not, in which module did things get bogged down?

- **Flow**
  Was the customer able to follow the logical flow of the interview easily?

- **Clarity**
  Note any questions of clarification the customer asks. Are there words they didn't recognize? Are there sentence constructions that seemed to confuse them? Did they have any difficulty understanding the scale?

Note on Language

Surveys are most effective when they closely reflect the actual language the customer uses rather than the jargon used by people working in the industry. Watch this aspect carefully in the testing phase. If respondents routinely translate your question into different words in their answer, this is an indication that the language needs refining.

The other things to watch for are words and phrases that are unique to your company. Value surveys are typically "blind" surveys. People are told that the research firm is studying an industry sector, and asked what company or companies they buy from. If the questions contain your trademarked language – you mention Aeroplan (unique to Air Canada), for example, rather than something more generic like "frequent flyer reward program" – then it's obvious to them who has commissioned the research.

Look for more on this topic in Step 4 – *Capture the Data.*

5. Finalize and Obtain Stakeholder Approval

This step is important and it must be handled carefully. Key decision makers who expect to use the data should see the survey and sign off on it before it goes to actual implementation. You don't want people rejecting the data later on because they didn't agree with the survey design.

You certainly don't want people telling you that they can't use what you've collected for decision making because you've missed something important on the survey.

But at the same time you don't want executives to act as amateur survey designers, pull rank and damage the survey. If you've taken care in the standards development phase to get alignment around the basic principles of design and solicited the opinions of stakeholders in the internal qualitative research phase, it should be relatively easy to get final sign-off and approval to begin surveying.

SUMMARY RECOMMENDATIONS ON SURVEY DESIGN

SAMPLING REQUIREMENTS

Precision Interval
- Mean score + or - 5%

Confidence Level
- 95%

QUESTIONNAIRE DESIGN

Mandatory Questions (to be included on all value surveys)
- Worth what paid for
- Overall rating of products, services, relationship or image (quality)
- Overall rating of purchase price, cost of ownership (price)
- Likely to recommend
- Likely to buy again/spend more

Modular Design
- Questions in logical groupings (experience with product, with service, relationship or image, price)
- Overall rating question comes last (review all critical elements before getting final ratings)

Optimum Length
- Transaction survey: In the 8 to 12 minute range
- Value survey: In the 15 to 20 minute range

RESPONSE WORDING

Value Questions
- How would you rate...from poor to excellent?

Behavior Questions
- How likely are you...from not at all likely to very likely?

RESPONSE SCALES, LABELS AND DEFINITIONS

Value Questions
- Ten-point scale where 1 is poor and 10 is excellent

Behavior Questions
- Ten-point scale where 1 is not at all likely and 10 is very likely

No Other Labels
- No labels attached to numbers 2 to 9 on the scale

SURVEY METHODS

Telephone
- Preferable for most consumer and business customer surveys

Web-based
- Less expensive than telephone, and becoming increasingly effective, provided you and your customers have the appropriate technology

Mail
- Third choice for consumer and business customer surveys

Face-to-face
- Appropriate in business-to-business situations where the target decision maker population is small

ATTRIBUTE IMPACT WEIGHT

Derived Impact
- The derived approach is preferred and is more predictive of customer behavior

Stated Importance
- Until sufficient data is available, stated importance is a good interim approach.

Step 4–Capture the Data:
Effective Survey Processes
chapter eight

This is a relatively short chapter about a very important step. Whether or not you have sufficient reliable data to work with through the rest of the process depends on how well you perform this step.

It's shorter than you might expect only because if you've read the previous two chapters closely and worked through all those tasks and issues, you're most of the way there. You'll have thought through how you want to segment your market, whom you want to sample and how you're going to get the list of names. You'll have designed a robust survey that will be meaningful to customers and give you actionable data.

Your next step is to think about how you're actually going to administer the survey to your sample group and collect the data. You need to consider:

- What you need in an outside market research firm
- Which vendor to engage
- How you plan to manage/monitor the survey process in partnership with that vendor.

We'll cover these three topics in this chapter.

Ten Steps to Mastery

Step 4: Capture the Data: *Effective Survey Processes*

1. Do Your Homework
2. Select Vendor
3. Manage and Monitor

Building in Quality Up Front

There are many purveyors of what people call customer value analysis. What differentiates Ray's customer value management approach in my mind is that he has a solid operational process laid out. You can see the steps, you can see the logic behind the steps, and when you drill down into any specific step – like developing the initial value Attribute Tree – you find meticulous planning.

Ray has built quality into this process up front. A lot of effort has gone into making sure the right questions are asked in the first place, through focus groups, validations, trials. As everyone knows, the place you build quality into any major engineering process is before there's a big expense. And in this process your big money gets spent doing the actual surveys.

- Dr. Nick Fisher

1. Do Your Homework

Managing the outsourcing of your survey processes is just like managing any other vendor relationship:

- The clearer you can be up front as to what your expectations are, the greater the likelihood you'll contract with the right organization in the right way to deliver what you need
- The better the material you give your vendor to work with, the more efficient and effective the vendor can be.

The two previous chapters dealt with making sure you have good material for your vendor to work with. I'll take it as a given that you have designed a survey process that reflects the most important drivers of customer value in your market and ties to your business processes. I'll also assume that you've thought through how you're going to characterize your survey sample and build your list.

In real life, of course, the process will not be an entirely linear one. While I'd urge you to get very clear on these two items internally before taking your thoughts out to an external vendor, there are clearly many vendors who will be able to assist your thought process by asking the right questions or making suggestions based on their experience. You may have a vendor already doing market research for you whom you want to bring into the conversation early on.

There are a few other pieces of homework I suggest you work through before deciding with whom to partner in this all-important data collection step.

Inside or Out?

You'll have noticed that I've already made the assumption you will be contracting the actual data collection to an outside firm. Nine times out of ten, I recommend this to my clients as the best course of action. There are two reasons for this:

1. **Administering a survey in an objective manner is a difficult task.**
   Most companies opt for telephone interviewing as the method most likely to ensure they get to the people they want to interview and capture the most useable data. It takes special skill and training to conduct a telephone interview well – to probe for the meaning behind the respondents' answers without biasing the result. It's a task best left to a professional firm with a good training program and quality control measures.

2. **No matter how hard they try not to, interviewers from within the company are likely to introduce a bias into the results.**
   Even if internal interviewers have the proper training and skill, they still have a vested interest in making sure the company gets ratings in the 8 or 9 range, not the 4 or 5 range. The smallest and subtlest variations in tone of voice can send this message to the respondent (more on this when we talk about quality monitoring).

If respondents know the interviewers personally, or know that they are employed directly by the company, there may also be a tendency to gloss over the bad news and emphasize the good. You're much more likely to get a full, objective picture if the customer knows you're using an objective third party.

The Business-to-Business Exception

I sometimes make an exception to my "contract-it-out" rule in a business-to-business situation, when the survey process is actually a series of one-on-one interviews with the most senior decision makers in 10 or 12 companies. This is as much a relationship-building opportunity as it is a data collection process, and you want to structure the data collection process to take advantage of it. My recommendations in this case are normally:

- **Do what you can to introduce a measure of objectivity into the process.**

Don't, for example, simply send the account team out to interview their customers. The team will have too much emotional investment in the outcome, and customers may feel constrained in raising issues specifically related to the team.

If you're going to use account teams to interview, have them interview customers they don't deal with directly. Another approach is to ask a senior marketing leader or other influential member of the executive team to conduct the interviews. In either case, you'll want to make sure the interviewers get thoroughly briefed in advance by the account teams so you can make best use of valuable executive time. You want to go in with a solid sense of what customers' issues or hot buttons are likely to be.

- **Get proper training on interviewing techniques.**
  While it's perfectly reasonable to use the interview to further a customer relationship, you still want to come back with reliable data. I generally recommend you use an outside consultant to train the teams in customer value management interview techniques, demonstrate the techniques to them by leading the first few interviews, and coach them through a few more interviews until they're completely comfortable with the process. It's important in these interviews to close the loop with customers, indicating how the information will get used and how they'll know what action has been taken.

- **Interview in teams of two people.**
  You need at least two people on the team: one to lead the questioning, and one to focus on capturing the responses on paper. The verbatim responses are especially rich in face-to-face interviews, and you want to get as much down as possible in customers' exact words. Unless special circumstances warrant a larger team, I'd suggest you send no more than two people, so the customer doesn't feel outnumbered and overwhelmed.

What Do You Need?

There are many, many players in the market research field. There are pure market research firms that are essentially call centers. There are market research companies that also provide consulting services. There are consulting companies that market themselves as research companies, but actually subcontract or "farm out" that work to call centers and use the contract as an entrée to sell their consulting.

There's nothing inherently good or bad about any of these types of firms. It's simply a matter of making sure you know what you're getting and getting what you need.

Selecting Your Partner

Selecting and using an outside source is much like a marriage. Think of it as a partnership or a strategic alliance – not a simple buy/sell agreement. Choose a vendor you feel comfortable with – someone you can trust to tell you what's really going on and not what they think you want to hear. Be willing to listen to each other.

- Davis Steward, Customer Opinion Research

If you have sophisticated market research and statistical analysis expertise in-house, there's no point engaging a consulting firm that's going to turn around and subcontract to an independent call center. In this case, you're better off contracting directly with the call center that is actually going to do the work. If on the other hand you need up-front help in sorting through some of the survey logistics – like how respondents will be screened for eligibility – or downstream help in analyzing and packaging the data, you're best to contract with a research firm that can provide you with these services as well.

As with any vendor agreement, the contract will set out a full description of the work: inputs, outputs, volume, compensation, deadlines, other expectations.

Who Will Manage?

I urge my clients to give a lot of thought to identifying the right in-house person or people to manage the vendor relationship. I said in Chapter Four that you want to have someone on your internal team with enough market research background to have credibility with an outside vendor and be able to deal intelligently with them. If you're farming out data analysis and econometric modeling, you still need an internal person with enough savvy to direct that effort and do a sanity check on the results that come in. You may find one person with both these skills, or you may need two part-time people assigned to the team to handle these aspects of vendor management.

Don't take this to mean that I don't trust the market research professionals to do their jobs! My point is simply that there are currently very few companies that specialize in the customer value management techniques and tools outlined in this book. Many have their own off-the-shelf programs that may or may not be aligned with customer value management. If you want to institute this customer value management approach, you're looking for someone who will partner with you to be sure you get data that will allow you to use the techniques and populate the decision-making tools. If you try to graft onto your customer value management initiative one of the many proprietary approaches that different companies have invented, things are going to get very messy.

So the bottom line for me is this: Be clear with yourself and your vendor that you are managing the data collection and analysis, and contracting with them for specialized assistance. You are not turning the process over to them to manage as they see fit. This is a key qualifier for the vendor selection process that I'll say more about in the next section.

2. Select Vendor

The list of needs you came up with in the "do your homework" task will form the core of your vendor selection criteria. Here's a generic checklist of things to think about in selecting a vendor:

Relationship
- Do they understand and are they willing to accept the parameters of the relationship as you've defined them?
- Do they agree that you own the data, not them?
- Can they supply data in an electronic format (such as ASCII) that you can manipulate internally?
- Are they willing to include senior executives from your company in the pretest?
- Are they open to having you or another senior executive drop in periodically to monitor live calls on a spot-check basis?

Performance
- Do they have the capability to reach a sufficient sample of your target market (whether defined by geography, demographics or other characteristics)?
- Do they regularly implement industry best practices?
- Are they equipped with CATI or other appropriate interviewing technology?
- Are they able/willing to supply weekly performance reports (calls completed, number used, % refusal rate, % completion rate, unusable/incomplete sample provided by company)?
- Do they have the capability to "lock out" for a specified period people who have been interviewed, to avoid over-surveying?
- How do they handle complaints or questions that arise when interviewing selected respondents?

Personnel
- Do they have rigorous training and performance management systems in place?
- Are interviewers supervised and periodically monitored by a senior interviewer?
- Is there a key contact who is fully briefed on the customer value management approach and responsible for keeping the work on track?

Security
- Do they comply with applicable privacy legislation and market research codes of practice?
- Do computer storage systems have adequate security and log-on procedures? Are servers backed up daily?

Note from a Change Agent: Vendor Relationships

I've had the privilege of working under contract with several corporations to help them get their customer value management programs up and running. In my experience, it's important to be very clear with your vendor from the beginning on the kind of relationship you're looking for. You'll want to put on the table questions like:

- *What quality standards will be complied with?*
- *How will we ensure non-sample error is minimized?*
- *Who exactly will be doing the work?*
- *What is the work plan, and is there room for flexibility?*
- *Can the call center be visited on an impromptu basis?*
- *What is the agreement on updates, turnaround times, follow-up work, additional services?*

When you're instituting a customer value management program, you need to choose a vendor who is very open. You want someone who is willing to learn about the customer value management approach and methodology, and willing to collect information in a way that's useful to you. You want to feel free to go on-site and talk to their interviewers, drop in for periodic spot checks on how the interviews are going, discuss any issues with them and work with them to fine-tune the script if necessary. For one managing director I worked with, the ability to visit the call center and listen in on live calls with his customer was the critical factor in vendor selection.

Many vendors are very comfortable with this kind of relationship. Some aren't. Some have a trademark proprietary approach that they guard closely. Their approach is to listen to what question you're trying to answer, design their own way to get there, and package the data for you. In most cases they continue to own the data and will produce reports for you on request. That approach works well for many companies' needs, but it doesn't work at all if you're seriously trying to implement customer value management.

You want to be clear that you own the data, and you want to have access to it in a format that allows you to run statistical analysis in-house if you have that capability in the company.

You want to make sure all the vendor's staff understand how important it is to collect information exactly to your specifications. Sometimes technicians will make changes when they're loading your questions onto their CATI system to reflect the technical requirements of their system or their standard practice. If a subcontractor changes the respondent profiles or industry segment sector codes without telling you, you can run into difficulty analyzing and comparing the data.

In one instance, for example, we found that the research company had substituted their standard "profile" questions for what we had given them. They had a check box for "officer of the company," but we wanted much more specific information. We wanted to know if we were talking to the managing director or a vice president and exactly what he or she was responsible for. That underscored for me how important it is to have absolute agreement from the vendor that nothing will be changed without your involvement and approval.

It's also a good idea to be clear with vendors as to what role you see them playing in presenting data to the executive team and discussing its implications. You may want some key people with you when you're working with the data, so they can answer any questions that arise as to reliability or approach. Then again, these may be highly confidential strategy sessions and it may be inappropriate for vendors to attend. It helps keep the relationship strong if there's no last minute misunderstanding on these fronts. As a change agent, your role is to avoid surprises for your company and the vendor.

If you're switching to a customer value management approach in a company that already has a longstanding contract with a market research vendor, then the challenge is to educate the firm as to what's going to change in the relationship. It may not be much, or it may be a lot. If you've outsourced survey design to them in the past, it could be a significant change. There may be changes in how we ask for information, how the contract is managed, how the data is managed, and so on. What's important is that you make it clear that the change is coming from top management, and why. If you've got a strong relationship with a good vendor, it's worth taking the time to explain the new approach and explore what it will take for both parties to make it work.

- Susan Moore, Market Insight

3. Manage and Monitor

I've learned from experience that a lot of little things can go wrong with the actual survey administration, even when you've designed a good survey and think you have a good sample. Sometimes survey questions that made sense in the design phase turn out to be turnoffs to respondents, causing high dropout rates in the middle of the survey. Sometimes you'll find that the people in your survey sample may not be able to give you reliable information about the questions you're asking. Or you may discover that poorly trained interviewers are introducing an unacceptable bias. While it's basic good vendor management to build into the contract a formal performance review and evaluation at an appropriate interval, it's just as important – if not more so – to agree on an ongoing monitoring process to catch these glitches before they become big problems that threaten the quality or reliability of your data, and your relationship.

I'll turn this part of the discussion over to my colleague Davis Steward, who for the past dozen years has run a company called Customer Opinion Research Inc.

Dave and I first worked together at AT&T, where we both had the privilege of learning from John Nemesh, one of the very early customer value management pioneers. John started designing customer opinion surveys back in the 1960s, long before this idea had taken hold widely. He championed the creation of Service Attitude Measurement, commonly known as SAM, in 1967, which later evolved into Telephone Service Attitude Measurement (TELSAM). In fact, Dave reminds me that John was involved with Bell Labs in creating the first CATI software. At the time, the general opinion was that the product was never really going to go anywhere and so it was sold. Now, of course, later generation CATI products are the instrument of choice for surveyors around the world.

Dave has been doing survey research for 30 years and customer value work for 20. Here's his advice as to what to watch for in the survey process:

> *Ray asked me how I would draw the quality branch of the Attribute Tree when it comes to drivers of value in the actual survey process. I said I would split the 100 points he gave me equally among three attributes: the survey design, the sample, and the calling center (the actual people doing the interviews).*

Dave's Attribute Tree for Survey Quality

	Design Impact Weight = 33.3%
Survey Quality	Sample Impact Weight = 33.3%
	Administration (Call Center / Interviewer) Impact Weight = 33.3%

> *Let me touch on what I think is important in each of these areas, and what to watch for during the actual survey process.*

> ### The Survey Design

> *A colleague of mine is fond of saying, "There is no statistical technique that will polish dirt." A lot depends on getting the survey design right from the beginning.*

> *Ray and I are in agreement on the basic principles of survey design. The questions should explicitly tie back to business processes the company can fix. The order of the questions should replicate customers' experience of the company. The survey should walk the customer through that experience to remind him or her of key points or feelings along the way, before asking the all-important, "Overall, how would you rate the experience?" question.*

At the same time, the survey must capture what's important to the customer about every step in that process – what benefits the customer derives from it. I've seen too many surveys that end up simply being tests of whether the process worked the way the company designed it, while ignoring the issue of whether the process added value to customers. Others test satisfaction with a random set of attributes, and don't bring back actionable data.

Those are the more technical aspects of survey design. It's equally important that the survey be interesting to respondents. People are most likely to complete the survey if they get the feeling along the way that they're contributing to helping the company better itself. If they don't see the theme – if it seems to them to be just a mishmash of questions – then they're likely to drop out before the end of the survey.

This is also the case if they don't recognize the language in the survey as something meaningful to them. (At the same time, you have to be careful that the survey isn't full of jargon unique to your company – language only your customers will recognize and understand.) I usually pitch surveys to about an eighth grade general understanding, and I make sure they sound like an interesting conversation, even if that means they're not always grammatically correct.

This is the kind of thing you're listening for when you pretest the survey and in your ongoing monitoring throughout the survey process. I always insist as strongly as I can that the client participate in the pretest. I can train interviewers how to ask the questions, but they may need more context on the business and on how the data are going to be used to really understand what's behind the questions they ask. I find it's really valuable to get very senior people involved at this stage. From our perspective, this gives us a comfort level that we're asking the right questions and getting information back that the client can use. At the same time, we find that the client learns a great deal just from listening to these few surveys.

The Sample

"It's always the sample," I'm known to say to my clients. By that I mean that it's always the sample that turns out to be more of a problem than we expect. This has a multiplier effect because sample is on the cost branch of the survey Attribute Tree as well as the quality branch. If I contact a lot of people who either don't pass the initial screening as eligible respondents, or who drop out of the survey partway through because they don't feel it's relevant to them, then it's going to take me a lot more time and effort to get a sufficient sample of completed surveys.

- Davis Steward

Sample Required for Modeling Purposes

One frequently asked question is, "How big a sample size do I have to have to be able to do useful statistical modeling with the data and use it to populate customer value management tools?" Every statistician will give you a slightly different rule of thumb.

Mine is approximately 50 responses for every variable. So if you have six different attributes on your tree as drivers of overall sales quality, ideally you're looking for a minimum of 300 responses. We've found that we can get decent regressions with as few as 70 to 80 responses, so long as we structure the survey in modules with the "overall how would you rate" question last, as both Ray and Dave have recommended.

That's why it's important to limit the number of attributes on a survey. If you've got ten factors driving satisfaction with repair, you're going to need 500 responses before you can get a decent sense of the extent to which satisfaction with each variable drives perception of overall value received from the repair experience.

- Rich DeNicola, Econometrician/Statistician

I'm continually surprised that in spite of much talk these days about customer relationship management and the availability of great tools for capturing customer information, few companies act as though they see their customer database as the lifeblood of their company. It seems they're more comfortable paying big money to advertising firms to help them attract new customers than they are investing small sums in keeping an up-to-date database that could help them retain current customers.

Although the first response I get when I start to talk about sample is, "We'll just go to our IT department and get that to you right away," we often find that it's not so easy to get accurate customer lists from a client. It's even more difficult to get lists of competitors' customers, although presumably many of these were in contact with the client company before they decided to purchase from a competitor. In a company that's really thinking about customer value management, as much information as possible is being captured about every individual who has any contact with the company, whether they end up purchasing or not. People point to the sales force as one source of information on customers, but you can't rely on the sales force alone to give you a valid random sampling of customers. Consciously or unconsciously, they're highly likely to direct you to the more satisfied customers. Billing records are usually a good source of information, but even then we find phone numbers that have been disconnected, area codes that have been changed and so on. I always feed this information back to the appropriate person in the client organization.

What's more telling is that I often find people directing me to "primary customers" who in fact don't consider themselves to be primary customers of my client. Often it turns out that they also buy (and buy more) from a competitor, or once bought from my client but have since switched to a competitor.

My point is that if you haven't been managing your customer database very closely, monitoring the survey process is an excellent place to begin. Even if you never do another survey, you can probably find good reasons later on to communicate with your customers (new product introductions, promotions, etc.). Use the survey process to get information up to date and think through how you can best maintain it.

The Call Center/Interviewer

The interviewer is critical. If you've designed a very poor survey or handed over an incomplete script, you can't blame the interviewer. But even the best survey can be ruined by a bad interviewer.

In my work, I think of interviewers as my customers. It's my responsibility as a survey designer to make sure I give the interviewers good material to work with, including a full script that walks them through every aspect of the interview. For example, I don't just say, "You must screen the respondent to make sure you have a decision maker." I'm responsible for laying out a full script that will elicit this information from the respondent in an appropriate way. All the interviewer needs to do is follow the script.

Following the script is not as easy as it might seem. One of the advantages of a telephone survey is that you can probe the respondent for more information if your first question elicits an incomplete answer. So if the person you're interviewing has just given the company a 4 out of 10 on a particular rating, you want to follow up with a question like, "What's the single most important reason you rated the company that way?" If the respondent replies with something like, "The service was just fair," you need to peel the onion further by asking, "What exactly about the service was just fair?" You're trying to get to the root cause – but you're trying to get there without leading the witness or attributing your own assumptions to the respondent.

If the person says, "I'd rate that an 8 or a 9," you need to be confident that your interviewer will follow that with, "Would that be closer to an 8 or a 9?" If the respondent won't answer, then the whole question gets rated "Don't know" or "N/A." We're not looking for the interviewer's best guess as to which the respondent might have chosen.

I can lay out all these techniques in a script, but it takes skill to follow them. Even very subtle signals from the interviewer can bias the response. I once was monitoring a survey and discovered that when the respondent gave an 8 or 9 rating the interviewer would say "Okay" as the transition to the next question. When the response was on the low end – say a 4 or a 5 – the transition statement was invariably "I see" rather than "Okay." That one little idiosyncrasy was enough to signal to the respondent that high ratings were okay, but low ones weren't. So now I make sure interviewers are trained on how to manage these transitions correctly.

Training is extremely important. I work only with facilities that have robust training plans for new interviewers, at least two to three days of training before they go live. I monitor them regularly on a spot-check basis to make sure: a) that they're following the script; and b) that it's working for them. If they're not following the script, that's a quality control issue that we need to confront and deal with. If they're following the script exactly and having trouble with high refusal or drop out rates, then it's my issue. What's wrong with the survey design? Are the questions too intrusive? Are they not compelling enough? Are we asking the wrong people the wrong things? The software can help by analyzing exactly when you're losing most people, and the interviewer can provide his or her views on what's going wrong.

- Davis Steward

What I hear both Susan and Dave saying in their accounts is that the need for vigilance doesn't end once you've designed a survey and contracted with an appropriate firm to administer it. While we've concentrated on telephone interviews here, many of the principles apply equally to in-person, web-based or mail interviews, although these methods are tougher to pretest and monitor.

Both the sponsoring company and the research vendor bear responsibility for monitoring interview quality and for investigating the cause of unacceptable refusal/drop-out rates before these become a big cost issue or data reliability problem. As Susan stresses, if you have a strong relationship based on agreed expectations, you'll be able to work together to overcome these issues and meet your goals.

An Aside from Ray: Asking the Right People

One of the things to pay attention to in the pretest and monitoring process is, "Are the questions I'm asking appropriate to the person I'm interviewing?"

I once worked with a company that got so excited about the "worth-what-paid-for" question they wanted to put it on every survey they did. Now, if you're doing a transaction survey on a recent installation for which there was no specific charge – or if the charge was recorded on an invoice that went to someone else – it's not very useful to ask the "worth-what-paid-for" question. If the person you're interviewing was happy with the installation, he or she is highly likely to say it was worth what was paid even if he or she has no idea what was paid!

If you're interviewing top decision makers, it's reasonable to suppose they have some idea of the cost involved, even if they weren't the recipient of the actual invoice. But at the transaction level it's important to remember that the respondent may not know much at all about any of the other steps in the Waterfall of Needs.

Let me end this chapter with an anecdote to illustrate my point. In many years of monitoring what works and what doesn't work in administering surveys, I've come across some interesting phenomena that I wouldn't have expected. One of these is that it seems if the people doing the telephone interviews are calling from a different country than the respondent's, the likelihood of people agreeing to take the survey goes way up.

I first experienced this when I was doing some work with Australia and New Zealand Telecom. We were having a hard time getting people in Australia to take the time to do a market perception survey. Everyone was too busy. When we tried making the calls to Australian decision makers from New Zealand – introducing each call with something like, "I'm calling from X market research firm in New Zealand and we're conducting a study of the telecom industry in Australia" – the response rate rose from something like 20% to almost 55%! It made each telephone interview a bit more expensive, but it was worth it.

I tried a similar tactic in the UK when I found we were having trouble getting past secretaries to the decision maker. We moved the base of our telephone interviews to France. When we told the secretary the call was coming from France (and this was indeed the truth), we got through most of the time. For whatever reason, it seems that the perceived importance of the study goes up if it crosses national boundaries.

The point of my story is that human beings are complex creatures, and the process of collecting their opinions is rarely as scientific and mechanical as some textbooks might lead you to believe. You've got to stay alert throughout the process and be ready to innovate to address whatever factor may threaten your goal of obtaining reliable and actionable data.

Step 5–Share the Results: *Reports Leaders Will Use*

chapter nine

This step is about making sure that the customer value data you're collecting impacts business decision making at the highest level. It looks at:

- What is included in the high-level report that is regularly put in front of officers and key executives
- The process of getting this report put together and distributed
- The importance of getting the report's audience to agree on a format and process that works for them
- The importance of sticking to the agreed-upon template and process for every report.

There are two key messages in this chapter. The first is, "Keep it simple." Too much detail actually lessens the impact of the data on this audience. The second is, "Choose a format and stick to it." If you don't, you risk confusing your audience.

Ten Steps to Mastery

Step 5: Share the Results: *Reports Leaders Will Use*

1. **Design the Template**
2. **Design the Process**
3. **Get Sign-off**
4. **Implement Consistency**

1. Design the Template

I talked at length in Step 3 about the importance of standards and consistency. The easier you make it for your audience to interpret the data you put in front of them, the more likely they will be to pay attention to it and use it. If they have to relearn every time what the numbers represent and how they're calculated, they may not make the effort. They certainly won't have as much confidence in the data.

The most effective officer-level customer value reports I've seen have four sections:

- Introduction
- Corporate Summary of Results by Business Unit
- Results by Market Segment/Product
- President-level Commentary.

Introduction

Typically the *Introduction* section provides context for people getting this report for the first time. It defines relative customer value and explains how it is measured. It may also outline the company's customer value performance objectives and how these compare to world-class scores. It describes the contents of the report and how the results should be read. The text of the *Introduction* usually doesn't vary from quarter to quarter, unless performance objectives or measurement standards change.

Corporate Summary of Results by Business Unit

Since the goal is to have customer value data used with the same discipline, passion and understanding as financial data, it's logical to model the format of customer value reports on financial reports.

As you develop a rich database of detail on attributes that drive customer value, their sub-attributes and impact weights, you'll be tempted to start adding detail into the officer report. Resist that temptation. In most companies, officers receive a one-page summary of key financial data each quarter. This summary page focuses on the key financial metric the company uses to track shareholder value – margin on income, for example, or return on invested capital – so that officers can see at a glance how the company is doing and which way business is trending. They're interested in the bottom line for the company and how each business unit is contributing to it.

The corresponding metric for customer value is CVA ratio. Remember that this is the number you get when you divide your company's score on the overall "worth-what-paid-for" question by the mean score of your competitors on the same question. The heart of the Customer Value Data report is a one-page overview showing CVA scores and trends by business unit (for companies that have multiple business units) and an overall CVA score (weighted average) for the company. Here's a sample:

Summary Quarterly Customer Value Results
XYZ Company
SAMPLE

Business Unit	Percentage of Revenue	CVA Results					CVA Trend Over 1 Year
		1st Qtr. 2001	2nd Qtr. 2001	3rd Qtr. 2001	4th Qtr. 2001	1st Qtr. 2002	
Unit A	48%	1.02	1.04	1.04	1.05	1.06	↑
Unit B	27%	1.03	1.02	1.04	1.02	1.03	→
Unit C	10%	1.06	1.04	1.04	1.02	1.00	↓
Unit D	7%	0.96	0.97	0.97	0.99	1.02	↑
Unit E	5%	0.98	1.00	0.99	1.00	0.99	→
Unit F	3%	0.92	0.97	0.97	0.98	1.02	↑
Company Overall	100%	1.02	1.03	1.03	1.03	1.04	↑
(weighted average CVA)							

I'd like to highlight three aspects of the report design:

- **Ordered by revenue**
  The order in which the business units appear is determined by percentage revenue, with the business unit representing the largest proportion of revenue at the top. Some companies I've worked with prefer to use market share rather than revenue, which works as well. The important point is that they are not ordered according to CVA score. Ordering by revenue or market share puts the emphasis where it should be – on the relation between CVA and how each business unit is doing in the market, rather than on how business units rank against one another on CVA score. Remember: It's not enough to beat yourself.

- **Overall weighted average**
  The overall CVA for the company is calculated by taking an average of CVA scores, weighted by percentage of revenue for each business unit.

- **Numbers, not graphs**
  The summary report consists of actual numbers, not graphs and trend lines. In my experience, executives tend to be more skeptical of what they see in graphs, since it's easier to manipulate the reader's impression with the graphics. A simple directional arrow in the last column is sufficient to visually depict the trend.

Detailed Results by Market Segment

Behind this summary page, I recommend you have backup detail that indicates what is causing the improvement or the decline in customers' perception of overall value. Is it related primarily to what they get (product, service, relationship quality) or what they pay (initial price and ongoing costs)? Is it driven by one market segment or spread across many?

While this section has more detail than the one-page summary, it is still high-level information. I don't recommend including data broken down by attribute and sub-attribute in officer-level quarterly reports. If there's a serious problem in a particular area and officers want to learn more about what's behind it, the relevant data can be packaged and made available to them. But in general, people at this level don't want to wade through pages and pages of detail. If you've done a thorough job of getting prepared (Step 3) – including getting sign-off on data collection guidelines and standards – they'll have confidence that the right data is being collected and used by the appropriate people.

Here's a sample of what this *Detailed Results* section of the report could look like, using an actual example from the insurance industry. The bolded headings are business units; the sub-headings are market segments. In this case, they've defined "market segments" as product lines. Other companies in the insurance sector might choose to break results down by regional market segments or by customer characteristics such as age groups or claim history.

Corporate Level
Detailed Results by: Product/Market Segment

SAMPLE

Product/Market Segment	Planned Annual Revenue	% of Rev	Current Quarter Results			
			Relative Perceived Value			
			Products and Services	Price	Overall (CVA)	CVA Trend Over 1 Year
Individual						
Life Insurance						
Annuity						
Medicare Supplement						
Health, Accident, Special						
Group						
Managed Health Care						
Life Insurance						
Dental Insurance						
Disability Insurance						
Retirement Plans						
Property and Casualty						
Homeowners						
Renters						
Condominium						
Auto/Boat						

Note on Coverage

I want to repeat here a point I made in Step 1 about how much of your business you want covered by customer value data. Generally companies set a target of having customer value data on the business units and market segments that account for 75% to 80% of their revenue. The return on investment in surveying customers that account for very small amounts of revenue is usually also small – unless that particular market segment is poised to emerge as a strategic growth area, in which case you would want to understand it thoroughly.

President-level Commentary

The very best reports I've seen contain a one-page analysis of each business unit's results, written and signed by the senior officer responsible for that business unit. The commentary gives the president's or managing director's view on why the results are what they are, what's behind trends and what the business unit is going to do to improve or sustain the scores. It may also include some analysis of key competitors in that market – their strengths and weaknesses, their strategy, the company's response.

In my view, it's critical that these commentaries not be written by market researchers or the customer value team. While these staff people will no doubt influence the president's views, it is the senior officer who's responsible. He or she must take accountability for the scores and commit to action.

2. Design the Process

Four key questions for the team to address at the outset are:

- Who should get the report?
- When should they get it?
- How should they get it?
- What's the process of getting the report populated and delivered on time?

Distribution

All of the officers of the company – that is, anyone who carries legal or fiduciary accountability for company actions – should get the report. In a large company this would include the heads of such corporate staff functions as information services, human resources and legal, as well as the heads of the business units and sales/marketing organizations.

In some companies, the report also goes to the board of directors. This serves both to provide them insight into the business and to give them confidence that the leadership team is making data-driven decisions.

Timing

Customer value data will have most meaning and impact if it is delivered at the same time as financial data. I always recommend that it be bundled with the quarterly financial results and go out as a single briefing package before quarterly review meetings or scheduled strategic planning sessions. It works well if the person responsible for the business unit's financial results is also responsible for doing the customer value report for that unit. Data that comes after these key meetings is not useful. The major decisions will already have been made, and they will have been made on the basis of an incomplete picture of the company's competitive position.

The principle holds true if you're collecting data on a six-month cycle rather than a quarterly cycle: Bundle the data with every second quarter's financial data.

Note on Reporting Frequency

I recommend that companies survey customers and report data quarterly if possible, or every six months if quarterly is not feasible because of cost or sample size. More frequent surveying usually doesn't bring much additional insight because most markets simply don't change that quickly. If you survey less frequently, you risk missing competitive moves that can seriously undermine your value position before you even know what has happened.

Distribution Media

The decision as to whether to distribute the report electronically or in hard copy will be based on company norms. I recommend that you choose the format in which the company's financial data is distributed, and follow the security protocols that govern the release of financial data.

Production Process

Companies usually have strict protocols for how financial reports get pulled together, checked and double-checked before the distribution deadline. The process for producing flawless customer value reports should be just as rigorous.

If the report needs to be sent out on the second Friday of the month following the close of a quarter so that officers have it for the regular third Wednesday review meeting, then your production timeline needs to back up from this. You'll want to establish cut-off dates by which all data must be collected, and assign responsibility for assembling it into the standard report format. You'll set up procedures for double-checking the accuracy of every number and making sure the data meets prescribed standards. If the report includes presidents' commentaries, then time must be allowed in the schedule and booked in each president's calendar.

Even if your company doesn't follow the practice of having the president or presidents write commentaries, you will want to build in time to review each business unit's numbers with the accountable officer before the report is issued. Business executives don't like surprises any more than customers do! If there's anything in the report that is potentially embarrassing or that will raise questions, you want to give the officer time to double-check and to understand what's behind the numbers.

Dealing with Errors

No matter how much effort you put into ensuring the accuracy of reports before they're released, occasionally you will find errors after the fact. I suggest that your process documentation include guidelines for dealing with this eventuality. Frequent reissuing of corrected reports undermines credibility. At the same time, you don't want leaders making significant business decisions based on data you know to be incorrect. Under what circumstances will the report be pulled and reissued? How will errors detected after release be reflected in the next quarter's report?   Think about this and discuss it with the leadership team before you hit a crisis.

3. Get Sign-off on Template and Process

As I said earlier in connection with data standards and guidelines, all my recommendations are based on what I've seen work well in the companies I interact with. If you're just starting to institute a customer value management business approach, my suggestions on report format and process are meant to short circuit the process of trial and error. If you already have a report and process that are working well for you, this chapter may give you useful suggestions for continuous improvement.

But what's most critical is that your report meets the needs and expectations of your company's officers. So as with the data guidelines, it's important to get sign-off from the people you expect to see and use the reports before you invest a lot of time producing them. Not just conceptual sign-off. I recommend that you actually design the layout of the report and show this to its audience for feedback. Even small improvements to the format can make a big difference to how easy reports are to read and understand.

If you have some data already, you can populate your sample template, but that's not really important at this point. It is, however, important that you set out your understanding of which business units and market segments will be included on the report. You want to be absolutely sure that the officers agree these are the key units and segments. You may want to do a sample president's commentary as well to get alignment around general approach and level of detail expected in these.

A List of Reporting "Do's"

- Resist the temptation to keep adding more. Keep the reports high level and simple.
- Get the data to officers prior to key business review or strategy planning meetings.
- Be absolutely certain that the report includes only data that you know is reliable and meets prescribed standards.

4. Implement Consistently

You've heard this from me again and again, so I'll be brief. Consistency brings credibility and speeds the process of getting people comfortable with reading and interpreting the data. Data that people understand and have confidence in will be used for decision making. If your report format, timing and process are haphazard or ever-changing, you're not getting the best possible return on your customer value management investment.

Step 6–Analyze the Data: Customer Value Tools

chapter ten

I've said several times that customer value management is about:

- **Choosing the value:** Deciding what value proposition you are taking to market
- **Delivering the value:** Making sure your business processes are aligned with your value proposition and working together to deliver value to customers
- **Communicating the value:** Educating the market on your value proposition.

I've also stressed my firmly held belief that if you try to do too many things at once you won't make a big impact on anything. The key to success is picking your priorities and working on a few things at a time.

Choosing, delivering and communicating value is not a one-time linear process. Decisions on priorities are made all the time in all sorts of venues: business strategy sessions, new product development planning, process owners' quality improvement meetings, marketing and advertising strategy workshops. The next two steps are about making sure that customer value data is packaged and available to these groups at the right time, and about teaching people how to use it to pick priorities.

In Chapter Two we introduced the basic tools of customer value management. In Chapter Eleven we'll look at a method of getting people comfortable with using these tools to make decisions. This is the "how-to" chapter, focused on the mechanics of using survey data to populate the core customer value management tools so that decision makers can work with them. It covers:

- **Slippery Slopes:** A tool for helping people understand what the absolute scores mean in the minds of customers, and what kinds of scores you need to win customer loyalty

- **Value Maps:** A snapshot of your competitive position in the marketplace, useful for planning both attack and defense strategies
- **Impact Weights:** The missing piece of information that completes the Attribute Trees you used to create your survey (important for understanding the extent to which each attribute drives overall perception of value)
- **Competitive Profiles:** A format for summarizing the most pertinent customer value information for informed decision making
- **Waterfall of Needs:** A visual to guide discussion on how business processes impact one another and overall perception of value.

Ten Steps to Mastery

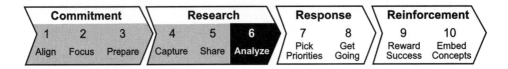

Commitment			Research			Response		Reinforcement	
1	2	3	4	5	6	7	8	9	10
Align	Focus	Prepare	Capture	Share	Analyze	Pick Priorities	Get Going	Reward Success	Embed Concepts

Step 6: Analyze the Data: *Customer Value Tools*

1. **Calibrate Data: Slippery Slopes**
2. **Understand Playing Field: Value Maps**
3. **Calculate Weighting: Attribute Trees**
4. **Summarize Results: Competitive Profiles**
5. **Link to Business Processes: Waterfall of Needs**

1. Calibrate Data: Slippery Slopes

The Slippery Slope is the simplest of the customer value management tools and one of the few that uses absolute scores rather than relative-to-the-competition scores. By itself, it doesn't really help you decide where to focus effort, and it's not something that needs to be continually front and center with decision makers. It is, however, a useful starting point for introducing people to the concept of customer value.

You don't need a history of customer value management to produce this chart. If you've been doing any form of customer research at all, you can normally find a way of creating a Slippery Slope using existing data. The value of the chart is that it helps answer some age-old questions: What is in customers' minds when they give us an overall value rating of 7 (or 6 or 8 or whatever)? How do we know whether they think that's pretty good or not very good at all?

What if 8 is in fact the top mark that most customers in this market are prepared to give – why are we killing ourselves trying to get a 9?

The Slippery Slope provides what market research people call a cross-tab. By showing how this absolute score relates to a key indicator of customer behavior, it helps calibrate your mind to what the numbers mean to your customers. It tells you which absolute scores equate to the delivery of superior customer value in the eyes of your customers.

How to Produce a Slippery Slope

The chart itself is very easy to produce:

- **X axis:** Plot the absolute score your customers gave you on an overall rating question. The question could be "overall rating on price," "overall rating on product," "overall rating on services" – anything like that. If your focus to date has been on traditional customer satisfaction measures, you can use the "overall satisfaction" scores to build your initial Slippery Slope and then move to value questions over time. I recommend sticking to the really important value or overall satisfaction questions here. Taking a subcomponent like "documentation is easy to read" and trying to correlate it to loyalty doesn't really tell you much, unless you know that this is a very strong driver of value and loyalty in your market.

- **Y axis:** Plot the percentage of your customers who gave you "top-box" scores on a key behavioral or loyalty indicator. "Top box" in my vocabulary means 5 on a 5-point scale, 9 or 10 on a 10-point scale (I recommend a 10-point scale). As I said in Step 3, the loyalty questions I like most are, "How likely are you to recommend the company to others?" "How likely are you to buy from the company again?" "How likely are you to spend more with the company?" "Likely" is a stronger word than "willing," since people may be willing to do many things (like retire to a villa in Tuscany) that they know they're not likely to do in the foreseeable future. But you can use whatever loyalty question you've been tracking and it should work.

Why "Top Box" Matters

When we were first developing customer value management techniques at AT&T, we were able to conduct some specific research on real-life customer loyalty behaviors and link these back to the response that customers had given in previous value surveys. We found that only customers who give a top-box score on a loyalty question have any significant probability of actually practicing the behavior in question – for example, buying again – in their future interactions with the company.

What you get when you plot these figures looks like the chart below. It's called the Slippery Slope tool because every time I've done this correlation for a company, I get a slope that falls off very quickly once you get past the highest overall rating scores, and totally flattens out at the bottom.

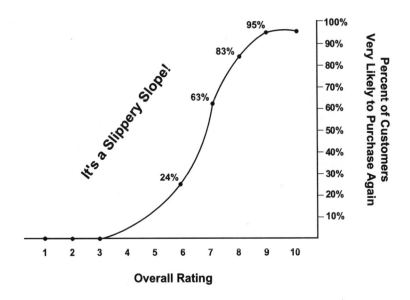

How to Interpret a Slippery Slope

What it says is this: Of the customers who gave us an overall rating of 6, only 24% are very likely to buy from us again. Of the customers who gave us a 7 rating, 63% said they were very likely to buy from us again. Or to put it another way, 37% are leaning towards buying from our competitors next time around. Only when you get to overall ratings of 8, 9 or 10 do you start getting customers demonstrating loyalty to the company. The message is clear: For your customers, an overall rating of 7 isn't good enough. If your goal is to reach 90% customer loyalty, then you need to be getting average absolute ratings in the over 8 range. If you don't get these rating, you'll find yourself sliding down that Slippery Slope and losing customers.

2. Understand Playing Field: Value Maps

The purpose of the Value Map is to give you a snapshot of the competitive playing field and your company's position on it. Earlier I likened it to the maps military leaders put on war room walls – the ones that show the position, strength and movement of their troops versus enemy troops and help them plan their strategy.

Value Maps can become very complicated and technically sophisticated. I always try to keep them as simple as possible, because to me their real value is in the story they tell about current reality and the "what if?" scenarios that can be spun out of them.

If you don't have all the data that I list in the next section, you can still build a notional Value Map based on the best knowledge that exists in your company as to your position in the market relative to competitors. Just estimate the importance customers place on "what they get" versus "what they pay" in your market, and how they view you and your competitors. It may not be totally accurate, but it can still be a useful tool to shape your thinking about competitive strategy. You don't have to wait until you have all the data.

Building a Map

To get a full-fledged Value Map that gives you a good picture of the competitive field, you need to have survey respondents naming actual competitors and rating each as an individual entity – not bundling together ratings of an amorphous "competition." Here's the information you need to build a more accurate Value Map:

- **Relative quality ratio:** How the market rates you relative to the competition on "what you got" (products, services, relationship or brand image – I sometimes use the short-form "quality" for all of these). This will be expressed as a ratio – with 1.0 being parity. You can pick this score up from your survey data (your average score on overall quality divided by your competitors' average score).

- **Relative price ratio:** How the market rates you relative to the competition on "what you pay" (initial price, cost of ownership – sometimes "price" for short). Again, you'll get this from your survey data.

- **Competitors' ratios:** How the market rates your key competitors on overall relative quality and overall relative price (their average scores divided by the average score for the other key competitors in the market).

- **Relative weighting of quality/price:** How much weight the market gives to quality versus price in rating overall value. If you've asked respondents to weight these two factors in the course of the survey (by splitting 100 points between them, for example), you can use their stated response as your importance weighting. To be more accurate, you should derive the impact weight from the responses to the survey. We'll talk later in this chapter about how you do that, in the context of assigning impact weights to items on your Attribute Tree.

How to Plot the Data

Here's how I recommend building a Value Map:

- **X axis:** Represents relative ratings of customer-perceived quality, running from low (left) to high (right), with 1.0 as the midpoint. You can adjust the outer ends of the scale to accommodate the actual data you're plotting. Normally the scale would run from about 0.90 to 1.10.

- **Y axis:** Represents relative ratings of customer-perceived price, running from high ratings (bottom) to low ratings (top) – again with 1.0 at the midpoint. It may seem counterintuitive to put the highest ratings on the bottom of the scale, but remember that what we're looking at here is how highly customers rate the company on the price value driver – not how high the price is. If we were looking at absolute price instead of customer perceptions of and satisfaction with price, we'd put "low price" at the bottom of the scale and "high price" at the top.

Technical Note

Charts created using the default settings of most software programs will have a y axis that is shorter than the x axis. If you're using such a program to create Value Maps, it's important that you manually square off the chart. The elongated x axis can distort the data and lead to faulty interpretations.

- **Plot scores:** Plot your company's scores with a single dot at the point where your relative ratings on price and quality intersect. Do the same for your competitors.

- **Fair value line:** Draw a "fair value line" based on the relative weightings your market assigns to price versus quality. More on this below.

How to Draw the Fair Value Line

The fair value line rotates around the center point of the graph (the point that represents 1.0 on quality and 1.0 on price) like the hands of a clock. If you draw in a vertical dotted line going straight up from this center point, and a horizontal line going straight to the right, you'll have dotted in a 90°angle. Here's how you calculate where to draw the fair value line:

- If your market puts equal weight on price and quality, then you want to bisect your 90° angle, to form two equal 45° angles.

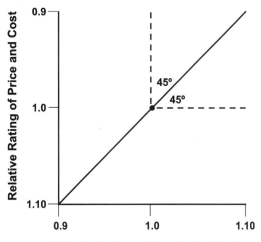

Relative Rating of Products, Services and Relationship or Image

- If your market puts 70% weighting on price and 30% on quality, you want to draw a line from the center point that is 70% of 90° (63°) from the vertical line and 30% of 90° (27°) from the horizontal line, as shown in the following graph.

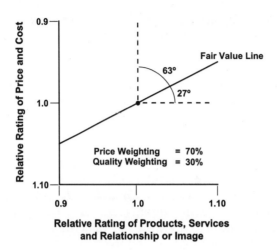

- If the opposite is true – if your market puts 30% weighting on price and 70% on quality – you want to draw a line from the center point that is 30% of 90° (27°) from the vertical line and 70% of 90° (63°) from the horizontal line.

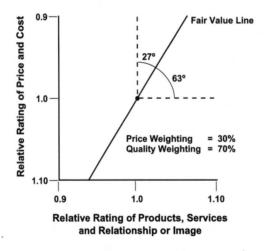

- Remember that a completely vertical line through the midpoint would mean that the market gives 100% weighting to quality. So the more vertical the line, the higher the quality weighting.

- A completely horizontal line through the midpoint would mean 100% weighting on price. The more horizontal the line, the higher the price weighting.

How to Interpret a Value Map

There are a few basic concepts you need to remember:

- Companies clustered along the fair value line are essentially at parity from a relative value standpoint, whether they're low-priced economy brands or high-priced premium brands. We call this area immediately surrounding the line the "fair value zone."

- Companies positioned in the lower left of the map are perceived in the market as economy brands (lower quality for lower price), while companies in the upper right of the map are seen as premium brands (charging a higher price for higher quality).

- Companies positioned to the right of and below the fair value line are in the "better value zone."

- Companies positioned to the left of/above the fair value line are in the "worse value zone."

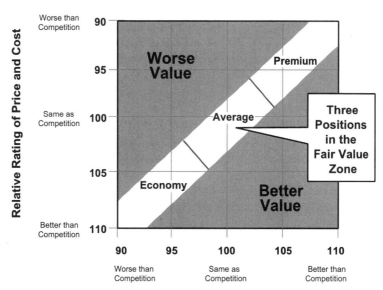

Relative Rating of Products, Services and Relationship or Image

It's very important that the fair value line be drawn correctly. Let me illustrate:

The Value Map below depicts a market in which customers give equal weighting to quality and price. The fair value line bisects the right angle formed from the midpoint of the chart to produce a 45° line. Company E is seen as a premium brand, with high quality and high price. Company D is perceived as having average quality and price, and Company C is known for charging lower prices for products of lower quality. Customers in this market consider all three to be charging fair prices for the quality received, and so companies C, D and E are all in the fair value zone, with CVA ratios ranging from 0.98 to 1.02. Company B, on the other hand, is considered a worse value vendor, charging high prices for lower quality goods. Company A is in the better value zone, charging lower prices relative to the high quality of the goods sold.

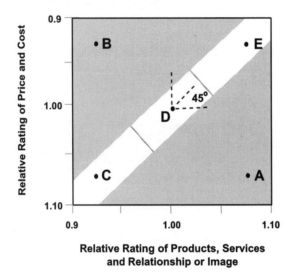

Relative Rating of Products, Services and Relationship or Image

Now let's assume that something happens to make customers in this market start valuing quality more than price. If they now weight quality as having 70% impact on their decision, with price dwindling to a 30% impact weight, the fair value line rotates counter-clockwise. Company E is now in the better value zone, while Company C has moved to the worse value zone. Their actual position on the map hasn't changed. They haven't changed their prices or their quality. All that's changed is customers are now placing a higher value on the quality that Company E offers, and place less value on Company C's lower quality product, despite that lower price (as shown in the following graph).

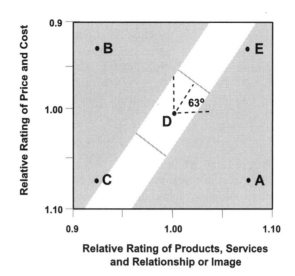

Suppose the opposite is true, and the market has shifted emphasis so that price (with a 70% impact weight) matters more than quality (with a 30% impact weight). The higher-priced Company E loses its competitive advantage and shifts into the worse value zone, while Company C moves into the better value zone because customers value its lower prices.

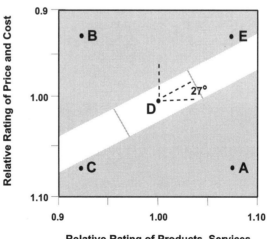

Armed with these concepts, you can learn to interpret Value Maps. It takes a bit of practice, because the goal is not only to understand what the competitive field looks like now, but also to think about what strategic moves you might make to move yourself into a better value position. You want to play out some "what if?" scenarios based on intelligence about your competitors' business strategies (are they about to launch a discount brand to undercut you in the marketplace?) or about new competitors who may be contemplating a run in that market.

If you're playing in a number of different markets, you can also use a Value Map to get a snapshot of how you're doing in each of these markets. Knowing, for example, that the products you're marketing to seniors are consistently in the better value zone, while products aimed at the teen market are languishing in the worse value zone, can help you chart an appropriate strategic course.

A Note on Value Maps

I like this approach to drawing Value Maps because it's simple and it produces the desired results. But I have to acknowledge that respected colleagues do it differently and also obtain useful results.

The statistician I worked with closely at AT&T, Rich DeNicola, likes to plot absolute average scores, not relative ratios. If you're doing this, I'd urge you to start the scale on the x axis at 4 or 5 on a 10-point scale – not 1. Very few people give scores of 1 to 4, and so if you put the entire 1 to 10 scale on the x axis companies will likely be clustered at the higher end and the competitive distinctions will be harder to see. Instead of drawing the fair value line manually using derived impact weight data from the survey, he runs a regression equation from the data on the chart looking for the locus of points for all values of price and quality for which the relative value is 1.0 and superimposes what he calls the "constant value line" based on this equation.

While Rich's approach would stand up better in a court of statistical law, we both have agreed over the years that my more approximate approach consistently produces a line that's so close to his it's equally useful for business decision making.

3. Calculate Impact Weights: Attribute Trees

The next few pages should probably come with a warning label that reads something like this:

WARNING

If you're severely allergic to statistics, you might choose to skip this section and get your econometrician/statistician to read it and tell you what you need to know.

If you're an expert in statistics, be warned that we've framed this discussion to be intelligible to laypeople. While it's been reviewed by experts to confirm the validity of the approach set out here, don't expect the depth of analysis you'd find in an expert article in a journal of statistics.

This section is about using statistical analysis to confirm and complete your Attribute Trees. You'll need this information in order to populate the Competitive Profiles we'll talk about next.

You were introduced to Attribute Trees in Chapter Two. In Step 3, we talked about using internal experts and customer focus groups to identify the key drivers of value for customers in your target market and the sub-attributes behind each of these main drivers. You'll remember I recommended you design your surveys in modules reflecting the main branches and ancillary branches on the Attribute Tree, focusing on the key value drivers for your market.

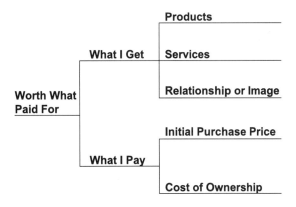

We also explored in Step 3 two ways of determining the weight customers give to each element of the Tree in determining overall value:

- **Stated importance:** For example, you ask survey respondents to split 100 points among a set of attributes. This can give you some idea of relative importance for the top level attributes, but gets cumbersome and makes the survey too long if you try to do it with every sub-attribute. It's a good place to start, but not totally reliable. When we do the statistical analysis, we often find that derived weightings will reveal that the most important determinants of overall value are quite different from what respondents have stated as most important to them.

- **Derived impact weights:** The derived impact method involves using statistical techniques such as multiple regression to determine the degree to which variation in the rating on an attribute influences variation in the overall rating. If you have enough data to produce reliable results, this is the preferred technique.

In my opinion, it's well worth taking the trouble to use statistical analysis techniques to derive impact weights. It's a key piece of information that makes the Competitive Profile (which we'll discuss next) a truly useful tool for turning data into action plans. There's no use allocating significant time and resources to improvements on an attribute that has little impact on how customers perceive the value of your offering.

This is where you need the help of an expert econometrician/statistician. I'll turn much of this discussion over to my colleague Rich DeNicola, with whom I've been associated for almost 15 years. I first met him at AT&T, when he was working in the market research organization of General Business Systems. At the time I was having econometric modeling done by outside consultants, but I knew I really needed someone inside the company on my team. I wanted to do more modeling and I wanted to have more control over how the modeling was done. Rich was a great partner in this effort. Over the years he has trained and supported members of my international network of colleagues and clients.

I've asked Rich to explain in his own words how he approaches determining impact weights for the each branch of the Attribute Tree, and to comment on some of the finer statistical points along the way:

Here are the basic steps involved in deriving impact weights from customer survey data:

1. Clean the Data

Typically, the data comes to me from an outside market research vendor in the form of an ASCII or Excel file. The first step is to "clean" the data. If the raw data is corrupted in any way, we won't get accurate results from the modeling. This has become less of an issue in recent years as data recording has become more mechanized, but still exists in areas where surveying depends on manual data entry.

For example: If respondents were asked to rate the company on a poor, fair, good, excellent scale, we start by putting numeric codes on each of these responses and changing all the alpha responses to numeric responses. We need to do this when data has been entered manually because often we'll find whoever was summarizing the data sometimes wrote "Excellent," sometimes "Exc" or "Exc." or just "E." We know that all of these are intended to mean "Excellent," but to the computer they're different responses.

2. Define and Run the Regressions

"Regression" is a mathematical technique that attempts to explain how changes in one variable, such as customer perception of quality, impact another variable, such as overall value. When we draw a standard Attribute Tree, we're assuming that overall value is a function of quality and cost, but we can't quantify that function: We can't say, "If we can improve quality by x% or x units (or cost by x% or x units), value will go up by x." That's what we're trying to find out by running regressions.

So we start by writing down all the regressions that will be required for the model we're trying to build. Each branch of the tree represents one regression. Normally we require 15 to 25 regressions to create an overall Tree structure that shows the relative weighting of each sub-attribute in relation to its main attribute.

We read the clean data into a format that can be manipulated by a statistical program such as SAS or SPSS, and run the regressions.

3. Normalize the Data

Here's where we get a bit technical. What the regression actually delivers is an equation that looks something like this:

Overall value = 3.0 +0 .4 overall quality score +0 .7 overall price score.

The 3.0 is an intercept term; 0.4 and 0 .7 are regression coefficients. From these regression coefficients, we can calculate a set of elasticities, one for each independent variable. By "elasticity" we mean the percent of change we can expect to see in the dependent variable if a related independent variable changes by a certain percentage.

What we end up with when we do this might be something like:

A 1% change in quality will drive a 0.3% change in value.
A 1% change in price will drive a 0.5% change in value.

Now, I can't imagine putting that kind of information in front of an executive and expecting him or her to use it to make decisions. For the purposes of business decision making, it's much easier to work with elasticities that add up to 100%, so we normalize them (make them add to 1, then multiply by 100 to get a percentage). In this example, we'd say:

$$\frac{0.3}{0.3 + 0.5} = .375 \times 100 = 37.5\%$$

$$\frac{0.5}{0.3 + 0.5} = .625 \times 100 = 62.5\%$$

So in "impact weight" language, we say that 37.5% of customer perception of value is driven by quality; 62.5% by price. And that's what we'd put on our Tree. The impact weights of any given set of sub-attributes always add to 100% or thereabouts (it will vary slightly due to rounding).

4. Test the Model

There are a number of ways to test the validity of the resulting model, but two are important to mention here. First I run a t-test to test whether the regression coefficients I'm getting are statistically significant. If this procedure suggests that a variable is not significant, we drop it out of the equation and rerun using just the variables that are significant. (Note that we don't drop it from the Tree. We leave it on and mark it N/S. See box below for more on this.)

Statistically Insignificant but Not Unimportant

Don't fall into the trap of thinking you can ignore a variable that the tests say is statistically insignificant. Remember that impact weights are telling you what attributes are most influential in driving changes in value or what sub-attributes are driving changes in the next level attribute. If a variable isn't changing very much at all, it's not going to enter into the regression in any strong way. But that doesn't mean it's not important.

Let me give you an example: This situation happened once when we were running a regression to assess perceptions of billing quality. Of the five to six variables that we were testing, one was courtesy. The results of the regression said that courtesy wasn't significant at all.

But intuitively this didn't make sense. We all know very well that if the people answering the phones and correcting your bill are discourteous, your perception of billing service quality is going to be low. That's just common sense.

When we looked at the absolute scores, we realized that the reason courtesy wasn't showing up as a driver of changes in perception was that we were consistently getting excellent ratings in this area. We were doing such a great job on courtesy that the ratings never varied. So while at that moment in time the variable was having no impact on changes in overall billing quality perceptions, we could be pretty sure that would change quickly if suddenly our courtesy ratings started to drop. Courtesy was not a significant factor in the regression model, but that didn't mean we could take our eye off the ball or become complacent. We needed to keep up the good work in this area.

The point is that statistical modeling can help you understand the data in a deep way, but its results can't always be taken literally. You have to look at them through the filter of your own common sense.

The other think I look at is the R-SQUARED, also called the coefficient of multiple determination. This is a number between 0 and +1 that measures how well the regression explains variation in the driven variable – at the first attribute level, for example, how well changes in quality and price explain the observed variation in value. This is also sometimes called the "model fit."

In our case, the nature of the data we're working with is such that when any variable changes in a positive way it drives positive changes in the related variables (e.g. if you increase quality you wouldn't expect value to go down). The closer R-SQUARED gets to 1, the better the model fit. An R-SQUARED of 0.8, for example, means that 80% of the variation in value is explained by the variables of quality and price. Typically we get numbers from 0.3 to 0.9. If the model fit is on the low side, we'll do some other tests to see whether there are sub-attributes on other branches of the tree which are impacting the attribute we're studying. For example, we might hypothesize that customer perceptions of cost of doing business are highly impacted by a sub-attribute we've identified as belonging to the perceptions of the sales process: how well sales people explain the costs up front. If the model fit improves when we include this variable in the regression, then our hypothesis is probably right.

A Hypothesis in the Form of a Hierarchy

When we first build an Attribute Tree based on our best knowledge of what drives value for customers, we're creating a hypothesis in the form of a hierarchy. When we run the regressions and determine impact weights we're testing to see whether the data supports our hypothesis. The techniques can't tell us our hypothesis is categorically true, but it can tell us whether there's evidence to support our theory.

The Tree defines a hierarchy in which attributes are driven by sets of linked sub-attributes (ideally no more than six or seven) which in turn are driven by sets of linked sub-sub-attributes if you like. When we run regressions, we're assessing the relative impact of this set of attributes assuming they're acting simultaneously on the next level attribute. Some people prefer to use bivariate techniques that assess the effect of quality on value, then separately assess the effect of price on value. I think it's more realistic to examine the effect of quality on value in the presence of the effect of price on value – because in the real world of commerce, the two are acting simultaneously on a customer's decision.

I've seen surveys where questions are randomly ordered – just thrown together one after another with no real regard to any relationship with the preceding or succeeding question. In my experience that doesn't work very well. If you hypothesize the hierarchical structure up front (based on focus groups and existing data), design your survey in modules that reflect that structure, and put the overall rating question pertaining to that attribute at the end of each module, you stand the best chance of getting robust models that are really useful for decision making.

Business Process		**Customer Need**	
	30% Product	Reliable	(40%)
		Easy to Understand	(20%)
		Features	(30%)
	30% Sales	Knowledge	(30%)
		Responsiveness	(25%)
Products, Services, Relationship or Image		Follow-Up	(10%)
	8% Application	No Problems	(10%)
		Easy	(25%)
		Right Coverage	(30%)
	10% Billing	No Surprise	(45%)
		Easy to Understand	(10%)
		Resolve on First Call	(35%)
	22% Claims	Progress Report	(25%)
		Fast	(35%)
		No Troubles	(10%)

Multiple Techniques for Multiple Regression

I use the Ordinary Least Squares (OLS) multiple regression technique for analyzing customer value data.

If you're a statistician, you'll know that there are other techniques, such as Multinomial Probit Regression (MPR) and Multinomial Logit Regression (MLR), that are more specifically designed to handle this type of ordinal categorical data set.

There have been discussions up and down the statistical literature about whether OLS should be used with ordinal categorical data and how valid it is. I won't try to summarize or defend or refute any of those arguments. I'll stick here to what I've learned from our experience with customer value data.

We decided to start with an open mind and try out the different options. We ran several different sets of models from different surveys using OLS. Then, we repeated the analyses using MPR. In 99% of these experiments, the ordering of influence of the driving variables was the same in both techniques. Technically, the results of an MPR analysis are interpreted in terms of probabilities. So while in OLS, you would say that sales has the highest impact weight, in MPR we'd say that a given improvement in the sales score increases the probability of getting an excellent score in the overall variable more than a corresponding increase in another attribute. The effect is the same for our purposes. When we ranked the attributes based on these probabilities and compared it to the ranking of attributes indicated by impact weights derived from OLS regressions, the lists were identical.

We looked at the advantages and disadvantages of each technique and came to the conclusion that for our purposes, OLS was the better option. Using OLS, it's easier to express the impact weights simply as percentages that add to 100, and to build Attribute Trees. MPR is much more difficult to interpret and explain to business leaders, since it talks about probability of occurrence rather than impact weight. I've found that most executives aren't really interested in the finer points of statistical analysis, because they're just looking for the one, two or three most influential items to work on. No matter which system you use, the three most influential items are going to be the same.

- Rich DeNicola

Because I'm not a statistician, I've always been very conscious of making sure that colleagues like Rich who do have this expertise are comfortable with my methods and the conclusions I draw from them. At the outset of this work, I had AT&T statisticians and market research people test and retest the customer value management approach we were using within the company and with strategic partners such as Telecom New Zealand. They confirmed that it passed the statistical reliability tests. But when I started applying the principles and tools more widely through my consultancy, I sought additional opinions from outside expert statisticians.

One of these was Dr. Nick Fisher, then a Chief Research Scientist in the Mathematical and Statistics Division of CSIRO, Australia's Commonwealth Scientific and Industrial Research Organization. He's since left to start ValueMetrics Australia, which we'll learn more about in Chapter Sixteen. Nick has been a statistical consultant and researcher for over 30 years, and is the author of over 100 research papers and books, including works on statistical aspects of quality management. Here's what Nick has to say about the customer value management approach:

> *I've examined Ray's customer value management approach from a technical perspective and it is sound. His thinking has very much influenced my own work in performance measurement – an area where business organizations on the whole tend to be very weak.*
>
> *He advocates use of a 10-point scale in surveying, which is sufficiently fine to enable the type of analysis he does. Most importantly, Ray adopts what I would call a pragmatic approach to analyzing the data and reporting results.*
>
> *One of the world's great statisticians, the late John Tukey, invented a notion called "portable power." Portable power is defined as "the power of the technique multiplied by the probability that someone is going to use it."*
>
> *People can fall into the trap of thinking that the more powerful the technique, the better. But the more powerful techniques can become very, very complex. You can have the world's most powerful technique, but if most people haven't got the means of implementing it it's not likely to be used. And if you can't turn the results into something meaningful for the people you expect to use this information, it's a total waste of time.*

> *Ray has developed a methodology that captures a lot of data without sacrificing the ability to convey to the leaders who own the data the key information they need to make a business decision.*
>
> - Dr. Nick Fisher

I like this idea of portable power. I have a great respect for people with expertise in statistics and have counted on my statistician colleagues to make sure that the customer value management techniques I use are rigorous and reliable. From time to time I've been persuaded to try out the "latest and greatest" new technique, and in general I've found that you don't get superior value from the greater investment. The more complex the technique, the harder it is to get busy leaders to understand and accept the data.

When I see the eyes of my audience start to roll back in their heads, I know that the stuff I'm presenting is a bit more magical than they want to deal with. I prefer to use the simpler, more accessible systems. At the end of the day, all we're looking for is the two or three attributes or sub-attributes that most influence the next level attribute. If we work on these, and find that value scores and market share go up – as we have again and again – that's reliable enough for me.

4. Summarize Results: Competitive Profiles

Once you've done this work, it's a simple matter to populate the Competitive Profiles, which are the most important input into decision making. I'm using the plural "Profiles" here, because you'll probably have a Profile on quality, a Profile on price, and additional Profiles on key sub-attributes. Over time, you'll find that these will probably be the only tools you put in front of decision makers. When you first start implementing customer value management, you need to show them Slippery Slopes, Value Maps, Attribute Trees and Waterfalls so that they get the conceptual basis behind the data. Once they've got it, Competitive Profiles give them the key information they need to pick priorities.

A Competitive Profile contains the following information:

- Attribute
- Impact weight of the attribute
- Your average score
- Average of your competitors' scores
- Competitive ratio (your score divided by your competitors').

Remember I said back in Chapter Two that using the Competitive Profiles to pick priorities is as much an art as a science. As Rich pointed out in the last section with his story about courtesy of billing services personnel, you can't ignore a factor simply because the impact weight says it's not significant. The Competitive Profiles give decision makers the absolute scores and relative scores they need to put that one piece of information in context.

Quality Profile

Key Purchase Criteria	Importance Weight %	Your Company	Competition	Ratio
Product:				
Understandable	18	7.4	7.2	1.03
Features	12	9.0	8.6	1.05
	30			
Service:				
Sales	30	8.5	8.1	1.05
Application	8	8.5	8.5	1.00
Claims	22	7.8	8.1	0.96
Billing	10	7.0	8.0	0.88
	70			

A Competitive Profile to guide decision making doesn't have to be anything more sophisticated than a simple table like the one above. For companies that wish to play out "what if?" scenarios from this data, there is software available to automate the process.[1] They're looking to answer such questions as: What if we improved our score on billing from 7.0 to 8.5? How would that impact our overall value relative to the competition? What improvement do we need to make on "soft cost" factors to achieve our target CVA ratio and move to the desired position of the Value Map? What if we combined this cost improvement with small gains on the key relationship items of communication and ease of doing business – what impact would that have?

5. Link to Business Processes: Waterfall of Needs

While the Waterfall of Needs is really just another way of depicting elements that also appear on the Attribute Trees, I find it useful for two purposes. First, as I said in Chapter Two, when you're just starting out on your customer value management journey it's great as a brainstorming tool. Asking a group of executives to draw a picture of how customers experience the company helps them start looking at their business from a customer perspective and thinking about hand-offs and interdependencies among business processes.

---

[1] *See **www.twovogels.com** for information on customer value management software.*

The Customer Waterfall of Needs

Sales
- Accessible
- Responsive
- Knowledgeable
- Follow-up

Products
- Reliable
- Features
- Easy to Understand
- Performance Record

Application
- Time Required
- Easy to Apply
- No Problems
- Get Right Coverage

Billing
- No Surprises
- Easy to Understand
- Timely
- Easy to Resolve Problems

Claims
- Progress Report
- Fast Resolution
- No Troubles
- Follow-up

Second, I've learned that it helps focus discussion around several key questions that I think should be asked as part of the priority-picking process:

- **Frequency of occurrence: How often do customers go through this experience?**

  The Competitive Profile may be showing that the quality and cost of repair services have a reasonably significant impact on overall value, and that repair is an area in which you're lagging the competition. But suppose that in your business, most customers go years without experiencing the need for repair. What happens when they do have a need significantly influences how these customers rate overall value. But if in a given year only 10% of the customer population experiences this need, do you want to put all or most of your resources into improving the repair experience? If billing is also a significant item, and it happens monthly, I'd suggest it's more important to fix that quickly and get to repair as time and money allow.

- **Multiplying impact: Are there upstream processes that, if they were improved, would automatically lead to improvement in other elements further down the Waterfall?**

  We've used an insurance industry example in this Waterfall, so let's explore that. You learned in the Suncorp case study at the end of Part I that a common customer peeve is that insurance policies – auto insurance as an example – are so complex that not even the internal claims people are 100% sure of what's covered and what's not. And yet this one aspect matters a great deal to people. They not only want to know what they're covered for, they want to know how premiums are calculated. If they just have a minor scrape to the car, they want to be able to decide whether it's a good idea to involve the insurance company, or whether that will just cost them more in the long run because their premiums will go up.

This is a communication problem that should be relatively easy and inexpensive to fix. If you look at the Waterfall of Needs, you can see how making the product – in this case the actual policy – easy to understand has impacts all down the entire Waterfall. You see the easy to understand factor there under product, but you can also see that better communication of what's covered and what it costs will impact people's perception of how knowledgeable the salesperson is, of how easy it is to apply and get the right coverage, how easy the bill is to understand, and how quickly their claims are resolved.

So from this one action you can get positive impact across multiple customer experiences. If you looked at the full Attribute Tree from which this Waterfall was derived, you'd probably find that the same action would likely impact customer perception of price and image as well. Most important, from the point of view of aligning business processes, if you choose to work on this one item you'll have people in different business units across the company working on a common issue: better communication of what's covered and what it costs.

This is a lot of information to absorb in one chapter. But I think once you've gone through a couple of cycles of using the survey data to populate these tools, you'll find that it's fairly intuitive and straightforward – and even the statistical analysis is not too complex in the hands of someone with the right knowledge and background. The key is to keep it simple and remember what the ultimate goal of all this work is: To help business decision makers pick the priorities that will produce the greatest improvements in customer value as quickly as possible with the least possible investment.

Step 7–Pick Priorities:
Action Planning and Implementation

I noted in Step 6 – *Analyze the Data* that the process of picking priorities in a business is happening all the time in all sorts of venues. The ultimate goal is to have the concepts and tools of customer value management so ingrained in people's hearts and minds that they wouldn't dream of making a strategic decision or taking action without first considering what the customer value data was telling them. Over time, if your initiative is successful, customer value management will simply be how people do business.

But to make that happen requires some out-of-the-ordinary effort up front. In the initial stages of your customer value management initiative, you'll need to decide how to train people to interpret and use the data. I strongly believe that the only way to get people to really understand, accept and act on the data is to have them roll up their sleeves and work with it. And I've found the best way to do this is through hands-on, action-learning workshops that take place as soon as you have a good set of data.

The basic design I use for these workshops takes people through the phases of understanding, acceptance and action. Two further steps – root cause analysis and alignment with other business processes – needs to take place before the "in-pencil action plans" produced at the workshop become set in stone and ready for implementation.

Ten Steps to Mastery

Commitment			Research			Response		Reinforcement	
1	2	3	4	5	6	7	8	9	10
Align	Focus	Prepare	Capture	Share	Analyze	Pick Priorities	Get Going	Reward Success	Embed Concepts

Step 7: Pick Priorities: *Action Planning and Implementation*

1. **Design a Learning Process**
2. **Create Understanding**
3. **Gain Acceptance**
4. **Plan Actions**
5. **Analyze Root Causes**
6. **Align with Business Processes**

1. Design a Learning Process

It's quite possible for people to understand the customer value management concepts, tools and results but not accept their importance. I know that while the group around the meeting table is nodding agreement, silent objections are running through the heads of many – questions like:

- I don't really understand what any of this has to do with me – why do I need to pay attention to it?
- This data doesn't agree with what I know to be true – why should I trust it?
- I already knew this – why am I wasting my time?
- That may be what the customer perceives, but the reality is much different – how can I change perception?
- I don't control the customer's entire experience of the company – how can I be held accountable for these results?

That's why I advocate starting with a structured, action-learning process that does more than help people understand the concepts and tools. It needs to address these silent questions and lead people to accept that it's important for them to understand and use the data.

But acceptance doesn't automatically lead to action. You may accept that losing weight or gaining weight or stopping smoking are important things for you to do, and still do nothing about them. Have you ever made an explicit resolution to do something, perhaps at the start of a new year – to the point of actually writing it down – and still not done it?

Following Through

I've always liked the dictum that British engineer Frank Price introduces in his book Right First Time: [1]

"No inspection or measurement without proper recording. No recording without analysis. No analysis without action."

If you're not going to follow through, why collect the data?

- Dr. Nick Fisher

All the time and money spent capturing and analyzing the data and helping people understand and accept it is wasted if it doesn't lead to action. So the workshop design I use actually gets people picking priorities and building action plans.

Workshops: The Critical Element

In my mind these experiential workshops are the make-or-break point in your customer value management journey. If you can't get your senior people to engage with the data and start using it to pick priorities you're in for a hard slog to embed customer value management into the business. If you skip this step altogether, I can guarantee you won't get maximum return on your data collection investment.

I've done hundreds of workshops in my time, and here's what I've found works best:

- **Start at the top**
  Start with a six-hour workshop session involving the CEO and senior leadership team. The output of this session will be a draft action plan (I call these "in-pencil action plans") focusing on high-level strategic issues such as cost and business relationships. Schedule this meeting as soon as possible after your data comes in. You want it to be fresh and timely.

---

[1] Frank Price, *Right First Time: Using Quality Control for Profit.* (Ashgate Publishing Co., 1994).

- **Cascade to intact teams**

  Have the CEO's direct reports lead similar workshops with the next reporting layer. The ideal is to have each workshop consist of a cross-functional group working with their own data, not hypothetical data or data that belongs to somebody else. You want to have all the groups represented that must work together to make improvements in a specific set of customer value scores.

  How many times this process of cascading to the next layer needs to happen will vary depending on the size and makeup of your organization. You want to reach at least the first layer of front-line management: the people who will actually be implementing changes to deliver better customer value. By the time you reach the middle management layer, the in-pencil action plans will be more focused on specific internal metrics related to one of the Waterfall elements.

- **Make participants work**

  While some material needs to be presented, the emphasis of the workshop should be on the participants' active exploration of the concepts and data.

The agenda for the workshop typically follows this flow:

Customer Value Workshop Agenda

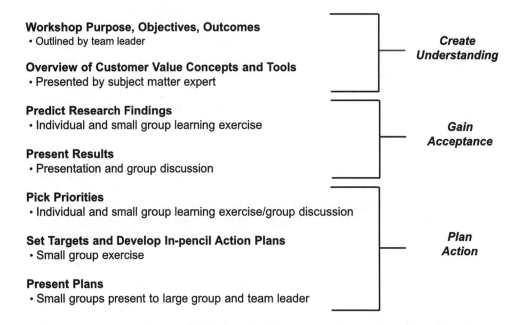

Workshop Purpose, Objectives, Outcomes
- Outlined by team leader

Overview of Customer Value Concepts and Tools
- Presented by subject matter expert

Create Understanding

Predict Research Findings
- Individual and small group learning exercise

Present Results
- Presentation and group discussion

Gain Acceptance

Pick Priorities
- Individual and small group learning exercise/group discussion

Set Targets and Develop In-pencil Action Plans
- Small group exercise

Present Plans
- Small groups present to large group and team leader

Plan Action

2. Create Understanding

Workshop Purpose, Objectives and Outcomes

It's critical that a senior leader in the company be present to talk about the workshop purpose, objectives and outcomes – either the immediate leader of the participating team, or someone from higher up in the reporting structure. If you give this task to an outside facilitator or customer value management expert, you're losing an opportunity to signal that the leader is taking personal accountability for the customer value data and sponsoring the performance improvement effort.

The exact wording of the purpose and objectives varies from business to business, but generally boils down to "understand, accept, act on the customer value data." The most effective workshops have as their outcome an in-pencil action plan and an agreed process for finalizing the plan, getting it approved and implementing it.

Overview of Customer Value Management Concepts and Tools

This is the presentation portion of the workshop, and it essentially covers the material contained in Chapters One and Two of this book: the fundamentals of customer value management and an overview of the tools. How much detail you get into depends on the time available and the needs of the participants.

You would generally get a subject matter expert to deliver this material for the senior leadership team workshop, because the credibility of the data depends on precise explanation of the technical aspects of customer value management. This could be an external facilitator or the change agent.

But you don't necessarily need an expert to lead every workshop through the cascade process. You'll remember that Paul Wondrasch at AT&T expected all his leaders to learn the material well enough to present it in turn to their teams, with a subject matter expert in the room to answer any questions that they couldn't address. The more people in the company you train to give a solid overview of the concepts and tools, the easier it will be to sustain the work over the long term. The important thing is that the workshops be led by people who are passionate about customer value and personally committed to the work. If the facilitator believes it's an academic exercise, that message will get through to the audience very quickly.

For this overview, I make sure that my sample Attribute Trees, Value Maps and Slippery Slopes are built around disguised or fictitious examples of a company that the audience will relate to. They should not specifically reflect data from the participants' company. If you use real data from the participants' company in this presentation phase, you risk having people derail the process by reacting to the numbers at an emotional level before they understand what the data means. (You'll use their data in the next phase.) At this point, you want the example to be from the same or a related industry (e.g. if it's a high-tech company, don't talk washing machines) so that people understand the language on the chart and are focusing on the concepts, not the numbers.

3. Gain Acceptance

Predict Research Findings

"Desktop research" is the term I use to describe collecting opinions from within the company as to how customers will likely respond to the survey. It's a good idea to have workshop participants actually take the survey before the workshop. This has three purposes:

1. **Increase their confidence in the survey process itself** and, by extension, the data. They'll see that the survey is professionally administered, clear and not onerous for the customer.
2. **Have participants experience the thought process a customer goes through** in responding to the survey. This will help them connect better to the data they see.
3. **Give you a snapshot of internal opinions** on how customers perceive the company's value relative to the competition to use as a starting point in the workshop. You'll have a high-level Attribute Tree pre-populated with mean scores from participants.

If you aren't able to do this prior to the workshop, start this section by showing them the Attribute Tree on which the survey is based. Have them take a few minutes on their own to write down what score they believe customers would give the company relative to the competition on each of these items. Collect the responses and populate the Tree with the mean scores.

The next portion of the workshop then usually follows this sequence:

- **Individual exercise**
  Ask people to spend about ten minutes thinking in silence about whether they agree with the group's view. Also ask them to divide 100 points among the attributes at each level of the Tree to indicate their relative weighting. Even if you have had the participants do the survey prior to the session, you won't have enough data to derive impact weights statistically, so you'll have to do this step in the session.

- **Small group working session**
  Break the team up into small groups and ask them to come to a consensus in the group on ratings and impact weights.

- **Large group discussion**
  Bring them back together to discuss what they've found and see if you can find consensus within the team.

Note on Reaching Consensus

Invariably I find that groups have more difficulty than they expect reaching agreement on what weight customers give the different attributes and how they're likely to rate the company. Often the first comment made when we come back into the large group is, "We didn't have enough time."

When we compare the results of their hurried consensus, we find that results vary widely from group to group. There's usually consensus on some items – these are the things they're aware of and have been focusing on. But in every group there are items that people haven't thought about much. This is where we see divergent views. At this point in the workshop I often hear comments to the effect of, "No wonder we can't make a decision around here. We're working from completely different views of the market!"

Present Results of Customer Surveys

Next we reveal how customers actually rated the company and the impact weight of each attribute. We also show the company's position relative to the competition on the Value Map, and what the Slippery Slope looks like when we correlate the overall performance rating with the chosen customer loyalty metric. The previous step has prepared participants to read these results much more thoughtfully and carefully than if they'd just been handed a report. The group discusses how the external customer view compares to the internal view, highlighting where they guessed correctly and where they were wrong.

In every workshop I've experienced there have been at least a few surprises that made people realize how important it is to actually ask customers rather than just guess at what they're thinking. In some workshops there are many, many surprises.

"Going Down Rat Holes"

Is this expression used in your company? It means taking a meeting off in directions that risk derailing the purpose of the meeting. Tactics used for preventing people from taking a meeting "down a rat hole" include "no rat hole" signs that participants can hold up at appropriate moments or rubber rats to throw in the general direction of someone who's heading for a hole. A rat-hole issue can be a very important issue. It's just that if the meeting goes in that direction it won't accomplish its objectives.

The issue of statistical methods and validity can be one big rat hole for this workshop. It's an extremely important topic because if people don't believe in the data they won't use it. But occasionally you'll get people in workshops who threaten to derail the workshop by spending hours delving into minute technical detail on the econometric models you've used and the assumptions behind them. Usually there's also a group at the other end of the spectrum who couldn't care less about the science behind the modeling but won't accept the results because they don't align with their intuition.

You have to be ready to deal with either extreme. Plan in advance how you surface these questions, recognize them as valid, and schedule time at a later date to address them in detail with those participants who are interested. You can't risk losing the entire group by going off into technical discussions that are of interest to only one or two people.

4. Plan Action

Pick Priorities

The next step is for the group to work with the data to identify priority areas for improvement. When I'm facilitating, I start this session by having them discuss where they want to be on the Value Map (relative competitive position) and on the Slippery Slope (overall absolute performance). If we have done correlations to financial indicators and have an idea of what improvement in customer perception of value is required to meet the business unit's financial targets, we can get pretty specific here about quantifying the improvements they need to make.

I then ask them to pick priorities, using the Competitive Profiles. They're looking for high impact items on which they're below parity against the competition and have room for improvement in absolute terms. They may also be looking for high impact items on which they're rated significantly higher than the competition and which haven't been featured prominently to date in advertising or other communication with customers.

Here's an example of how a group might think this through. Their starting point is a Competitive Profile that looks like the one reproduced below, except that the Priority column is blank as they begin the discussion.

Note that this Profile captures the high-level view of the overall drivers of value. In this case, the three factors driving customers' perception of overall quality (what they get) are products, services and relationship. The impact weights of these three factors add up to 100%. The 60% figure beside Overall Quality on the table indicates that 60% of customers' perception of value is driven by what they get. Similarly, the 40% beside Overall Costs indicates that 40% of customers' perception of value is driven by what they pay. The three factors driving cost perception in this example are initial price, ongoing costs, and customers' ability to justify the costs.

Competitive Profile

Attribute	Impact Weight	Our Rating	Competitor Rating	Competitive Ratio	Priority
Overall Quality:	60	7.8	7.8	1.00	
Products	25	8.0	7.5	1.07	C
Services	40	7.5	8.0	0.94	I
Relationship	35	8.0	7.8	1.03	H
Overall Cost:	40	7.2	7.2	1.00	
Initial Price	25	7.0	7.3	0.96	H
Ongoing Costs	30	8.0	7.0	1.14	C
Ability to Justify Costs	45	6.8	7.2	0.94	I
Overall Value	**100**	7.6	7.6	1.00	
Priority Legend: C = Communicate I = Improve H = Hold					

The group's discussion:

The bottom-line story from this profile is that we're at parity with our competitors, with an overall CVA of 1.0. That's not good enough. We want to create a competitive advantage and win market share. So what can we learn from the detail in the chart about how to do this?

Let's start with the first level quality attributes – customers' perception of what they get from us. We have a very good rating on products, at an 8.0. We know from our Slippery Slope that this is a good place to be. The competition's a little worse, and that gives us a nice competitive ratio of 1.07. With a 25% impact on the overall quality rating, it's the least important to customers of the three quality attributes, but it's not insignificant. Our priority here is to invest in communicating to the market that our products are better on average than those of our competitors, to reinforce this differentiation.

Now let's look at the services attribute (things such as sales support, billing, technical support and so on). Our rating is modest at a 7.5. The competition is better (8.0) and this gives us a competitive ratio of 0.94. The services attribute has a high impact weight, and we have a significant competitive disadvantage. This is clearly a priority for improvement. Once we've finished analyzing this Competitive Profile, we'll look at the next level Profile on services, to get a better sense of where exactly we need to focus service improvement to gain competitive advantage.

On the relationship attribute, the news is good. Again we have a very good score of 8.0. The competition's pretty good too, with a 7.8, but we have a modest advantage. The best strategy for us is to focus our improvement efforts on the services attribute, but make sure we hold our position on relationship.

Now we'll look at the overall cost side, which is a significant driver of value with a 40% overall impact weight. Here it's easy to spot the top priority for improvement quickly, because the attribute with the highest impact also has the lowest rating and competitive ratio. Providing customers with enough information that they can justify the cost of doing business is rated at a 6.8, which is the lowest score on the chart, and one of those scores that barely makes the grade as "good" (which we know is really "bad"). The competitors are doing better than we are on this attribute. Fortunately not tremendously better, but better enough that our competitive ratio is a 0.94. With an impact weight of 45%, clearly this is an item that must be improved.

Now what about price, since price is always important to customers? Look at the customers' perception of the initial price. It's a significantly weighted factor at 25, but not the most important factor. The score is a 7.0, which is not great, but the competition isn't much better and our competitive ratio is 0.96. There are good business reasons why we don't want to get into lowering our initial pricing structure. We want to "hold" on this attribute.

And we don't really need to address initial pricing, because when we look at customers' perception of ongoing costs of ownership, there we're doing significantly better than our competitors, with a competitive ratio of 1.14. If we were to invest in communicating this good news story to customers in the right way, we should be able to positively impact their ability to justify costs – which we've already established as our first priority for improvement on the cost side.

So the decisions are pretty clear: Focus on improving services and the ability to justify costs. Communicate the good news stories on products and ongoing costs. Hold our current position on relationship and initial price.

I usually ask people to do this analysis individually first, then discuss in small groups, then reach consensus as a team. It's been my experience that at this point in the workshop, groups that earlier had great difficulty coming to consensus on customer perception of the company now move very quickly to about 90% agreement on priorities for improvement. I believe this is because they're now working from a common data set, and because the way the data is organized makes it relatively easy to see opportunities.

Create In-Pencil Action Plans

Once they've chosen the priorities as a group, we split into small groups again to create a first-cut action plan for addressing each priority. Teams discuss how much improvement they want to target in each area and how to get there.

Some groups find it difficult to make the leap from picking priorities to choosing specific actions. Other action-oriented groups may try to jump immediately to an "in-ink plan." It's important to stress at this point that you're not expecting them to make a firm commitment here. This is a first brainstorming on what we could do to drive improvement in the chosen areas. It's too early to do a carved-in-stone plan. The group has just seen the data for the first time and hasn't had a lot of time to analyze it. They haven't yet taken the all-important step of finding the root causes of the issues.

Don't Get Stuck Debating Priorities:
It's Actions that Really Matter

One of the exciting things about the customer value management approach is that it delivers objective data and analysis. This factual evidence allows us to rise above the morass of subjective opinions, conflicting anecdotes and political power plays when deciding where to focus our limited resources to improve the business.

That's not to say that the availability of rigorous customer value data dispenses with the need for healthy debate and balanced judgement. It doesn't. Occasionally, the statistical analysis of our customer survey data fails to identify clear-cut "winners" for the one or two highest level attributes. A potential scenario could be several different attributes, all receiving roughly similar mean scores on the ten-point scale. Then suppose that these same attributes all have roughly equal impact weights. To top it off, there may be no statistically significant differences between us and our main competitors on these attributes. Now what? This is the point where we really do need to have a productive and open discussion about the best way to go forward. Educated judgement calls will need to be made.

In such situations, workshop participants may find themselves stuck in disagreement. A prolonged debate about which one or two items are really the top priorities for improving customer value starts to heat up and loop around on itself. It can be uncomfortable and feel as if we're slipping back into the same old style of arbitrary decision making that we thought we'd left behind. Unless the facilitator (or someone else) recognises what is happening and intervenes to prevent it, a form of "gridlock" can occur and no agreement will be reached. If this lasts until after the workshop is finished, further progress will probably be stalled until a higher authority makes the decision.

The unfortunate scenario I have sketched here is avoidable...provided we don't lose sight of the bigger picture. The key is to remember that the attributes listed in our customer survey data are almost never entirely independent of one another. For example, making a service encounter faster is rarely possible unless we also improve other closely-related attributes, such as accuracy and process complexity. Very often, it really doesn't matter exactly where we choose to start. Just like a woven cloth, once we start pulling on a thread it all starts to unravel. That's the end-to-end nature of most business processes. Tackling a "downstream" problem inevitably forces us to look "upstream" for the root causes. Or, tackling an "upstream" issue invariably benefits everything further "downstream."

The good news is that the customer survey data always gives us a very good idea of which "clusters" of related attributes offer the greatest opportunity for leverage, even if there isn't a definitive rank order of importance for each individual attribute.

So, don't agonise about picking exactly the "right" one or two priorities for improving customer value.At the end of the day, it is only action that ever matters. If you choose something to work on that is clearly important to customers, even if you can't be sure that it's the "most" important item, then that's far better than not acting at all.

- Ilmar Taimre

The workshop we're describing in this chapter is about learning and taking a first stab at picking priorities, not about final decision making. The product that's expected at this point is some initial ideas and a plan for:

- Putting the right cross-functional team in place to explore the ideas further
- Getting at root causes of the issues and proposing solutions to address these
- Developing and testing trial solutions
- Identifying the right measures of success
- Bringing a proposed "in-ink plan" to a future meeting for discussion and approval.

Present Plans

The session ends with the groups presenting these plans back to the larger group and setting out the process by which these draft plans will turn into real action. If the senior leader who kicked off the workshop hasn't been able to attend the entire session (ideally he or she has), then it's critical that he or she returns to hear these plans and give people the authority to move ahead on next steps.

If all goes as planned, the workshop will be a significant learning experience for participants. First they'll have been taught in a safe way, using someone else's data, how to read and interpret the numbers. They'll have experienced the survey and the thought process customers go through when determining ratings and impact weights. They'll also have had a chance to analyze their own data, surface their own assumptions and compare them with what customers actually said. They'll know what to look for in picking priorities, and they'll have begun the process of moving to action.

Ilmar's story clearly illustrates that this process isn't cut and dried and doesn't always work perfectly. Yet, as he states, "at the end of the day, it is only action that ever matters." This is a critical point because, in my experience, nine times out of ten these workshops are the turning point for customer value management deployment.

5. Analyze Root Causes

Before people launch into implementing solutions, it's important to make sure you're solving the right problem. Sometimes this involves sitting down with your process metrics and immersing yourself in the details of process flow, inputs and outputs, hand-offs, decision points and metrics. Sometimes it's as simple as some basic root-cause analysis to make sure you understand the underlying cause and aren't solving a problem that doesn't exist. For example, an investigation into incorrect addresses on mortgage statements might go something like this:

1. Why are customers complaining about mortgage statement addresses?
   Because the address details are incorrect.

2. Why are the address details incorrect?
   Because they are incorrect in the statement system.

3. Why are they incorrect in the statement system?
   Because they are entered incorrectly into the system.

4. Why are they incorrectly entered?
   Because the entry screen is hard to use.

5. Why is the entry screen hard to use?
   Because there are no instructions on how to use it.

Sounds simple, but if you don't go through a "five-whys" questioning process like this, you might find yourself investing a lot of money with little effect.

Don't Solve the Wrong Problem!

Here's an anecdote I heard some years ago that illustrates how easy it could be to solve the wrong problem if you don't do root-cause analysis first. A premier resort hotel that was a destination of choice for people from around the world learned from their customer data that they had two weak points: 1. Customers were complaining that their rooms didn't have the view they'd asked for; and 2. Customers wanted their room to be available whenever they arrived, even if they arrived early morning from an overnight flight.

Management's first thought was that they were going to have to make a major investment in building new additions onto the hotel so they'd have more rooms and rooms with the right views.

But their root-cause analysis suggested some simpler, less expensive solutions. They instituted a practice of having the customer service staff call customers right after they checked in to inquire about the views from their room. Eventually, they learned that most of the customers with complaints about views were on the ground floor. Turns out that the groundkeepers, intent on beautifying the building from the outside, had let the shrubbery grow tall. From the customers' perspective, however, the shrubs were not the pool view or garden view or lake view they had requested. When they replaced these with smaller shrubs that didn't block the view, the view ceased to be a major source of customer dissatisfaction.

Similarly, the issue with rooms not being ready was largely solved with some retraining of the housekeepers on the computerized room tracking system. Housekeepers were supposed to call a number when they finished turning around a room and punch the room number into the computer. What many of them didn't know was that they had to wait until they heard three beeps before they hung up. The rooms were actually ready for guests, but not showing up as such on the front desk system.

6. Align with Other Business Processes

I said at the beginning of this chapter that ideally over time the customer value management data will be integrated into the regular business planning processes. If in the initial stages, however, your action-learning workshops are happening in parallel with other processes, before you absolutely pin down priorities it's important to consider:

- **The overall business strategy and plan**
  Checking customer value data against the value proposition that you think you're taking to market is a very important thing to do. If the key elements of your value proposition are coming out with high impact weight percentages and you're getting high ratings, then your strategy is on track and the discussion is about how you grow your advantage.

  If you're focusing on things that are not proving to be of high value to your target market, it's time to revisit your strategy. If you're getting very low ratings on the things you're touting as strengths in your value proposition, there's a good chance your internal processes are out of line with your strategy and you have some work to do on that front.

- **The budget**
  The name of the game is to improve value in the market as quickly as possible with the least amount of investment. If you know there are things you can implement quickly and cost effectively, start there – even if they aren't at the top of the list from an impact weight perspective. Sometimes a small investment in improving communication with customers so that they better understand what they're getting and what they're paying can have a significant impact across the entire business system.

- **The marketing/advertising strategy**
  I've seen companies advertise that they have the best repair service on the market, only to find out that they're actually scoring lower than the competition on this attribute. It may be that the right thing to do is to invest heavily in making the repair reality live up to the advertising. But it may be better to shift the advertising strategy to focus on an aspect in which they're beating the competition.

  The same holds true if you find that your advertising is focusing on something that doesn't turn out to be an important driver of value for your customer base. The question I get all the time in this situation is, "Can we shift the impact weights? Can we convince the market that an attribute where we really shine actually does deliver value to them, even though they don't see it yet?"

My answer is always a qualified "yes." It can be done in many instances, with the right advertising strategy and a big advertising budget. It also takes time. So it's not the first place I recommend that people go. Start with the low-hanging fruit, and look for quick wins. But there's no reason why changing impact weight shouldn't be part of your longer-term strategy, if you have the budget to support it.

Changing Impact Weights: An Example from Sprint

This story is getting pretty old now and may seem strange to the younger generation of readers. Years ago, nobody minded having a bit of noise or static on a long distance telephone line. In fact the research we did at AT&T showed that having a little bit of noise on the line was a good thing, because if you didn't hear anything at all when someone put you on hold, you didn't know whether you'd been disconnected. This was before the days of "music on hold" and before the need to send data over phone lines made lack of noise a required feature.

Then a company called Sprint started to expand their network with the latest fiber-optic cables and digital switching. The new technology didn't produce the amount of noise that the old electromechanical systems and plain wire on telephone poles did. But they found that this feature wasn't really having any impact on their market share because a quiet line was not high on the list of people's value drivers.

Sprint turned the whole equation around with a very slick advertising campaign. I remember one telephone commercial where they showed someone in the US talking to someone in Japan. The person in the US dropped a pin on the desk, and the person in Japan stopped and said "What was that noise?!" They made a big deal over the fact that their circuits were so quiet you could actually hear the proverbial pin drop. And because the AT&T network was definitely noisier than Sprint's, they started to see the impact on ratings and market share. They had changed the impact weight in the market's perception of value.

Step 8–Get Going
Engagement Strategies

I've emphasized before that while I've broken the concept of mastering customer value management into ten steps for the purposes of clarity and focus, it's not strictly a linear process. It's especially important to keep that in mind in this chapter, in which we'll look backward to earlier steps and forward to later steps.

This chapter focuses on the engagement process that actually begins the first time customer value management is mentioned in the company and continues as long as new people are brought on board and up to speed. We shine a spotlight on it here because this is a critical moment in the process. You've shared your first set of high-level results with the leadership team and you've trained a core group of people to understand, accept and use the data for action planning and implementation. Now is the time to establish expectations as to how this data will be shared and used in the company on an ongoing basis. Investment now in getting the leadership and key players fully engaged increases the likelihood of sustaining the initiative over the long haul.

Whereas Steps 6 and 7 both had a "how-to" slant – how to populate the tools, how to run an action-learning workshop – here we'll look at some strategies to deal with what might be considered "softer" aspects:

- Engage the leadership (calibrate the data for them, make meaningful comparisons, stay visible)
- Engage key players (create understanding and acceptance, nurture a sense of collective ownership across business units)
- Look for early wins, and determine how you're going to deal with the inevitable resistance to change.

Ten Steps to Mastery

Commitment			Research			Response		Reinforcement	
1	2	3	4	5	6	7	8	9	10
Align	Focus	Prepare	Capture	Share	Analyze	Pick Priorities	Get Going	Reward Success	Embed Concepts

Step 8: Get Going: *Engagement Strategies*

1. **Engage the Leadership**
2. **Engage Key Players**
3. **Look for Early Wins**

1. Engage the Leadership

While engaging the leadership entails a lot more than sending out the occasional report, that's a good place to start. Step 5 was a practical look at how to design and distribute customer value reports that convey the key data points to leaders clearly and concisely. In that chapter, we talked about setting an expectation that reports will appear regularly just before established business planning meetings, and will maintain a consistent format.

"Regularly" to my mind means "quarterly," since in most large companies I'm familiar with the leadership team meets quarterly to look at financial and operating results, analyze them within the business context and adjust strategies accordingly. The ideal in my mind is distributing a quarterly customer value report, in the format previously described, along with whatever other data (such as quarterly financials) goes out in advance of these meetings.

If it's not feasible to produce a full set of competitive ratios each quarter, I'd urge you nonetheless to present some type of customer value data for each meeting. Same advice if your leadership is in the habit of meeting monthly: You want to take advantage of every opportunity to keep some aspect of the customer value story in front of them.

If you've nothing of substance to report, then you don't want to waste their time with a rehash of old news. This is not about data for the sake of data. But the expectation that there will be something to report at least every quarter in itself helps keep momentum going. You might present follow-up data from transaction surveys. If the previous quarter's customer value report indicated a problem or an opportunity in the area of repair, for example, it makes sense that you'd follow up with a report on transaction surveys done to hone in on the critical repair process issues. If you've already determined what business process needs to be fixed and established internal metrics and targets, then your focus for that quarter can be on progress toward those targets.

You don't need to wait until you're able to produce a full-fledged quarterly customer value report to start educating your leadership team, though, and you don't need to confine yourself to quarterly communication once you have reached this stage. Seasoned champions and change agents have a knack for spotting opportunities to put interesting pieces of information in front of the CEO, president or other key influencers, packaged in a way that gives them new insight into what drives customer value and why customer value is important to the business.

This might be a tidbit passed on verbally over lunch or during a meeting. It might be an article or study forwarded with a few key paragraphs marked and your own observations added. It might be a single chart or graph that you've created from your data that looks at things in a new light. Every leader has his or her own unique passions and ways of looking at information, and part of a change agent's challenge is to figure out how best to push the right buttons to keep customer value management high on the leadership agenda. Strategies that I've found work well with most leaders include:

- **Calibrate their minds**
  Particularly in the early days, it's important to give leaders ways of putting the numbers in context and understanding what they really mean. Because leaders don't have the kind of historical perspective for customer value figures that immediately tells them whether earnings per share of $0.37 is good or bad or indifferent, they really need this calibration. And, depending on their personality and confidence levels, they may or may not feel comfortable asking for it.

  A good starting place is this simple chart:

Performance Level	CVA	Relative Quality Ratings	Relative Price Ratings
World Class	> 1.10	> 1.15	>1.08
Above Parity	1.03 to 1.10	1.03 to 1.15	1.03 to 1.08
Parity	.98 to 1.02	.98 to 1.02	.98 to 1.02
Below Parity	< .98	<.98	< .98

Because it is so important to be able to put CVA and the relative quality/price ratios into some kind of context, I've invested considerable time in studying the PIMS [1] database of companies of varying sizes in a variety of industries around the world and comparing what I found there with what I've seen in my consulting work. Based on an analysis of the normal distribution of CVA scores and the relation to financial performance, I believe this chart gives a solid indication in most instances of how to interpret the numbers.

What this chart gives you is industry-wide generalization. To give more specific guidance on what excellence looks like for your company in your market, the best tool is the Slippery Slope created as part of Step 6. That chart graphically depicts what kind of absolute overall ratings you need to earn customer loyalty – however you choose to measure loyal customer behavior. It also alerts you to the "danger threshold": the point at which you're at risk of losing too many customers and jeopardizing the business.

- **Link customer value results to business results**
  Anything that demonstrates correlations between customer value data and financials or other key business metrics captures the right kind of attention. Simple charts showing CVA ratios tracking to market share or revenue over time are often all that's needed to get leaders engaged in customer value management. For businesses in which there is constant change, such as the cellular phone market described later in a case study of Vodafone New Zealand, it may be more important to show how changes in CVA relate to metrics like customer retention or percentage of new customer wins. If there's value for your business in producing more sophisticated charts demonstrating the complex correlations among key factors across the value chain, you can graduate to those over time. You'll see some examples of how companies have made the business case and linked customer value to business results in the case studies at the end of each part of the book.

As your work on impact weights progresses, you'll get clarity on which internal measures are strong predictors of customer value ratings. Simple reports tracking performance on these process measures and what happens to value ratings as a result are great ways to engage process owners.

- **Compare with key competitor scores**
  The critical score in my approach to customer value management is the Customer Value Added ratio. Remember that the CVA ratio is:

[1] *Profit Impact of Market Strategy database housed at the Strategic Planning Institute.*

The average perceived worth of your company's products and services
divided by
The average perceived worth of competitive offers

The point I'm stressing here is that it's the average of <u>all</u> your competitors' scores – not any one best-in-class competitor. In my work over the years, I have consistently been able to demonstrate a relation between this score and a company's market share. I've <u>not</u> been able to consistently demonstrate a relation for companies that want to look at their score only as it relates to the score of one best-in-class competitor.

I therefore don't recommend trying to do complex market share correlation studies that focus on one best-in-class competitor. That having been said, in any given market there's probably one serious competitor you want to understand in greater depth. You can do this by comparing your absolute scores to this competitor's scores in a simple table, or by producing a Value Map (as described in Step 6) that shows your competitive position in relation to quality and price perception.

What is not useful is trying to compare your scores on individual attributes to best-in-class scores on each attribute. I've seen companies try to do this, and I've never seen much useful insight or action come out of it. What you end up doing is comparing yourself to a hypothetical market superstar. While you want to know who is best in class on the limited set of attributes you've chosen as your focus for the purposes of benchmarking and learning from them, trying to beat on all fronts a company that doesn't actually exist doesn't strike me as the best use of scarce time or money.

- **Look at percentage of highly dissatisfied customers**
This isn't the most uplifting way of engaging leaders, but it is an important conversation. If you have a high percentage of highly dissatisfied customers (which I usually define as people who give you absolute ratings below 6), then you have some immediate issues to address. These customers aren't just going to be disloyal, it's highly likely that they're out there negatively influencing otherwise loyal customers or potential customers. You need to find out quickly what's causing these very low ratings and do something about it. Often you'll find it's one badly-broken process that can be fixed without a major overhaul of the company.

These thoughts will no doubt spark your own ideas as to how you can package data so that it's meaningful to business leaders and get it in front of your leadership team. Remember it's not just a matter of producing tidy reports and sending them off. You're looking to create opportunities for dialogue that will keep leaders actively engaged in the customer value work, deepen everyone's understanding of what the data is saying, and prompt innovative ideas for action.

Engaging Leaders: A Change Leader's Perspective

Every book on change I've ever read says the critical success factor is enlisting the support of the leadership team and keeping them involved. That makes sense to me. Unfortunately the books rarely tell you how to do this.

The truth is they can't give you a formula or a framework, because what works in one business at a given moment is just as likely to fail somewhere else, or even in the same business at a different time. In my experience, the key is knowing how to pick your moments: when to push and when to back off.

You need to understand the business agenda very thoroughly. You need an insider's view of the leadership team dynamics: how decisions get made and who plays what role in making things happen. You need to know what individuals are passionate about and what makes them lose sleep, because it's really about being able to capture their hearts and minds. You need to recognize entry points when they open up, and be prepared to leverage them. I don't think you can learn any of that from a textbook. It's partly intuitive, and it partly comes with experience. It's definitely a "soft" skill.

The part about being prepared, though, starts from making sure you've got a really sound business case. I've known people with very good ideas – I call them "zealots" – who seem to believe that the business will grab their idea and run with it if they personally believe strongly enough that it's a good thing to do. In most organizations there are more good ideas floating around than there are resources to invest. You've got to be able to show that the change you're advocating is fundamental and will benefit the business more than other approaches the company might take.

In the case of customer value management, the arguments are pretty clear. The senior officers and the board of directors are responsible for creating shareholder value. Yes, we've seen instances recently of business leaders losing sight of long-term value and manipulating financials for short-term gain, but that doesn't change the fact that in our system they are legally accountable to act in the best interests of shareholders.

Now, if you take things down to the simplest possible level, how is shareholder value created? Shareholder value is entirely dependent on the behavior of customers. There are lots of things we can manipulate in relation to costs and price and processes that have an impact on shareholder value, but if customers don't buy our products, then it doesn't matter what else we do. We have no chance at all. It's customer behaviors that generate shareholder value, not what they think or what they say, but what they actually do.

At a minimum, we want them to stay with us. If we do a good job for them, they'll also recommend us to others, start spending more with us, treat us as a preferred supplier or maybe even decide to deal exclusively with us. And they aren't stupid; they shop around. They'll behave the way we want them to only if we're providing better value than they can get elsewhere. The Slippery Slope chart Ray uses – I've used it in three businesses now – tells that story very clearly.

It makes intuitive sense that customer value and loyalty create shareholder value, but it's important to be able to <u>prove</u> it using a company's own data. When Jean Monty at Nortel Networks asked me to take the lead on a customer satisfaction initiative in the mid-90s, I didn't have to convince him that it was important to pay attention to customers. He had been CEO of one of Nortel's largest customers and made a big thing about how much he had felt taken for granted. He was determined to make Nortel more customer focused, while maintaining our historical strength in R&D and product excellence.

But even though he was convinced it was the right thing to do, he got very excited when we were able to prove it. We started with a simple chart that correlated the past four or five years of customer satisfaction scores with our share price fluctuations over the same period. That clearly showed how closely the two were related: a 90% correlation. Over time we were able to do much more sophisticated analyses showing that motivated and knowledgeable employees earn customer loyalty which in turn drives shareholder value. This research allowed us to isolate those factors which had the most impact across the value chain, and told us where to focus.

You've got to keep finding new ways of telling your story so it stays current and relevant. And you've also got to recognize when the right thing to do is to back off because there are other pressures on the business. That doesn't mean letting things slide. It's a great opportunity to make significant progress on an issue or gain new insights that you can put use to engage the leadership again at the right moment.

- Adrian Horwood, Vice President Global Marketing and
  Business Development, Celestica Inc.; formerly Vice
  President Customer Satisfaction, Nortel Networks

2. Engage Key Players

I've stressed before that even in large corporations, customer value management initiatives can be driven by a very small core team. What I mean by that is you need only a few people with the right mix of skills to build the business case, design the survey, manage the vendors, analyze the data, and take the lead on communication and action planning. Actually making changes happen in the organization, though, requires many, many people. In fact, it takes just about everybody in the company.

The Kordupleski Cube™

I like to use a cube diagram to show people the three sets of processes that contribute to the overall goal of creating value for customers.

On the front of the cube are the customer-facing processes: sales, delivery, installation, user training, repair and billing. These are the integrated processes that together make up the customer's experience of the company. I've been calling these the Waterfall processes throughout the book, because if something goes wrong at the top of the falls – if a salesperson makes an error in a quote, for example, or forgets to tell the customer there's an extra charge for delivery or training – then the problem is really bad by the time it hits the person handling the customer's billing inquiry at the bottom of the falls. It's very hard at that point for the billing inquiry staff to create a satisfied customer.

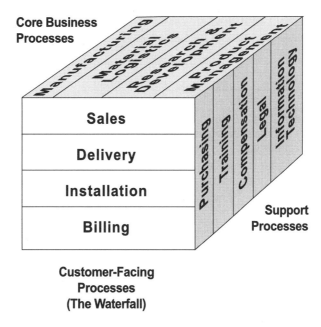

On the top of the cube are the core business processes. For an original equipment manufacturing company, these are things like product management, R&D, supply chain or materials logistics and manufacturing. Service firms would have a slightly different version of the cube, but it would still include core business processes like product design, development and packaging.

On the side of the cube are the support processes that are often called "business functions": purchasing; HR processes like hiring, firing, training, rewarding; legal processes related to the writing of contracts and purchase agreements.

So while the focus in customer value research tends to be on measuring satisfaction with the transactional customer-facing processes and understanding how they impact customer perception of value, it's important to understand how the core business processes and support processes impact the customer-facing processes.

To continue with the billing inquiry example: The problem with the billing may result from a poor decision made by a product manager to design a very complex pricing structure for the product. Or it may stem from a purchase agreement drafted by legal that wasn't written in language the customer understood. Or it may be that there isn't really much of a problem at all, but the person trying to handle the inquiry hasn't been properly trained and doesn't know how to resolve the customer's concern.

Like Rubik's cube, all these processes need to be aligned and working together as a system to create customer value.

People and Process

One of the things I like about customer value management is the emphasis on identifying the underlying business processes that impact customers' perception of value, and the people within the company who impact each process. If you leave out the people dimension in process flowcharting, then that's a problem, because as Dr. Myron Tribus points out, it's in the interaction between people and process that the problems occur.

Customer value management also forces organizations to break down barriers between departments. Processes cross many boundaries, and there's got to be a "right of way." It's important to identify who is accountable for the outcome of that process, and ensure that they have the skills to get people working together across organizational boundaries to produce the right experience for customers.

- Dr. Nick Fisher

Building a Winning "System"

I want to reinforce this last point about the importance of all the pieces working together as a system by quoting from a book that I really enjoyed.

It's written by Phil Jackson and Charley Rosen and it's called *More Than a Game*.[2]   Phil Jackson's name will be well known to anyone who follows basketball in the United States. He's now coached teams to win world championships a record nine times.

Six of these championships were won by the Chicago Bulls, and he had a definite advantage there with the great Michael Jordon on the team. But the interesting thing was that Michael Jordon had been on the team before Jackson became coach, and the team wasn't winning championships. Jordan himself was playing well and widely recognized as one of the best players in the history of basketball, but that wasn't enough. It was Jackson who taught them to work together as a team and win.

---

[2] P. Jackson and C. Rosen, *More Than a Game* (Fireside, 2002)

The six Chicago Bulls championship wins under Jackson's coaching might have been considered a fluke if it weren't for the fact that in the next coaching job he took – with the Los Angeles Lakers – the same thing happened. With two fantastic players – Shaquille O'Neal and Kobie Bryant – playing at the top of their game, the team hadn't won a championship before Jackson arrived. Jackson has now led them to the NBA championship three years in a row.

Not surprisingly, a lot of business leaders are interested in understanding Jackson's secrets for winning, so he's now on the lecture circuit and writing books. I want to focus on what he has to say about why it's important to think of a basketball team as a whole system and what it does for you if you do, because I think the principles are the same for customer value management.

More Than a Game
By Phil Jackson and Charley Rosen

It's the system that counts because:

1) It provides clear purpose and direction with implicit goals.
2) It trains and educates new people, who in turn learn how they can contribute.
3) It rewards unselfish behavior, which in turn renews the system.
4) It makes for easier transition through times of change.
5) It provides a context within which a leader can integrate all the skills of the team. (p. 165)

When I think about these statements in the context of customer value management, here's what occurs to me:

1. **It provides clear purpose and direction with implicit goals.**
   When customer value management is understood and implemented as a system, it also provides clear purpose and direction. It makes sure the entire company understands that the purpose of the business is to create value for customers and to do so better than the competition. It sets direction and goals in terms of targets for relative improvement compared to the competition, and for absolute improvement on processes.

   I'm not sure why Jackson talks about "implicit" goals. Perhaps it's because in basketball there's one explicit goal, which is to win, and what he's getting at are the goals related to how the team plays that will make this happen. In a solid customer value management system, the goals and targets are explicit and specific.

2. **It trains and educates new people, who in turn learn how to contribute.**

   When individuals are hired into a company that's using customer value management principles and measures, their colleagues know exactly how to explain to them what the company is trying to do and how the process they're responsible for interacts with other processes. They also are clear on which two or three key measures it's most important to deliver.

3. **It rewards unselfish behavior, which in turn renews the system.**

   One of the most common roadblocks to implementation of customer value management is an unhealthy concern about "protecting turf." When I see individuals drawing a box around "their" territory and looking for very narrow performance measures within the confines of that box, I know we're in trouble.

   I'm equally concerned when I see people trying to find the one individual who is dissatisfying the customer on the assumption that if they somehow fix that person all will be well. While it's true as I've said that one person can dissatisfy a customer all alone, I also believe strongly that it takes a whole team of people to fully satisfy a customer.

4. **It makes for easier transition through times of change.**

   These days it seems organizations are constantly changing and reinventing themselves. Whether driven by market conditions, new leadership or a desire to improve performance by reorganizing, change is a critical, inevitable and often disruptive force. It's tempting during times of change to sit back and wait to see how things shake out. People may be waiting to find out who their new boss will be or what direction the new leader will take. They may be waiting for the outcome of a key strategy decision. But in the meantime, they're missing opportunities to create value for customers.

   In companies with a strong customer value management orientation, it's easier to keep your eye on the ball during transition times because you know what your customers want, what your competitors are doing and what you're doing to deliver value better than they do. Changes in leadership or organization structure may result in different business strategies or different ways of delivering value to customers, but at least you know in the transition time that what you're doing is creating value for customers. And you know that no matter what changes when everything shakes out, what you did was not a waste of time.

5. **It provides a context within which a leader can integrate all the skills of the team.**

   This takes me back to the Kordupleski Cube, because I think that's exactly what Jackson is talking about here. If you understand the team as an integrated system of aligned processes working together toward a common purpose, you can explain to people both the unique role they play and how it fits into the larger whole. Both are critical, because if you understand how you integrate with the whole, you're better placed to find ways of improving performance across the system.

   And yet in my experience many people get focused on their own little world and rarely think about the big picture. They make process improvements that make them look better – shaving some time off the step in the process that they control, for example – but if that time saving means more time spent later on in the process, then the customer doesn't benefit and no value is created. That's why it's so important to find shared measures across groups that clearly relate to their common purpose. That's what we'll talk about in the next step.

A Customer Value Council

Because it's so important to get all these teams working together across boundaries, large companies I've worked with have found it important to create a formal vehicle to engage key players from across the business units in a sustained way. How exactly this is set up and who will be involved will vary depending on your organization's structure and size, the degree to which business units operate autonomously, and the goals of your customer value management initiative. But in my experience most companies want to have one senior leader driving customer value in each business unit and keeping that unit connected to the overall corporate effort. The council should connect business unit teams with people leading the key customer-facing and support processes.

The mandate of this central council or forum typically includes things like:

- Serve as a catalyst for change to implement customer value management tools and techniques across the company
  - Build and communicate the business case
  - Recommend implementation strategies to business unit leaders/ process owners
  - Ensure leaders/process owners understand, accept and use customer value tools and data
  - Drive data collection/analysis and action planning activities within the business unit

- Promote alignment and consistency across business units
  - Ensure corporate standards and guidelines are followed across the company, to enable data roll-up and comparability
  - Ensure consistency of messages in communication/education efforts
  - Share best practices to accelerate organization-wide learning.

Building Shared Ownership: A Change Leader's Perspective

One big challenge faced by a change leader in a large corporation is that you can't make anything happen without the support of your peers and their teams. As a small corporate group you can serve as a catalyst, but you need strong champions in every part of the business who actually drive the change there. You need to get alignment among a diverse group of people who don't report to you. A lot depends on your personal credibility. People must see that you're committed to a collective business agenda rather than a personal agenda. It also helps to have some formal structure to encourage collective ownership of the initiative.

I've implemented customer initiatives in a global high-tech company and a major Canadian bank. In both instances, it was important to set up a council that brought together key players from all of the business units and some of the corporate functions. We tried to meet monthly – quarterly at a minimum.

The council can't be window dressing: People will see through that very quickly. While as change leader you need to get the ball rolling on educating and guiding the team, very soon the team starts taking collective ownership for shaping the agenda and implementing change. It helps in the early stages to bring in some outside experts to teach the team and get the dialogue going. Anyone inside the organization comes with some personal baggage that may impact how different individuals hear and respond to their message. Objective third parties with practical experience in customer value management add immense credibility.

- Adrian Horwood

---

3. Look for Early Wins

It's a fact of life that not everyone is going to be 100% behind this effort from day one. In fact, there will never be 100% support. In every change effort there are early adopters and ambassadors who embrace and actively support the change. There are fence-sitters who adopt a wait-and-see attitude, and who may or may not be won over in time. Then there are the skeptics, and always a few actively hostile people who will never believe that the effort is bringing value to the company. They will work hard on all fronts to undermine the effort.

You can't take this personally. If you've remained focused on customer value rather than your own personal agenda, put effort into getting teams collaborating across boundaries, and you consistently bring accurate and actionable data to the table, don't beat yourself up because some – even many – individuals don't agree with you.

Everyone has his or her own strategies for dealing with conflict and resistance. You should know that it will be there and be prepared to deal with it. Personally, I choose to look for early wins and not get distracted by the naysayers. I focus my efforts on those pockets of the company where there is "pull" from the senior officers and real commitment to this work at all levels. If you achieve, document and celebrate business success there, over time the word will spread and others will come on board.

Step 9–Reward Success: Recognition Practices

I like to think in terms of "Reinforcement, Rewards, Recognition" (a new take on the "three Rs"!) because the phrase reminds me that rewarding people for making improvements in customer value is about much more than compensation. We will talk in this chapter about setting appropriate targets and tying achievement to cash on the table for employees if they meet them. But we will also talk about three Cs:

- **Clarity:** Using customer value management to clarify for employees the company's purpose and how they contribute to it
- **Collaboration:** The fact that the creation, delivery and communication of customer value depends on collaboration among different units or departments – and the resulting need to balance individual/functional rewards with team/cross-functional/company-wide rewards
- **Creative recognition:** Non-cash ways (such as performance reviews, promotion practices, special assignments, visibility in the company) of reinforcing customer value management principles and recognizing those who are successfully applying them in the business.

This is a critical chapter for all the senior leaders in the company to read carefully and think about. The best-designed customer value management program in the world will fail if this piece isn't done right, because at the end of the day you're relying on your people to implement it. And people pay attention to those things that the company's reward system says are important. They look both at the explicit or hard factors ("How much do I benefit financially if we meet these targets?") and the implicit or soft factors ("Who is getting promoted/getting the most interesting assignments?" "Who is being celebrated in the company culture?").

Unfortunately, in my experience there's a certain element of "damned if you do; damned if you don't" attached to the whole issue of who, how and what to reward. If you don't put money on the table, people who are skeptical of the leadership's commitment to customer value management will see this as a sign that it's not really important. People who believe that it is important will be disappointed. But if you design your reward program in the wrong way or put the wrong measures in place, you can sometimes make things worse.

First, there's a danger of getting people so focused on trying to manipulate the numbers that they'll forget what it's all about – learning from the data how to create greater customer value. You'll hear John Pelligrino talk about that in the Mead Corporation case study at the end of Part II. A real-life story from AT&T at the end of this chapter illustrates another common pitfall: giving each department its own performance measure without giving adequate thought to how these departments have to work together in an end-to-end process to deliver value.

As with most things, there is no one right answer that will work for every company. In this chapter I'll outline my own thinking on the topic, and give you some guidelines for determining what approach has the greatest potential to embed customer value management into your culture.

Ten Steps to Mastery

Commitment			Research			Response		Reinforcement	
1	2	3	4	5	6	7	8	9	10
Align	Focus	Prepare	Capture	Share	Analyze	Pick Priorities	Get Going	Reward Success	Embed Concepts

Step 9: Reward Success: *Recognition Practices*

1. Decide Whom to Reward
2. Decide What to Reward
3. Set Appropriate Targets
4. Decide How to Reward

1. Decide Whom to Reward

The most common pitfall companies fall into is deciding that since this is about customer value, only customer-facing employees should have their rewards tied to it. They focus only on the delivery aspect of my three-part arrow (choose, deliver and communicate the value). Even then, they fail to recognize that there's a set of processes going on in the background that is either helping the customer-facing people deliver value or hindering them.

If people were clear that the purpose of the company is to create value for customers and to do this better than the competition, they'd be taking a more holistic view. They would recognize that choosing the value involves the leadership team, the business strategy team, the marketing team, the R&D team and so on. Communicating the value clearly involves the brand management and advertising teams.

If you skipped Step 8 – *Get Going*, go back now and look at the Kordupleski Cube. I use this graphic to visually reinforce the fact that companies are three dimensional. For the effective delivery of value to customers, it takes excellent people working through excellent customer-facing processes and seamlessly supported by more excellent people working through excellent core business and support processes.

So to my mind the question of who should be included in any reward scheme tied to customer value management is easily answered. It takes the entire company to satisfy customers, so the entire company should be included.

2. Decide What to Reward

The most common way to tie customer value management to cash in the pockets of employees is to institute a performance bonus based on achieving certain targets, or to factor these targets into an existing bonus plan that also includes financial and perhaps people-related targets.

It would be easy to make the leap from my statement that everyone should participate to the conclusion that if the company's goal is to improve CVA from 1.02 to 1.04, then everybody in the company should have 20% of their bonus potential (or whatever percentage the leadership deems appropriate) tied to delivery on that target.

In my experience, that usually doesn't work. I find it's quite a stretch for the people who answer the phone in the billing inquiry center to understand how they can make a CVA of 1.02 move to 1.04, without mapping out some intermediate steps and targets that connect their work directly to the overall CVA score. Let me illustrate what I mean.

Customer Value Management System

Value Survey	Transaction / User Survey For Mission-critical Processes	Internal Metrics / Process Measures

```
                                    Features
                          Products
                                    Ease of Use
                                    Applications        Bill      Accuracy            ➡ % Billing Inquiries
                          Services  Claims             Itself     Timely              ➡ % Issued within X Days
Worth What      What I Get          Billing    ➡ Billing          Easy to Understand  ➡ % Billing Inquiries
Paid For                  Relationship                 Billing    Accessibility       ➡ % Abandoned Calls
(WWPF)                    or Image                      Inquiry    Knowledge           ➡ % Calls Requiring Supervisor Hand-off
                What      Initial Price                 Service    Resolution on First Call ➡ % Resolved First Call
                I Pay
                          Cost of
                          Ownership
```

Three Key Ratios		
Customer Value Added (CVA)	=	$\dfrac{\text{Your Customer Value (WWPF)}}{\text{Competitor Customer Value (WWPF)}}$
Relative Rating: Products, Services and Relationship or Image	=	$\dfrac{\text{Your Customer Rating of Products, Services and Relationship or Image}}{\text{Competitor Customer Rating of Products, Services and Relationship or Image}}$
Relative Rating: Price and Cost	=	$\dfrac{\text{Your Customer Rating of Price and Cost}}{\text{Competitor Customer Rating of Price and Cost}}$

Remember that in Step 5 – *Share the Results* I recommended putting together a high-level quarterly report for senior officers of the company that focused on a few key metrics:

- Overall CVA score for the company
- Overall CVA score by business unit
- For each market/product segment:
  - Overall CVA score
  - Relative perceived value: products, services, relationship or image
  - Relative perceived value: initial price and ongoing cost of ownership.

These are the key metrics derived from the value surveys as depicted on the left-hand side of this diagram. The senior officers are accountable for these metrics and should be evaluated based on their success in delivering targeted improvement in these numbers. I therefore normally recommend:

- That the leaders of each business unit be measured both on their own CVA score (since they are accountable for that) and the overall CVA score for the company (to reward unselfish behavior and encourage the team to work together to deliver value to customers). For example, if you've decided that 20% of a president's or managing director's bonus is going to be tied to CVA, you might have 10% tied to the business unit score and 10% to the corporate score.

- That leaders of product/market segments (if you're large enough to have segments within business units) be assessed on their segment scores and the overall corporate score.

As you work your way towards the right of the diagram to the front lines, you can usually identify leaders and groups who have a significant impact on each of the main attributes you're tracking through your value surveys. It takes a bit of thought and work, but I recommend:

- That you assess members of your management team based on relative or absolute improvement in ratings on the attribute they most impact, as well as on the corporate score. So, again assuming that 20% of a bonus is tied to customer value management, the leader of the billing department might have 10% tied to how customers rate the company on the billing attribute, and 10% to the overall corporate CVA score. Whether your targets are for relative or absolute improvement depends on what's more important to your business strategy. For example, if your relative scores are high but absolute scores low because your competition is weak, you may want to focus on improving absolute scores in anticipation of new competitors seeing the opportunity and entering the market.

Many companies stop here – at the management level – in their thinking about tying rewards to customer value management. But if you're doing transaction surveys, you have a significant opportunity to motivate people on the front lines to make improvements in the key internal metrics you know ultimately drive the corporate CVA scores.

Follow the chart through to the right-hand column. In this example, through transaction surveys we've discovered what drives customer perception of value in relation to billing. On the bill itself, it has to do with accuracy, timeliness and ease of understanding. With respect to the billing inquiry service, customers are looking for accessibility, knowledge and resolution on the first call. This is very specific, actionable knowledge, to which you can tie quantifiable internal process measures.

Connecting the Dots

Think how powerful it is, then, when you tie pay potential for a front-line person in the billing inquiry service to achieving improvement in percentage of calls resolved in the first call. You know how much that sub-attribute impacts the billing attribute, and how much the billing attribute impacts perceived value of products and services, and so on. Working through the chart from right to left, you can show calling center employees how improvements that they make in the "resolved first call" metric help drive overall CVA for the company – or at least the business unit in a large company. Now you can tie part of their pay to an overall business unit or corporate score and part to a "calls resolved" metric, and the targets have some meaning. The reward can be a bonus or a performance measure that impacts future assignments and salary increases. The result is the same: Employees understand what they have to do and why, and they have a financial incentive for doing it.

The art of it all is creating the right mix of individual/functional metrics and shared metrics that reward the unselfish behavior that makes the system work. Shared metrics might be metrics around an internal process which several functional groups touch or influence. They might be business unit metrics or they might be company-wide metrics. This is where your customer value management team needs to sit down with the appropriate leaders and compensation experts to talk about where you most need to make improvements and what specific behaviors you need to drive to win in your current business context. (See the "Common Purposes and Shared Measures" story at the end of this chapter for an example of how not to assign measures.)

It's much easier, of course, to give everyone one high-level CVA goal and leave it at that. But you'll miss a powerful opportunity. I strongly believe in using the knowledge you've gained through the customer value work to choose the right performance metrics for each group. You will see the benefit in greater employee alignment around a common purpose and commitment to doing the right thing for the customer and the company.

3. Set Appropriate Targets

Once you've decided what you're going to reward – what metrics you're going to use to assess the performance of different individuals and groups – how do you go about setting the right targets?

Since the right targets for internal process measures are specific to each company's business and context, I'll focus here on the three key ratios of customer value management. A good process for thinking through what's appropriate can look something like this:

- Calibrate your minds: What do the numbers actually mean?
- Revisit your company/group's vision and values: What does that tell you about where you should aim?
- Look at benchmarks for what's realistic in one year
- Compare this top-down exercise with what's emerging from the bottom-up process
- Consider links with other elements of your balanced scorecard.

Calibrate Your Minds

We talked about this in Step 8 – *Get Going* in the context of engaging the leadership team and helping them interpret the data. The first thing to remind yourself before you start setting targets is what world-class relative customer value or CVA scores generally look like across the industry.

Performance Level	CVA	Relative Products and Services Ratings	Relative Price Ratings
World Class	> 1.10	> 1.15	>1.08
Above Parity	1.03 to 1.10	1.03 to 1.15	1.03 to 1.08
Parity	.98 to 1.02	.98 to 1.02	.98 to 1.02
Below Parity	< .98	<.98	< .98

Anywhere above 1.03 is a decent place to be. In our research, a CVA score of 1.03 is associated with an average ROI of around 25%.

These are rough guidelines rather than strict predictors, since so many factors influence CVA, including how you've segmented your markets and how many competitors you have. But they'll give you a general sense of where you want to be relative to the competition.

The tool that tells you what the absolute numbers mean is the Slippery Slope. I won't include one here because you've seen it in earlier chapters, and you must use the actual Slippery Slope for your company for this to be meaningful. It will tell you what absolute scores you need to be getting on the "Overall, how would you rate...?" question to get the kind of customer loyalty (by whatever measure you've chosen) you're aiming for.

Occasionally, in some markets, it is possible for a company to get quite high CVA scores, as high as 1.10 or more, but still have quite low absolute scores on "worth what paid for", say around 6 or 7 out of 10. In such cases, the company is almost certainly not really "world class" at all, but simply the "best of a bad lot." On every Slippery Slope chart I've seen, when you reach the 6 or 7 level, you see a big falloff in customer loyalty.

If a company is getting high CVA scores but low absolute scores, then probably that company and maybe even the entire market are experiencing very high levels of customer churn. In this situation, it is probably better to focus the primary target on improving the absolute scores, and use the relative CVA score as a secondary indicator, remembering that a high CVA score is not the only thing that matters. High levels of customer turnover can be an enormous drain on company resources, as sales teams are constantly struggling to replenish all the customers who have defected over the last performance period. In this environment, actually growing the customer base seems like an impossible dream.

Revisit Vision and Values

One of the things that most excites me about customer value management is that it allows you to attach some quantifiable measures to the aspirational statements in your strategic plans and company literature.

Say your company vision and mission contain statements such as the following:

> *"We will, relative to our competitors...be perceived by customers and staff as the best wherever we operate..."*

> *"We have a strong customer focus and build relationships based on integrity, superior service and mutual benefit."*

The next conversation after you've calibrated your minds would be focused on what being the "best" really looks like to you in actual practice. You might come up with some more specific statements of principle, such as the following:

- **We aim to be either number one or two in all markets.**
  It's probably not realistic to be number one in every market in which you compete. But if you really want to be the best and if you've not achieved at least second place in a key market by a reasonable target date, you should probably be thinking about changing the leadership of that market team or exiting the market altogether.

- **CVA parity is the minimum acceptable threshold in all markets.**
  Again, you may want to set target dates by which this threshold should be achieved in each market.

- **We should aim for world class where it has most impact.**
  Nobody can be world class in everything. But if you want to be known for superior service, you should aim to be getting world-class ratings on service attributes in the markets where this will have the most impact.

- **In achieving our CVA targets, we will not compromise financial and people-related targets.**
  You should ensure that a balanced scorecard philosophy prevails, precluding any suboptimal approaches to increasing CVA (such as dropping prices below acceptable levels for your business model).

- **We cannot afford to have too many highly dissatisfied customers.**
  High-performing companies do not exceed more than 2% to 2.5% of customers overall who are highly dissatisfied (e.g. overall absolute ratings on value ≤6), although in individual markets this percentage may be higher for short periods of time.

- **We know what score we need on overall value** (insert whatever absolute number your Slippery Slope indicates) **in order to achieve acceptable customer loyalty and "willing-to-recommend" behaviors.** You know this from your Slippery Slope.

For each of these, you would then look at what specific quantifiable targets these principles translate to and compare those targets to where you are today.

Note on Data Collection Targets

Most companies launch their customer value management programs by picking the top priority markets and gathering data for those. Over time, they expand their program until they're collecting data for the market segments that make up about 80% of their revenue. As discussed earlier, it rarely makes sense to have data for every market. It takes too much time, money and effort to cover very small product lines or markets that are low priority for you.

As you're expanding the customer value management program in the first few years, it may make sense to set "coverage" targets and use these to measure the performance of your customer value management implementation team. For example, a reasonable target for this team might be to have data covering 70% of revenue by the end of the first year.

Realistic One-year Targets

At this point in the process, once people have determined what improvement they need to make to reach their desired state, they often ask me, "But is that realistic?" Over the years I've worked with my colleagues to put together some guidelines or benchmarks on how much improvement is feasible in a year.

CVA Ratio (Relative WWPF Score)

Current Performance	Achievable with Focus and Commitment	Possible with Some "Stretch"
> 1.10	Hold it	Get a little better?
1.03 to 1.10	Add .01 to .02	Add .025 to .03
0.98 to 1.02	Add .02 to .025	Add .03 to .035
< 0.98	Add .025 to .03	Add .035 to .04

Relative Score on Products, Services and Relationship or Image

Current Performance	Achievable with Focus and Commitment	Possible with Some "Stretch"
> 1.15	Hold it	Get a little better?
1.03 to 1.15	Add .02 to .03	Add .03 to .035
0.98 to 1.02	Add .02 to .035	Add .035 to .04
< 0.98	Add .025 to .035	Add .035 to .04

Relative Score on Price and Cost of Ownership

Current Performance	Achievable with Focus and Commitment	Possible with Some "Stretch"
> 1.08	Hold it	Get a little better?
1.03 to 1.08	Add .01 to .015	Add .02
0.98 to 1.02	Add .01 to .02	Add .025 to .03
< 0.98	Add .02 to .03	Add .03 to .035

Shifting Absolute Attribute Scores

Current Performance	Achievable with Focus and Commitment	Possible with Some "Stretch"
> 9	Hold it and focus on improving another attribute	Improve if nothing else left?
7 to 9	Add 0.5 to 1.0 point	Add 1.0 to 1.5 points
5 to 7	Add 1.0 to 1.5 points	Add 2.0 points
< 5	Add 2.0 to 3.0 points	Add 3.0 to 4.0 points

The general rule is the higher your current score, the harder it is to improve. If you have a CVA ratio of 1.10, you're probably already getting a lot of 9 or 10 out of 10 ratings on the "worth-what-paid-for" question. You can't expect to do much better than that. Conversely, if you're getting absolute ratings of 5, you're clearly doing some basic things wrong and should be able to make dramatic improvements by focusing on making corrections.

Top Down/Bottom Up

What I've described in this chapter is a top-down process that starts with the company vision and mission. If you're following the implementation approach I'm recommending in this book, you will also have had workshops going on in which groups look at the data, pick priorities and suggest improvement targets.

At some point the two processes will come together. The top leadership will negotiate with front-line management and agree on where the focus will be and what targets will be factored into the compensation system. Remember that if you saddle any given group with a long list of targets, you're less likely to make any significant improvement than if you pick a few priority items and focus people on them.

The Balanced and <u>Linked</u> Scorecard

Many companies have embraced some form of balanced scorecard approach and set targets that relate to customers, employees and other stakeholders (such as communities) as well as financial targets. Fewer companies actually see these targets as linked. Normally the process of setting financial targets is separate from and parallel to the process of setting customer targets.

But if you've mined your data and understand the correlations between CVA and financials, you should know how much improvement you need to make in CVA to gain a point of market share, and what revenue that translates to. You should be able to calculate back from your revenue or market share commitments and determine what your CVA target needs to be.

If you have a rigorous "people value" or "employee value" program in place, you may even be able to determine what you need to achieve in your key people value indicator to get the CVA score you need to meet the financial targets. If you have enough data and do the right correlations, you'll find the elements of the scorecard are not balanced so much as linked in causal relationships.

4. Decide How to Reward

So far in this chapter we've been focusing primarily on using cash to motivate and reward improvements in customer value. Often companies tell me they do this in the first few years of implementing customer value management, but then gradually it becomes less important to have the CVA targets tied to compensation. That's because after a few years of seeing how CVA impacts financials, people accept customer value management as a driver and lead indicator of market share and revenue gains. While there's still a definite need for CVA and key process targets, it's sufficient to base the bonus program on financials because people understand the link.

At that point, it becomes even more critical to make sure that other important mechanisms in the company are aligned with and reinforcing customer value management. Employees will watch the following very carefully:

- **Performance reviews**
  Are targets related to customer value management central to performance reviews? Is there a clear expectation that employees will understand how the work they do creates value for customers and what they need to do to create better or more value?

- **High potential/key resource criteria**
  Many large companies have a formal process for assessing their top talent and deciding whom to fast-track into important positions. Are the criteria used in these assessments aligned with what customers say they value?

Getting Explicit About Relationship Skills

One of the things that has struck me is how few companies include the relationship skills that customers say are so important as criteria for promotion or "key resource" designation. They generally focus on things like business acumen, leadership, communication skills. These are all important, but they miss a critical aspect: relationship skills.

Everywhere around the world I've had the opportunity to work, certain themes come up whenever we drill down into what customers want in a business relationship:

- accessibility
- knowledgeable people
- promises kept
- follow up
- do it right

- responsiveness
- promptness
- kept informed
- no surprises

Sound familiar? Isn't this what you're looking for in any relationship with important people in your life (except that a surprise is usually welcome on your birthday – and a surprise gift at any time!)?

As a father, I learn this from my kids all the time. They need me to be there for them, to say "sure!" when they want me to play with them, and to know enough about Ninja turtles or Harry Potter or whatever other game they're into at the moment to be a competent participant. They expect me to show up on time when I've promised – but if there's a good reason why I can't, they're okay with that so long as I let them know. I'll never forget my young son challenging me, as my mind was wandering to work while I was supposed to be playing with him, with, "Dad, are you thinking work or are you thinking kids?" They know when you're not doing it right.

When you think about it, relationship management skills are important not only in dealings with customers, but with colleagues, people who report to you, suppliers, business partners. To my mind, they're a critical element of any "top talent" profile, and to my knowledge, they're seldom explicitly assessed.

- **Promotions/assignments**
  Are the customer value management exemplars in the company getting the promotions or plum assignments, or are they being shuffled off into unimportant positions? Is competence in using customer value management to drive business decision making included in the profile of what's expected from leaders in the company?

- **Visibility**
  Most companies have their heroes. They may not be officially designated as such, but these are the people who are profiled in the company newsletter or quoted on the internal website. People come to them for opinions or help when they're trying to launch a new initiative. Stories about what they've done and said are used to help new hires understand what type of company they've joined. Are your company's champions of customer value management among the heroes?

In the long run it is these reinforcing mechanisms that will make customer value management a way of doing business.

LEARNING FROM HISTORY:
COMMON PURPOSE AND SHARED MEASURES

An early experience at AT&T taught me how it's possible that individual people or units within a business can be performing well according to their own performance measures, but collectively producing a suboptimal process that is dissatisfying customers.

It all started when the president of General Business Services learned that only 50% to 55% of the 5,000 orders the division was writing each month for telecommunication systems were being installed on time. The time interval required to recover from these delays was as high as two weeks.

It didn't make sense. The news we were hearing from leaders responsible for key aspects of what we called the "provisioning" process was good. Sales figures stood at 110% of quota. Materials management reported shipping 95% of orders on time. No problems had been reported with information and ordering systems. But still only half of the systems ordered by customers were being installed on time.

I was appointed to lead a task force to figure out what was wrong. We brought together people representing all the key steps in the provisioning process – setting installation dates, manufacturing, shipping, installing systems, submitting the order completion data required for billing, and training customers to use the systems – as well as the information technology experts.

What immediately became clear was that each person could tell the group exactly what he or she did, but no one could say how it all fit together. Each person saw his or her team as the center of the process, but had no picture of how what the team did impacted other steps in the process to either help or hinder the cause of on-time installation for customers.

When we started thinking about all these pieces as one cross-functional process designed to install orders on time, it was fairly easy to identify the problems.

Problem #1: Shortfall in Number of Systems Manufactured

The sales compensation system provided an incentive for salespeople to make conservative sales estimates, thereby increasing their chances of making or exceeding their quota. But the same estimates were being used to determine the number of systems to be manufactured in a given period. Since the product management team was measured and rewarded on success in keeping factory costs low, they would sometimes reduce the estimates for the factory from the sales teams' figures, in case sales fell short of predictions.

On paper the factories were meeting their target of manufacturing 95% of systems ordered by the promised date (a realistic goal, given dependency on suppliers for parts and components). But when the sales people reached 110% of quota, as they often did, there was actually a net shortage of at least 15% – even more if the product management team had reduced the sales estimates to ensure their costs didn't run over.

Problem #2: Orders Late from the Start

The cutoff time for the sales branches to submit orders was 10:00 p.m. local time. It was deliberately set late to make sure that the branches would receive credit for any sales signed that day, since that made a difference to how they were rewarded.

Sales orders were then forwarded to the provisioning system. The cutoff time for that system to receive orders, however, was deliberately set early – 6:00 p.m. local time – to allow the system to forward orders to the material services centers before 6:00 a.m. the next morning, which is what they were measured and rewarded on.

The result: Thousands of orders each day were late from the start.

Problem #3: Incompatible Information Systems

We discovered that incompatibilities in the information systems were also contributing to delays. For example, the system that processed the sales orders allowed a delivery address of up to 25 digits. But when it sent the record to the provisioning system, the address got truncated because that system allowed only ten digits. Information required to deliver orders to multi-tenant buildings or multi-building campuses was getting lost, and so were the orders.

Problem #4: Overpromising

Our standard was that small equipment would be installed two weeks from order, and large equipment four weeks from order. If, however, customers demanded an earlier installation date during the negotiation process, the incentive for sales was to promise it to them, since salespeople were rewarded on closing sales, not delivering on time. At least 5% of all orders were being submitted with "please expedite" instructions, without any consultation with the installation teams as to whether this was feasible. The installation team's performance target was that 95% of orders would be installed on time. These promises to customers of early installation meant that 10% of orders were now at risk of being late, and that's assuming that installation was meeting its 95% target, which clearly it wasn't.

Problem #5: Sales Order and Billing Errors

The installation team was also struggling with the fact that orders submitted by the sales teams were often inaccurate or were changed by the customers in the middle of the process. This caused installation delays.

Problem #6: Shipping Incomplete Orders

Employees at the material service center were evaluated and rewarded on the number of parts they shipped on time, not the number of complete orders. If they had five out of six parts required for an order, they would ship the five. On paper, their performance looked pretty good: parts shipped on time 95% of the time. But the customer still had to wait for the sixth part before the system could be installed.

The Net Impact on Provisioning

So while many of the individual units were at or near their specified performance objectives, the net result was late installation for customers half of the time. While each upstream function was optimizing its own performance based on what management had said was important, at the bottom of the Waterfall the installation team was delivering poor results and customers were suffering.

Common Purpose and Shared Measures

In one year, we managed to raise the number of installations completed on time from just over 50% to over 85%, and reduce the time required to recover from delayed installations from two weeks to one or two days. The most important factor in this turnaround was agreement among the presidents and vice presidents that everyone who touched the process would work toward a common purpose and be measured and rewarded on the same thing.

The common purpose was to deliver customer value by installing systems on time. Everyone working in sales, product management, manufacturing, information systems or installation would share two performance measures: installation within the defined standards, and time required to recover from a delayed installation.

That motivated the teams to understand what role they played in the end-to-end process, and how what they did contributed to or hindered on-time delivery. New reporting systems were instituted, root causes of problems were sought, and success in improving the process was rewarded through both monetary and nonmonetary means (awards, prizes, recognition in newsletters and meetings). By the end of year one, we realized we had done the best job we could possibly do in optimizing the current process. To move from the 85% we had achieved to our goal of 95% on-time delivery, the teams would have to work together to simplify and redesign existing processes.

I won't pretend it was easy: Getting business units that are used to thinking of themselves as independent working seamlessly across boundaries is usually difficult. People needed to develop new process management and quality improvement skills. Managers had to give up some control. But the common purpose and shared measures motivated people to make it work, and both they and the customers benefited.

Step 10–Embed the Concepts:
Sustainment Strategies
chapter fourteen

I'm continually surprised to find how short attention spans are in some companies. Time and again I've seen people get excited about a new idea or business technique, invest significant money and effort into selling the concept within the business and applying new tools, then get distracted by another idea or technique and walk away from the first initiative before it's had a chance to prove its worth.

I don't mean to suggest that companies are right to get stuck in a rut and never try anything new. But if employees' first reaction on hearing of a new initiative such as customer value management is to ask whether this is the next "flavor of the month," I take that as a danger signal.

Companies have to be ready to change course quickly as business conditions change, and should always be open to considering new ways of doing things. But when it comes to business fundamentals like measuring and managing shareholder and customer value, they should be prepared to commit to long-term, sustained effort. This chapter looks at techniques for ensuring that the concepts and tools of customer value management are embedded into the business and don't become just another passing fad. We'll explore methods of:

- Keeping leadership commitment visible
- Integrating customer value management into ongoing business processes and systems
- Integrating the customer value philosophy into ongoing people processes and systems.

Ten Steps to Mastery

Commitment			Research			Response		Reinforcement	
1	2	3	4	5	6	7	8	9	**10**
Align	Focus	Prepare	Capture	Share	Analyze	Pick Priorities	Get Going	Reward Success	**Embed Concepts**

Step 10: Embed the Concepts: *Sustainment Strategies*

1. **Keep Leadership Commitment Visible**
2. **Integrate into Business Systems**
3. **Integrate into People Systems**

1. Keep Leadership Commitment Visible

I talked earlier about the role of the business leader champion and how critical it is to have leadership support and visibility. In fact, in my experience, where successful customer value management programs haven't been sustained in a company, it's usually because the executive champion changed jobs or left the company. New leaders come in with a desire to put their personal stamp on the role. They sometimes feel a need to distance themselves from initiatives strongly associated with the last leader – no matter how successful these initiatives might have been in business terms – or they simply don't see the need to learn a new approach.

Leaders contribute to the successful implementation of a customer value management approach in many ways. One really important way is by talking about customer value at every opportunity.

Employees take their cue as to where they should focus from listening to their leaders, both the top leadership of the company and their own immediate manager. Ideally they're hearing from both levels that the purpose of the business is to deliver value for customers, because ultimately that's what drives shareholder value. They're getting the message that it's therefore important for the company to be systematic and disciplined about measuring and managing customer value. They're learning how the company is doing this and what results are being achieved.

If the philosophy of customer value management is new to your company, you're probably starting with only a handful of people who have enough passion and understanding to speak with conviction about the topic.

Throughout this chapter, we'll be looking at ways of expanding the cadre of people who can serve as ambassadors of the work, and of integrating the message into existing business processes and education vehicles. At the start, you need to have:

- A clear and compelling message
- Leaders delivering the message
- Vehicles for getting the message out.

The Message

At some point in your schooling, I bet you were assigned the task of writing up a news story by answering six questions: Who? What? When? Where? Why? How? If you're just introducing the concepts of customer value management in a company, the most important question to address in leadership communication is that fifth "w": why? I've seen programs get tarred with the flavor-of-the-month brush before they've even got started. Why? Because the communication about the program focused on how "cool" the tools and techniques were and neglected to mention the business problems they were intended to solve. Tools and techniques that are an end in themselves rarely have staying power.

So leadership level communication about customer value management needs to start from the "why?" and go on to the "what?" From my perspective, the main messages are:

- The purpose of the business is to find a customer need and fill it better than the competition
- If customers perceive the value you deliver to be greater than the value your competitors deliver, that will lead to greater value for shareholders down the line
- It's therefore important that you understand how to measure the value you deliver relative to the competition and get better at managing that value
- You intend to collect and use customer value data with the same discipline, passion and understanding you give to financial data.

People will also want to know the "who" – who's driving and committed to this work? These are the bare bones messages and they look pretty dry laid out like that. The more you can tie this conceptual framework to actual business issues and the real-life experience of employees in your company the more compelling the message will be.

In many companies, there are "burning-platform" issues that have prompted a new or renewed focus on customers: declining market share, declining profits, new competition in the market, a change in market dynamics. Whatever the hook that got the leadership team interested in exploring this work in the first place, it's likely the same hook (or a version of it) will help employees at all levels understand that customer value management is addressing an important business issue.

If you have historical data that demonstrates the link between customer value and business success for your company, that's a strong message. If you don't have it at the outset you can cite examples from companies similar to yours, then build your own business case over time. If you have or have had other customer-focused work going on (customer satisfaction, customer relationship management, Total Quality Management), make sure you're clear on how customer value management fits into the picture (see Chapter Fifteen for ideas on this.)

The Communicator's Dilemma

The most powerful communication is often deeply personal. People tend to remember messages best when they're stated clearly and simply, then brought to life through a story from the speaker's or writer's experience. This is especially true when the audience can connect an element of the story with something in their own experience.

If you're leading communication strategy for a customer value management initiative you have a dilemma. As more and more people take up the story and become advocates for the work, it becomes more and more likely that messages will get corrupted. If different people are defining key terms like "customer value" and "customer satisfaction" in different ways, at best the impact of the communication effort will be weakened, and at worst you'll have a very confused population. Your job is to keep messages consistent and keep people "on message."

But if you script everything out and insist that people follow the script you have different problems. Nine times out of ten it will sound wooden and dull and totally disconnected from the speaker. Best case: Your audience will tune out. Worst case: They'll dismiss it all as corporate propaganda.

In my experience the happy medium is to provide people with a basic set of messages and coaching (if they need it) on how to make the communication their own. You might create a one-

or two-page "message board" that lists the four or five key messages to be communicated and provides bulleted examples or "proof points" under each.

If your company tends to use a lot of charts or overheads, it's wise to create a basic presentation that sets out the main plot of the customer value management story in bullet point and graphic formats. Presenters can then add slides or commentary as they see fit. You can even attach speaking notes to each slide that suggest methods of illustrating key points on the chart, without actually providing a script.

- Dr. Janice Simpson

The Messengers

You'll know you've succeeded in embedding the concepts into the company when every employee can tell the customer value management story with clarity and conviction. But since that's not going to happen overnight, I suggest you start at the top and make sure the CEO is a strong and vocal advocate.

Your work will pick up momentum quickly if people hear directly from the CEO that it's a priority. If the culture of your company is such that an official announcement, launch or kickoff of the work is in order, you definitely want the CEO's voice heard there. But don't make the mistake of thinking that a launch statement is all that's required. You need a strategy for ensuring that the key customer value messages are embedded in all major communication from the company's leader, both informal and formal.

In Chapter Three I used Paul Wondrasch as a role model of a great executive champion. I noted then the symbolic things that send strong signals about the importance of customer value management – things like what he asked about first when he visited branches (customer data versus financials) and where customer data was positioned on his staff agendas (first versus last).

In the early stages of the work, you want to make sure that the focus on customers is front and center in all top-level communication on company purpose and business strategy. Over time, as you start using customer value data to help you pick priorities, you want your CEO to make the link explicit between what customers have told you they value and where you're focusing improvement efforts. You want to be sure that announcements of performance targets and results include customer value metrics.

If the CEO is the main champion of customer value in the company, communicating its importance and place in the company strategy will likely come naturally. If the main champion is another top business leader, then part of that person's role is to make sure the CEO understands the key role he or she plays in communicating to the leadership team and to the employee population as a whole what customer value management is and why you're doing it.

If you have the CEO, the champion, the change agent and the change team all expert at telling the customer value management story at this high level, you'll have a good starting point for keeping the leadership commitment visible and sustaining customer value management over time.

The Vehicles

At the risk of stating the obvious, I'll point out that you want to take advantage of every possible vehicle at your disposal to keep the leadership's commitment visible: regular letters from the CEO, in-person or webcast presentations, town halls, company newsletters or websites, electronic chat rooms. Find out the CEO's schedule for communicating within and outside the company, and drop him or her timely reminders that this would be a great opportunity to get such-and-such a message across.

Some leaders have people they look to for help in pulling together speaking notes and presentations or for communication coaching: an employee communication specialist, an executive assistant, an operations manager or an outside coach. It's worth taking the time to build a relationship with these people, educate them on customer value management, and ensure they have access to the latest and greatest customer value data and key messages.

2. Integrate into Business Systems

The more thoroughly customer value management is integrated into your business systems, the less susceptible it is to changes in leadership or business context. Goals to strive for in this area might include:

- Product development teams routinely use customer value data to determine features to incorporate into new products
- Advertising and marketing people use customer value data to shape their messages and plan their strategy
- TQM, Six Sigma or other quality/process improvement teams determine their focus from the Attribute Trees and Competitive Profiles
- Key CVA metrics and their correlation with business results are routinely included in reports to the board of directors

- Customer value data is required from each business unit as an input to the business planning process.

Let's take this last point as an example. Large organizations generally have a structured business planning cycle. A senior officer – often the CFO – sends out a template outlining information required from the business units as part of this process. Your goal is to make sure that the template requires CVA scores and targets, Attribute Trees and Value Maps, Competitive Profiles and strategies to improve competitive position. You'll want to work with the business planning team to be sure they understand how this information is used to make business decisions, and reject any submissions that don't fulfill the customer value data requirements.

See in the charts to follow (extracted as samples from a larger chart package) how one company built the requirements into the template used by each line of business, business unit and region to submit data into the strategic planning process. Note that the template includes an "employee satisfaction" measure, (ESAT) putting it on a par with customer and shareholder value measures. It also forces the businesses to link the drivers of value to internal and external measures.

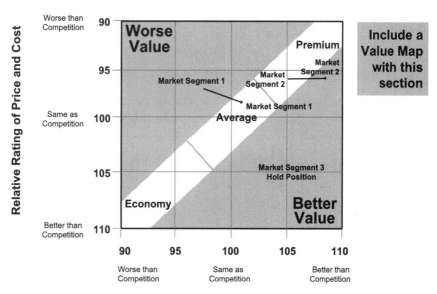

Example
Strategic Plan Value Map

Leadership Goals and Objectives

Mission Statement

Primary Strategy (for BUs only, please check one)

☐ Harvest   ☐ Build / Grow   ☐ Maintain

Leadership Objectives

e.g. Market Share, CVA, Customer Loyalty, Employee Satisfaction

Include a Goals
Matrix with this section

Business Unit Goals

Year	Market Share	CVA	Customer Loyalty	ESAT	Other
Current Year	25%	.99	28%	28%	
Year One	34%	1.03	48%	48%	

Value Proposition

Market Segment "X"

```
                                          Reliability (45%)
                         Products (40%)   Ease of Use (45%)
                                          Features (10%)
           Quality (60%)
                                          Sales (30%)
                         Services (60%)   Order Fulfillment (25%)
Worth What Paid For                       Customer Service (35%)
Value Proposition                         Billing (10%)

                                          Initial Cost (35%)
           Price (40%)
                                          Life Cycle Cost (65%)
```

Include a Value Tree
with this section

Name of Business Unit or Region: ** Tree structure and weights are examples.*

Example
Competitive Quality Profile

Key Customer Experiences	Importance Weight %	Business Unit Name	Competition	Ratio
Product:				
Reliability	12	8.6	8.0	1.08
Ease of Use	6	8.0	7.8	1.03
Feature Set	12	9.0	8.6	1.05
	30			
Services:				
Sales	30	8.3	8.1	1.02
Order Fulfillment	10	8.3	8.3	1.00
Billing	15	7.9	8.1	0.98
Customer Service	15	7.0	7.0	1.00
	70			
Overall Rating of Products and Services		8.1	8.0	1.01

Include
Competitive
Profiles
with this
section

Example
Quality Tree and Metrics

Product and Services Value Proposition		Customer Focus		Internal Measure Quantity · Timeliness · Quality	Example Survey Questions
End to End Business Process		*Customer Need*		*Internal Process Metric*	*Survey*
		Reliable	(40%)	% Repair Call	
	Product 30%	Easy to Use	(20%)	% Calls For Help	
		Feature Set	(30%)	Functional Performance Test	
		Knowledge	(30%)	Supervisor Required	
	Sales 30%	Responsive	(25%)	% Proposal Made On-Time	
		Follow-Up	(10%)	% Follow-Up Made	
Total Quality	Order Fulfillment 10%	Delivery Interval Meets Needs	(30%)	Average Order Interval	Did the interval they provided meet your needs?
		Order Complete	(25%)	% Complete	Was the order complete?
		Delivered When Promised	(10%)	% Meets Due Date	Was the delivery on-time?
	Customer Service 15%	No Repeat Trouble	(30%)	% Repeat Reports	
		Fixed Fast	(25%)	Average Speed of Repair	
		Kept Informed	(10%)	% Customers Informed	
	Billing 15%	Accuracy, No Surprises	(45%)	% Billing Inquiries	
		Resolved on First Call	(35%)	% Resolved First Call	
		Easy to Understand	(10%)	% Billing Inquiries	

Include Process Metrics with this section

3. Integrate into People Systems

Because it's so critical, we devoted Step 9 to embedding customer value management into one key "people system" or human resource process: the reward and recognition process. We talked about both monetary and nonmonetary ways of reinforcing customer-focused behavior and creating a customer-focused culture. We touched on the all-important performance management and promotion/advancement processes.

There are other important people systems to consider in your sustainment strategy. All the things we said about promotion, for example, apply equally to recruiting. One of the easiest ways to build an organization focused on customer value is to make sure that the people you're hiring instinctively "get it," are naturally aligned with your vision of customer value management, and have the right skills to make the vision reality.

Training and employee communication are other critical reinforcement mechanisms, and your sustainment strategy should include getting key players in these areas on board with your team and your messages.

Employee Training

You probably won't want to hand over the customer value workshops to an internal training department even if you're large and fortunate enough to have one, because these are not generic open enrollment courses. They're intended to be working sessions that bring together intact teams to start the process of implementing improvements in their business, and they need to be led by the business leader and customer value management experts.

You do, however, want to build the philosophy of customer value management into your new employee orientation, and more in-depth exploration of the topic into your management training/leadership development programs. You want to make sure that knowledge of customer value management concepts and tools becomes a core competency expected of all who take on leadership roles.

If the company's employee training and development programs talk a lot about shareholder value but never mention customers, employees will notice the disconnect between what they're learning in formal training and what they're hearing from their leaders about the importance of customer value management. You'll want to audit the major training programs to make sure that customer value management is presented as an integral part of how you do business. You probably won't go into a lot of technical detail in most programs, but you do want to make sure that every employee understands the definition of important terms, what key metrics like the CVA ratio are and how they relate to shareholder value, what performance objectives the company has tied to customer value, and what's expected of them in relation to customer value management.

If your business requires a large number of people with expertise in customer value management, then you might want to build a specific in-depth technical course to ensure an ongoing supply of the talent you need.

Employee Communication

We've already touched on the importance of keeping leadership commitment to the program visible. If employees never hear leaders mention customer value after the initial program launch, they'll soon decide it wasn't really important. But the high-level leadership message is only the beginning.

It's just as critical to communicate to employees what customers value, where the company is strong, and how it's working to improve, as it is to communicate to customers. Employees need to understand the results and the priorities that have emerged from the results to effectively plan their own time. Remember too, that customers' perceptions of the company are as much shaped by their interaction with company employees as by the official advertising campaigns. Think how much more effective as external ambassadors of the company employees can be if they're totally up to speed with what customers value.

A comprehensive communication strategy involves many players and many vehicles. It has customer value advocates throughout the company looking for every opportunity to get on meeting agendas or speak at conferences or workshops. It has the employee communication staff interviewing the champion and change agent regularly for internal newsletters or websites. It definitely includes regular publication of data and continual mention of progress against customer value targets and internal performance measures. It may have a website focused on customer value management or a dedicated customer value management section on existing business unit websites.

It may even have an electronic chat room or a discussion group where people can learn more about customer value management. The goal is to integrate the story into existing communication vehicles as often as possible, to reinforce the message that this is not a stand-alone program to be stopped at will, but an integral part of how you do business.

Note from a Change Agent: Enlisting Advocates

I truly believed in this work but I also needed to make sure that this wasn't a case of me imposing my personal agenda on the company. So I started keeping a running list of people within the company who were advocates or potential advocates of the work. Advocates were people who were actively using the customer value data to make decisions and excited about how this was helping their business. I counted as a potential advocate anyone who came to me to learn more about the work and what it might achieve. These people were important allies in getting the word out.

Over time, I decided to set up the "Ambassador Program." I made sure that I had someone on the business strategy team for every region, every category and every brand who had been trained in the customer value techniques. That meant that all business leaders had someone within their reach that they could call on for help in implementing customer value management. The Ambassadors also had responsibility for training others on the team. I found this approach very useful for spreading the word.

- Shawne Howell

How you do this will depend on the communication norms and processes in your organization. I suggested in Chapter Four that it's useful to have someone on the customer value implementation team who is knowledgeable about communication and training, and linked to the infrastructure in your company. It may simply be a matter of getting the right person in the company – a chief learning officer or corporate communication leader – to devote a portion of his or her time to staying connected with the customer value management team and work.

It's also a matter of becoming disciplined about capturing and profiling success stories. Company culture is both shaped by and reflected in the stories that people tell one another about the company. If you start hearing employees gathered in formal or informal situations telling one another about innovations that provided greater value to a customer, you'll know that you're making progress in creating a customer-focused culture.

To round out our discussion of the *Ten Steps to Mastery*, then, we're going to look at the stories that people I've worked with relate about how customer value management has been tried and proved successful in their companies. I've asked business leaders from opposite ends of the earth (New Zealand and the United States) and from widely divergent businesses (medical equipment, telecommunications, paper and packaging) to describe in their own words how they've used customer value management and what's been most important to them. Within each story I've provided context and some of my own observations as well.

Roche Diagnostics (New Zealand)

case study

I consider Adrienne Taylor to be both a champion – intent on influencing her colleagues at Roche Diagnostics to apply the customer value management business approach – and a hands-on change agent with practical experience in using the tools to deliver business results. When I first met Adrienne, she'd just taken the sales and marketing manager role for the diabetes division in what was then Boehringer Mannheim New Zealand. That was in 1996.

Like other companies that have embraced customer value management as a way to turn around a business decline, the diabetes division of Boehringer Mannheim was experiencing a dramatic loss in market share. Until the early 90s, they had 75% to 80% share of the market for glucose meters and strips: the equipment people with diabetes use regularly to test their blood sugar and manage their condition. In 1992, a Japanese company, using New Zealand as a test market, launched a competitive product. By 1995, Boehringer Mannheim's market share had dropped to just under 50%. For a company committed to being a leader, not a follower, this meant an all-out effort was needed to regain the competitive edge.

This is the story of how Adrienne's team at Roche Diagnostics used customer value management tools and techniques first to stem the decline, then reverse it. When we spoke in mid-2002, market share was back up to 70%. You'll also hear the voices of David Shieff and Deborah Hill, who along with my colleague Rodger Gallagher of Customer Value Management New Zealand worked closely with the diabetes division team to make this happen. But let's start with Adrienne's account of how she became interested in customer value management:

> *When I heard Ray speak in 1996, I had just completed some traditional market research which unfortunately hadn't given me the depth of information I wanted about what was really*

driving the behaviour of our end customers – the people who actually use our glucose meters to monitor their diabetes. After Ray's speech I came back to my divisional manager and told her I'd discovered the solution!

Except that I had a problem: I had just spent a lot of money on market research without getting the results I needed. I didn't really have any research budget left to do customer value analysis (CVA), but I knew I had to. So I presented a case to my divisional manager to reallocate some money within my budget.

The trade-off seemed very clear to me. At that time we had a database of about 18,000 people – 13,000 of our customers and 5,000 of our competitors' customers. We were spending quite a bit of money communicating with these people, but we didn't have any real evidence that this was a good investment. So I decided to spend less money for one year on this communication and use the freed-up allocation to fund the CVA work. Part of the driver there was that I wanted to be sure we were getting a good return on the communication investment.

- Adrienne Taylor, Manager Diabetes Care, Roche Diagnostics

The Japanese product was creating a problem for Roche Diagnostics with a group of key influencers in their markets: health care professionals. The main differentiator of this product was the strip that's inserted into the meter and collects the blood sample. The Roche Diagnostics strip required the user to hold a finger over the strip and drop the blood sample onto it. The competitor's strip drew the blood sample into the strip – a technique that required less blood. Health care professionals saw this as an important advance and stopped recommending Roche Diagnostics' product to their patients. Deborah explains the importance of understanding the end user:

You can segment the market for the glucose meter and strips into two categories: people newly diagnosed with diabetes, and long-term meter users.

Newly diagnosed people with diabetes are heavily influenced by the health care professionals they come into contact with as they're learning about their condition. All this is new to them.

They're trying to absorb a great deal of information in a short period. It's only natural that they rely on the professionals. They'll probably buy whatever meter they've been using at the hospital.

But as they learn to live with diabetes, they become much more knowledgeable and opinionated about their treatment. They join support groups, compare notes with other people with diabetes, read articles about advances. They're less dependent on people in the health care profession. This group of very sophisticated consumers also represents the greatest revenue potential for the company.

What we realized when we started to work with Adrienne and her team was that we had never directly asked the end users what was important to them. We knew what the health care professionals thought was critical, but not what the actual users thought. That recognition gave us the focus for our CVA study.

- Deborah Hill, Director, Unconventional Wisdom (a CVM NZ associate)

I'll let Adrienne pick up the story again from here:

The first wave of customer value data challenged all of our internal paradigms. We thought we knew how our products were perceived in the market. But when we went out and actually asked people what was important, it turned out that the things we thought were important weren't important to customers at all. For one thing, we found that quality was just expected. Customers assumed that any meter on the market was going to do the job. They were more interested in price and the long-term cost of use.

We also realized that while we'd been focusing exclusively on the product, our customers were more concerned about their relationship with the company. Our communications were designed to convince people that we had the best possible product. But our customers cared most about how the company would support them if something ever went wrong with their meter.

People with diabetes depend heavily on the meter. It puts them in control and allows them to manage their health. They want to do business with a company that has a great warranty and will act quickly to get them a replacement meter should anything go wrong.

- Adrienne Taylor

The experience of finding out there's a big gap between what you think your customers are thinking and what your customers actually tell you they're thinking can be very difficult for people. It's easy to let defense mechanisms kick in and start blaming the survey design or the researchers or the way the data was presented. Roche Diagnostics New Zealand's diabetes team and their country manager chose instead to accept this new information and use it to change their market strategy. The first step was to refocus their communication on the things that mattered to customers. Deborah explains:

> *The irony was that Roche Diagnostics was offering a de facto lifetime warranty on the meters, but had never made a big deal about this in their advertising. In an ad hoc way, the practice of providing a loaner meter if a meter broke down had developed, even after the official warranty had expired, and the defective unit was replaced as quickly as possible. The company knew how much people depend on these tests.*
>
> *If you think of the three-part arrow that Ray uses in his presentations – choose the value, deliver the value, communicate the value – the situation here was that Roche Diagnostics was actually delivering the value in the form of a lifetime warranty, but hadn't consciously chosen it and wasn't communicating it. The data told them that this was a critical element of their offering.*
>
> - Deborah Hill

Acting on the results from the CVA data, the diabetes team focused first on retention of current customers and halted the market share decline.

Phase two was an active customer acquisition strategy. One of the things the data had told them was that the initial purchase price of NZ $120 to NZ $150 was a definite barrier for people who might be considering switching brands of meters. Since the ongoing sale of the strips accounted for a large portion of the company's revenue, it made good business sense to offer special discounts to encourage long-time users of competitors' products to switch to Roche Diagnostics. The introduction of a new strip that matched the competitors' technology solved the issue the health care professionals had with the product and put them back in competition for referrals to first-time users as well. This put them squarely in a "better value" position, and market wins accelerated even more.

The team did a second wave of data collection in 1997, the results of which told them they were on the right track They've since done a third wave and are about to launch a fourth. Their CVA scores rose from 1.10 to 1.21 to 1.24 in the three waves. The unusually high scores are partly a function of the focus on their target market of sophisticated long-term users of glucose meters. Had the health care professionals been included in that first wave of data, clearly the numbers would be lower. But the dramatic improvement is impressive, as is the achievement of gaining back over 20% of market share after the drop to below 50%. David talks about how building relationships contributed to the success:

I didn't fully realize the significance at the time, but Adrienne's decision to build this database of end users and call it a "club" was the beginning of a CRM strategy. The concept of customer relationship management wasn't really in people's thinking here at the time and still isn't common. The purpose of the club at the start was to learn more about consumers, not to build a relationship with them, but later on it gave the team the means to build the relationship.

Initially the club and the CVA work were two separate streams of thinking. One of the things we were questioning around the time we started the customer value work was whether the club was really making customers more loyal. When we talked to people with diabetes about it, what seemed to be coming back was that it was a "nice to have." People didn't strongly associate the club with the company and didn't see it as an important element of the value proposition. That was confirmed in our first wave of data collection.

But the club has turned out to be a key enabler of customer value management and over time the two initiatives have been integrated. When we started the customer value work, the club database had around 18,000 people in it, about 5,000 of whom were buying from the competition. This gave us a great source database from which to draw our survey sample. Now called "Extra Care," the database has grown to include 50,000 people – more than half of the 80,000 New Zealanders we estimate regularly use glucose meters. In fact Adrienne has the largest medical database in the country.

Now it's consciously being used as a very powerful and cost-effective tool for communication with customers. It allows Roche Diagnostics to take the "We'll look after you for life" message to end users one-on-one. The club is a great way to get across the message that we're a company that will stand by each and every customer.

What Adrienne is doing – building direct relationships with consumers – is unusual in this business because the channel is traditionally through health care professionals and pharmacies. Customer value management has provided her with a clear line of sight to end users and helped her decide what to do to build value for them.

- David Shieff, David Shieff and Associates (a CVM NZ
  associate)

I asked Adrienne whether they hardwire customer value management to the compensation system at Roche Diagnostics New Zealand – so that employees are rewarded in cash for improvement in CVA scores. Her response was that while they did this for her senior management team for the first three years, customer value management has now become so much part of the organization – the way they think – that she doesn't really feel it's necessary any more. Her team is small and has bought into the need to do this work, and she has the country manager's support. The concepts and tools of customer value management are becoming entrenched. Once you really understand that customer value drives business results, you don't need a separate CVA target built into the compensation system.

Adrienne has become a strong champion of customer value management with the Roche Diagnostics teams in Asia Pacific and Europe, and other divisions have now begun to apply the concepts, with positive results. I'll leave the last word on the Roche Diagnostics experience to her:

To summarize what customer value analysis does for me: It's given me absolute clarity on what I need to do to run my business. There's no question about whether customer value analysis is worth the investment. I believe it is essential.

- Adrienne Taylor

Vodafone (New Zealand)

case study

This case study is drawn from the cellular telephone market in New Zealand. It tells the story of how Bell South Cellular (purchased by Vodafone shortly after the story begins), applied the concepts of customer value to become a serious force in a market dominated by Telecom NZ.

Two things strike me as particularly interesting about their journey. One is that they've honed in on the fundamentals of customer value management – seeing the business through customers' eyes and understanding that customer perception of value relative to the competition is what counts – while never hesitating to adjust the customer value management framework and methodology to their needs.

The second is that, like Suncorp (and Mead Corporation, as you'll read in the case study coming up), they've put a strong focus on internal measures that impact how customers experience the company – in this case, service quality measures. As I hear their story, I think, "Here's a company where customer value management is truly integrated into how they do business." It's definitely not a stand-alone program sitting on the edge of the action.

I first started tracking the story in 1996, when my colleagues Rodger Gallagher and Deborah Hill in New Zealand were asked to work with Bell South Cellular. The cellular markets were being opened up to increased competition and Bell South wanted to start surveying the market to understand their competitive position. I'm going to jump ahead in time a bit to hear what Graham Maher saw when he took on what he describes as a chief operating officer role with the company after it was purchased by Vodafone in 1998:

> *The purchase of the Bell South Cellular New Zealand business*
> *was a first for Vodafone. Our previous growth had been entirely*

from winning licenses or partnering with people to build networks. Our original thought was that we would make the business conform to the usual Vodafone model: one entity running the network, and another acting as a service provider for cellular customers.

But when we got in there and looked at the business, we realized that it was truly an integrated business, with both of these arms operating together in one environment. And we decided to leave it like that.

Bell South Cellular had enjoyed a very good business in New Zealand, but at the time it was going backward and was losing a lot of money. They'd been trying to sell the business for some time, and things were rather in a tough position. But I found that there were some really good things going on.

For example, one of the gems I found was that the technology department was incredibly customer focused. I couldn't figure out how this had happened. It was quite unique in my experience to have technology people with a really sound understanding of how what they do impacts customer value. I was really intrigued and wanted to work out what we could learn from that. As it turned out, we learned a lot.

The first thing I learned was that some of the strategic guys in the marketing area had been using the customer value management approach. And the same approach had been adopted and used by the technology group.

The next remarkable thing I learned was that the approach was showing significant results. When we bought the company the prevailing view had been that their coverage wasn't very good, and that's why Telecom NZ was winning away business. Using the customer value methodology, we were able to completely change this perception in the marketplace, without spending much more money. We did that by gaining an understanding of what customers really meant when they said that they valued coverage, and by making some adjustments to our network to align with those needs.

- Graham Maher, Managing Director, Vodafone Australia

Graham had picked up on a very important point here. When the first market research came in saying that coverage and the dropped call rate were two key drivers of competitive advantage in the market place, it was easy to conclude that Bell South Cellular would never be able to catch up with Telecom NZ, which had a bigger network, without massive capital investment in building a network to match.

Subsequent customer value surveys focused on getting behind these high-level attributes to find out what customers really had in mind when they were rating Vodafone and the competition on quality. My colleague Rodger Gallagher explains what they learned:

> *When people in this market talk about calling quality or coverage, it seems that what they really mean is:*
>
> - *The ability to make and receive a call when and where they want. They are relatively forgiving in rural areas, but absolutely expect to be able to initiate, receive and maintain connection of a call within a known coverage area – within towns or cities, and on major routes.*
> - *That calls, once established, will be free of distortion. They won't have robotic voice characteristics and the voices won't break up or be interrupted.*
> - *That network services will be available where the supplier has promised. Within publicized coverage areas, customers absolutely expect no disruption to service (dropped calls).*
>
> *The bad news was that Vodafone was trailing the competition on all these factors. The good news was that they could address these issues without the massive network investment that the single quality attribute "coverage" had implied. With this level of precision in their understanding of what matters to customers, Vodafone engineers were able to fine tune their existing network to better meet customer needs. The changes they made – changing the radio frequency and boosting the amplifier – were relatively inexpensive and had a big impact on customer perception of how well Vodafone rated against the competition on quality.*
>
> - Rodger Gallagher, CVM New Zealand

That was one early success story. Another interesting example of how customer value data is used for business decision making in the company stems from some competitive pricing issues Vodafone was running into a few years ago. Telecom NZ's strategy for fending off competition from Vodafone was to drop their peak rates. The result was that while Vodafone's off-peak rates were the same as those offered by Telecom NZ, their peak rates were 40% higher. Vodafone's dilemma: Do we need to drop peak rates to stay competitive, and can we afford to do so?

What they learned from the customer value data was that peak rates were not the most significant driver of customer perception of price value. Vodafone has been able to stay competitive by coming up with some innovative offers that drive up customer perception of value, such as a "three-day weekend" pre-pay card that gives customers off-peak rates from Thursday at 7 p.m. to Monday at 7 a.m., discounts on pre-paid cards, a flat rate to access voice mail.

Shawn Henry, who leads the corporate customer satisfaction program, credits the sophisticated modeling they're now doing for their ability to come up with cost packages that customers rate favorably:

> *At the beginning, the standard econometric modelling was spot on for what we needed. In the early stages you need focus. But we've progressed to the point of having designated "owners" for each of the main attributes: quality, service and price. These attribute owners want a much more comprehensive, holistic view and more in-depth analysis to help them determine the right course of action.*

> *Straightforward linear regression tells us what impact each of a set of independent variables has on a dependent variable like quality. The more elegant approach we're taking now – it's called structural equation modelling – allows us to understand the relation among the independent variables. With econometric modelling, you're looking for the four or five things that will have most impact on overall value. You still see that with structural equation modelling. But you also see two or three sub-attributes that sort of stick together, so that if you act on them together there's a kind of halo effect and you have a much more powerful impact across the board.*

> *If you look at ongoing cost, for example, within that cluster are things like the cost of our plan, ongoing minutes, the cost to access voice mail and several others. We found that there's a*

really tight correlation across all of these variables. Now, some of them are easier to act on than others, so this kind of understanding helps us determine which combination of actions in the cost arena will have the most impact. And once we sorted that out and made the changes, we've seen nice increases in these attributes – in the neighbourhood of 10% to 12% increase in absolute scores.

- Shawn Henry

The approach Shawn is describing is more complex than most of the companies I work with need. But it works for Vodafone, and gives the attribute owners responsible for monitoring trends and setting strategy a wealth of information to work with. As Rodger points out, it also helps even out some anomalies inherent in the cellular market:

The cellular market is very dynamic and the players have huge advertising budgets. One of the things we found when we were doing only linear multiple regression was that impact weights would shift significantly depending on the theme of the most recent advertising campaign.

That was confusing for people. When you use the structural equation model and take into account the correlations among the variables, you don't get such huge fluctuations. This gives people more stable data to work with in setting their marketing strategy.

- Rodger Gallagher

I think it's great that Vodafone has stepped up to doing this more complicated analysis and has designated "attribute owners" to analyze the data and implement strategies for action. Over time, the customer value data has developed a reputation for credibility with the leadership team. Here's what Graham had to say on that front:

Once I understood the customer value approach I became passionate about it and started talking about it across the company. I saw how powerful a tool it was and wanted to teach the rest of the organisation how to use it.

But it's not enough to be passionate about it – you've got to prove it. And we were able to prove that our CVM score is a lead indicator of our market share. In fact, after a while we were predicting market share a quarter out, based on the CVM data, within 1% accuracy all the time. Of all the ways we have to predict churn, again the CVM score has turned out to be the most accurate (also within 1%). Based on the current CVM score, we now know what the immediate future holds for the business. We now believe that.

In fact, when we first proposed putting CVM into our bonus structure, there was some push back from several members of the board on the concept of including such a "soft" measure – unlike the "hard" financial measures. But our financial director at the time, Philip Edwards, said, "The CVM score is more rigid and correct than any of our financial scores."

- Graham Maher

At the same time, Vodafone has avoided the trap of falling in love with statistics for the sake of statistics. While the "elegant" analysis is giving good direction to strategists and the CVM to market share correlations are serving as a "heads up" to business planners, when it comes to determining internal process measures designed to improve customers' experience of the company, the approach they're taking is both simple and practical. Chris Green, customer relationship management (CRM) project manager, explains:

Many people equate CRM with a piece of technology, but that isn't right at all. To me, the measurement and use of customer satisfaction information is one part of the CRM jigsaw puzzle. And so early on I got heavily involved with the CVM work.

There was a lot of interesting information going around the business about CVM, but I think it's fair to say that the majority of people in the organization didn't understand what it was they did that had an impact on CVM. And that was a dangerous place to be, because we'd just put CVM into the staff bonus structure.

So, we'd told people that the scores we got on CVM would have an impact on their bonus, but they didn't really understand what they could do to improve them. And that's what I set out to change.

> *The problem we started with is that customers' perceptions of our business and how we deliver value to them rarely fit with how we organise and run our business. So you can't look at one department or process and say, "You alone drive that attribute." One process could have an impact on many of the CVM attributes, and one attribute can be impacted by many processes. You've got a kind of many-to-many relationship going on, which is a horrendously complex thing for people to get their heads around. They ask, "Well, if I do this, will I see an impact here?" And the answer usually is, "You may see it here, or you may see it there or there or there."*

- Chris Green

Let me interject for a second to point out that what I hear Chris describing here is the classic Waterfall. I've talked before about how no one function or step in the Waterfall can totally deliver customer satisfaction – but any one can both impact customer satisfaction with that process and cause further problems in related processes downstream. He goes on to explain a simple approach to choosing where to focus that cuts through this complexity:

> *When I was a consultant working on customer value research back in the UK, I tried to get clear statistical linkages between CVM scores and processes. And I discovered that this is really a very inexact science – in fact it's more art than science. We tried to see if there were any correlations between improvement in process scores and increases in customer value scores. The answer was, "Yes, probably," but you've got lag effects and all sort of things going on, so it's really hard to cut through the statistical jungle.*

> *The approach I took at Vodafone was to not even try to prove these linkages statistically. We established as an intuitive principle that the work our staff does must ultimately have an impact on customers' perception of the value they get from Vodafone. We looked at the data, and used our common sense to think through what things we could do to impact the attributes that were showing up as highly important to our customers. We got a list of 25 or so processes, then did a cull, selecting those for which we believed that variance in performance would likely drive variance in customers' perception of value.*

> *We did it intuitively rather than scientifically or statistically. I think it's dangerous to try to make customer value management too scientific, because what you're actually measuring is customers' perception – what's inside their heads. There are so many other variables that we can't control. It's an incredibly useful tool, but I think it's dangerous to reduce it to a simple mathematical equation and get lulled into a false sense of security. There's a lot of "art" involved.*

> - Chris Green

I'm with Chris in his caution against reducing customer value management to a mathematical equation, and I like his simple and practical approach to determining the right internal process measures to focus on. There is indeed an art of interpreting customer value data that is grounded in common sense and good judgment, that takes into account the broader business context, and that develops with practice. I've seen CVM scores track closely to market share for months on end, only to suddenly get out of whack because of a significant discontinuity in the business or the market as a whole. The challenge in my mind is to put enough rigor into the capture and analysis of customer value data to make it a credible tool for top level decision making, without falling into the trap of leaving out the human factor and thinking about the delivery of value as an entirely mechanical process.

But let's get back to looking at how they used the measures they chose to get people focused on customers. Here's Chris again:

> *I felt strongly that we needed to express the Service Quality Measures (SQM) we chose from the customers' perspective. We used to say things like, "Our performance measure is that 98.4% of calls don't get dropped." But that's a Vodafone view of the world. What the customer cares about is, "Did MY call get dropped?" What we should be measuring is how many times the service fails, not the percentage of time the service is delivered as it should be.*

> *So now we have big SQM boards all over the place, on every floor, in every office, and each one contains about 14 absolute measures of service failure, worded from the customer's perspective – measures such as:*

- *My call was dropped x times*
- *My call was blocked y times*
- *My bill was late*
- *My e-mail wasn't responded to within three hours.*

People were a bit resistant to measuring absolute numbers of service failures, because the business is growing and the volume of transactions is increasing. But since our goal is to make sure every Vodafone customer has a world-class experience of the company, that's what you have to look at.

The board shows numbers for this month, last month and the previous month so we can track whether or not we're improving. Then we have one overall percentage that indicates whether service failures have gone down or up over the previous month and by how much.

We have a little cartoon character face on the board. If you put it up one way it's a bloke with a big smile on his face; if you turn it the other way, it's a grumpy looking person with a big frown. So depending on whether we've improved or got worse, the character is wearing either a smile or a frown. And what we say is it's all about "turning the frown upside down."

If I hadn't seen it with my own eyes, I wouldn't have believed how motivational this approach has been for the people actually working "at the coal face," working directly with customers in customer service, supply chain management, sales. The numbers of service failures have been coming down unbelievably quickly in a lot of areas, because people are thinking about the impact they have on the customer experience and they're absolutely focused on improvement.

People in technology who run some of the computer systems, for example, now see the impact of the computer going down in terms of the customer experience. They can actually see the difference in the service numbers when this happens. They didn't really understand before how much of a difference they could make to customer perception of value.

- Chris Green

It's this kind of story that backs up Shawn Henry's assertion that CVM has become totally integrated into the business at all levels. Chris is talking about what happens at what he calls the "coal face": the people who directly impact customers in their day-to-day work. At the most senior levels, the results are presented formally once a quarter to all the top managers in the company. Shawn puts out interim "pulse reports" to track trends in between. The group presentation is followed up by separate two-hour sessions for the business markets people, another for the consumer markets people, and another for other interested parties. More in-depth sessions looking at the results of statistical analysis are run for the attribute owners, who then use the results to set strategy and implement action.

Because the company has been growing, the concepts have now been built into the new hire induction course, and special workshops are run every year or couple of years to give new people a deeper understanding of the tools and techniques.

I think one of the reasons why customer value management has taken hold at Vodafone is that they've made it their own. It's not "Ray's tools" or "Rodger's technique" – it's the way Vodafone does business. Here's how Shawn puts it:

> *I think this is an excellent, rock solid framework. At the same time it's malleable – not an off-the-shelf product. We've stayed true to the framework, but made it more "Vodafonesque." I still think there's some tweaking we want to do to make it more robust for us. But what makes it so powerful is that we're dealing with people who are willing to work with us to personalise it and make sure it has the right impact on Vodafone's business.*

- Shawn Henry

I asked Graham Maher, who's now managing director of Vodafone Australia and involved in translating the customer value management concepts into "people value" initiatives there, what the bottom line was for him. I told him that many of the companies I work with like the conceptual framework, but worry that it will take a lot of resources, energy and money to make the work pay off. His response:

Yes it does, and it's worth it. You don't do it unless you're very, very committed. You've got to be serious about this and put everything you've got into doing it. You can't just talk about it. It takes time and effort and money from everyone in the organisation, and it's got to be led by the senior people.

The whole Vodafone New Zealand case study is fantastic. The only reason that this business was able to achieve what it did after we purchased it was that we focused on people and customers. That's it. Otherwise, it's the same business it was when it was losing money.

- Graham Maher

In 1997, when the customer value work began, Vodafone's net-adds/win market share rate was 19%. It rose to 30% by June 1998, to 42% by 1999, 60% by 2000 and more than 70% by 2002. Impressive results for a company that has incorporated the concept of delivering customer value into how it does business.

Mead Corporation (United States)

case study

Early in 2002, Mead Corporation completed a merger of equals with Westvaco, creating an $8 billion corporation headquartered in Stamford, Connecticut. MeadWestvaco is a leading global producer of packaging, coated and specialty papers, consumer and office products, and specialty chemicals. The company operates in 33 countries, serves customers in about 100 countries, employs approximately 30,000 people worldwide and manages more than three million acres of forests.

When I first started working with Mead in late 1996, it was quickly growing into a $4 billion company with close to 14,000 employees worldwide. It had about 40 business units each serving a different market, reporting into ten division presidents.

A Learning Organization

What continues to impress me about Mead is the company's ability to grow, learn and change without throwing out what is good and valuable and productive in its heritage. It is truly a "learning organization." I've seen so many companies assume that when a new buzzword gets coined or a new approach established they need to forget everything they've been doing and start again from scratch. Proponents of customer loyalty, for example, sometimes talk as though anything having to do with customer satisfaction is outdated and therefore wrong.

In Chapter Fifteen, I'll talk about my belief that concepts such as customer satisfaction, customer loyalty, customer relationship management and total quality management can all build on one another to create a more in-depth understanding of how to create value for customers. In this story, we'll follow Mead's evolution from a commitment to quality to a focus on customer satisfaction to a customer value management approach. I get a sense from the story that they've managed to maintain the best of each discipline along the way.

Mead is a company that cares about history. On its website, the company history starts at 1846, when Colonel Daniel Mead and some partners first formed the company that would become the Mead Paper Corporation in 1881. So it's not too surprising that when I asked Wally Nugent (now retired), the key executive champion of customer value within Mead in its early stages, to tell their story, he started by taking us back to mid-80s – 1980s, that is!

> *In the mid-80s, I was asked to move from my role as group executive in charge of four divisions to take on a corporate position leading purchasing, logistics and marketing for the company. Now, our divisions were very autonomous and did their own marketing, so my job was to look for potential synergies across all divisions – what we could be doing as a company to get ahead of the game.*

> *At the time, our industry as a whole was not all that savvy in the field of marketing, and I would say Mead was running in about the middle of the pack. Like so many others, we were very wrapped up in the quality movement, and putting a strong focus on cost, technology and manufacturing processes. While there was a lot of activity in these areas through the late 80s – lots of training in quality improvement tools, lots of quality improvement initiatives underway – at the end of the day we weren't seeing significant bottom-line impact. And we finally figured out that this was because the whole thing was driven by our desire to improve our internal processes, with little or no focus on markets or customers. We were making great improvements – by and large on things that customers didn't value.*

> *It's almost embarrassing now to admit how long it took me and my colleagues to figure out why we weren't seeing financial results from the quality improvements we were making. In hindsight it was ridiculous to be doing all this stuff and not really asking ourselves whether we were grounding our improvement initiatives in things that would make a difference to our customers. But that just wasn't our mindset back then.*

> *In about 1990, I became interested in customer satisfaction and started going out to meet with other companies that were doing this kind of work. Most were willing to share what they were learning – Milliken, for example, really helped us a lot – and pretty soon we had a fairly simple customer satisfaction survey*

system in place. We started by piloting the system in a few business units that were particularly interested in the new thinking about customer satisfaction.

Those early pilots were extremely revealing and, frankly, extremely exciting. In every case, the management team learned they had grossly overestimated how they were viewed in the market. The surveys helped the team identify where they should focus performance improvement efforts to gain competitive advantage.

In 1991, our CEO retired and our president, Steve Mason, took over the reins. He had a drive to transform Mead from what we were – above average in the industry, but not a major leader – into the best performer in the forest products industry. The framework he put forward to achieve this goal had three legs:

- *Customer satisfaction*
- *Productivity improvement*
- *High performance organization (attracting and retaining the best people, building team skills, creating effective reward systems, etc.).*

I was particularly gratified to see customer satisfaction right up there – first among equals if you like. We committed to doing a customer satisfaction survey for each of the more than 40 business units every year. Division managers were charged with taking substantive corrective action based on the surveys, and we tied a significant amount of their incentive compensation to this. Over the next five years or so, we made very credible progress in most of the business units. Mead's overall performance relative to competitors improved significantly over time.

But for some reason, in the mid to late 90s, our progress hit a plateau and support for it started to waver.

- Wally Nugent, retired Mead executive

This is the point at which I first learned of Mead's customer satisfaction journey and was invited to help them take the next steps. When it became clear that techniques that had served Mead well for five years were no longer delivering results, Wally started searching out people who could bring him up to speed on the latest thinking on customer satisfaction and value. He attended conferences, searched the literature, did benchmarking. In the process, Wally was directed to me, and eventually he asked me to do a presentation to their senior team about the customer value management approach.

Getting the Focus Right

But before we launch into the next stage of the journey, let's get another perspective on what was happening to the customer satisfaction initiative and why it hit a plateau. This one comes from John Pelligrino. If Wally is the champion of the customer value work in my terminology, John is the change agent. For the past five years he's been the director of customer satisfaction measurement for Mead (and now for MeadWestvaco). He was with the packaging division for 20 years prior to that. As director of organization development for the packaging team, he had helped facilitate a lot of the customer survey work in that division. Here's what John saw happening in the mid-90s:

We had started out with a very simple survey process: a couple of means, some stated importance. We had people rate importance on a scale of 1 to 10, but since there was nothing preventing them from rating everything as important, that was of limited value. The system as a whole served us very well at first, but by 1997 we all realized we needed to make some changes.

That's when Wally pulled together a team from across the company to try to improve the process. I was the packaging division representative.

One thing that I felt was wrong was that the process had evolved into what you might call a "beauty contest." I strongly believe that customer satisfaction measurement should never be purely a scorecard effort – with the emphasis on getting the best score, looking good against your colleagues, and getting praise from the corporate parents. If that happens, it's too easy for people to get distracted into arguments about whether we're surveying the right competitors, the right customers (i.e. the ones likely to give favorable responses) or asking the right questions.

I tried to get people to worry less about the scores. Yes, we want to know how we're positioned against competitors; and yes, I believe that customer satisfaction and value scores are linked to profitability. But the real goal of the surveys was to learn something about what we needed to do better to have customers rate us higher on value and loyalty. It was the learning aspect that was getting lost. In focusing on the scores, we were missing insights into what we needed to do to grow our business. That's what we got back to when we adopted the customer value approach.

- John Pelligrino, Director, Customer Satisfaction Measurement

Wally makes a similar point, although it's framed in different terms:

I'm a proponent of customer satisfaction work – it's critical – but it should be preceded by value proposition work. Unless you're very clear on what market you're trying to serve, what value you're trying to bring to the market, what you're really trying to achieve, you're wasting your time. You can be doing great work in customer satisfaction, but if the organization isn't really clear on the value proposition, you're working on a bed of sand.

- Wally Nugent

When I introduced the customer value management approach to Mead, several things seemed to click for them. Here's Wally's view:

Seeing the customer value management approach was a breakthrough for me. First, it clearly showed that just making progress relative to yourself isn't enough. You've got to go beyond your current customer set and survey non-customers before you can be sure you're making progress. This clicked with me and the team adopted it pretty much carte blanche.

The other area where it particularly helped us was in our thinking about how price, relative to products, service and relationship, fits into the whole customer satisfaction equation. We kept getting all wrapped up in this and we knew we weren't getting it quite right. Our reaction when we heard Ray's approach was, "Here's a much better way of doing it."

- Wally Nugent

John's answer to why the customer value approach seemed right to them focuses more specifically on some of the technical aspects:

> *Some elements of the new approach tied very closely to our old method and we saw it more as an enhancement than an entirely new approach. We could start from the same attributes and ensure continuity in our tracking. Where we had focused in the past on stated importance for each of the attributes, we could now also derive impact weights using statistical analysis.*
>
> *We were taken by the concept of "value" as a proxy for how a customer makes a buying decision. It was important to us that Ray's statistical methods were open methods that we could do ourselves and adapt to our own circumstances. We were very clear that we didn't want any kind of "black box" analytical process.*
>
> *A lot of market research firms have their proprietary analytic method and they won't crack the formula for you. They'll tell you what the data suggests, but not how they came to that conclusion. Now, I wasn't about to stand up in front of a group of managers and say, "You ought to do this" with no better rationale than, "That's what the consultant told me to say." I'm not saying that these research companies are doing anything wrong. But for us, if we couldn't completely understand the formulas that made us arrive at a result, we weren't going to use that method. Our managers weren't going to go with a result that they couldn't dissect themselves if they chose to.*
>
> - John Pelligrino

Adapting the Roadmap

What's been exciting for me is watching how Mead has taken the customer value management "roadmap" and made it their own, incorporating the best of their previous approaches, and adjusting the methodology to suit their business. They continue to track customers' stated importance for each major attribute (now measured by having customers split 100 points among a group of attributes) in addition to derived impact, and include this metric on their versions of the Attribute Trees and Competitive Profiles. This additional data helps them analyze which attributes are truly "entry tickets" and which have the potential to be "competitive differentiators." This is important because they've learned that exceeding customer expectations on entry ticket items does not usually contribute significantly to customer satisfaction and value, even though falling below expectations on these items can become a major source of dissatisfaction.

To calculate their impact weights, they have had good success with a different statistical analysis technique from the one I usually recommend (see Step 6 – *Analyze the Data*). John explains below why Normalized Pairwise Estimation (NPE) is better suited to their purposes than Ordinary Least Squares (OLS), and how they make sure that the ratios they present to decision makers are put in context:

> *One of our challenges is that we have a lot of niche businesses in very unique market segments where our sales channels are business to business. So we don't have potential customer samples in the 100K range – often it's more like 20 to 30 businesses. With target groups this small, many of our surveys are actually full census surveys, not random samples.*
>
> *We're also fairly selective as to which non-customers we survey. We want to make sure we're talking to people who could conceivably be prospects, whose needs are in general alignment with our value proposition – not just anybody out there.*
>
> *You normally need at least 60 to 70 observations to do the OLS regressions that Ray recommends. That's usually not possible with the size of our samples. We've done some OLS regressions and got a reasonable R^2 with fewer than 50 responses, but I still have some concerns about reliability.*
>
> *With NPE, you can get a reasonably solid model with as few as 20 observations. Even where we have a larger sample, this allows us to break the data down into smaller market segments and model for those segments.*
>
> *The other element of customer value management that gives conservative statisticians heartburn is our use of ratios to give us a single number that indicates how we're doing against the competition. I understand that calculating ratios from interval data is a statistical "no-no" – since the ratio can vary a lot based on where it's positioned on the scale. If we score a 2 and the*

competition scores a 1, for example, then our competitive ratio is 2.0; whereas if we score a 9 and the competition scores an 8, our competitive ratio is 1.13.

In reality, you seldom get scores at the bottom end of the range, and when you do, you use your common sense to interpret the ratios appropriately. I pair the ratios with what are sometimes called "stop/go" charts – charts that put the ratios into the context of absolute scores. If we're scoring 9 or 10 on a 10-point scale on an attribute, it's colored green. A 7 or 8 would be yellow (satisfaction, but no delight) and anything below 7 would be red (an at-risk item that we really need to look at). If you're not looking at absolute scores as well as the ratios, you can end up with the "cream of the crap" phenomenon. You may be beating the competition, but all that means is that you're the least hated of the available options.

- John Pelligrino

Measuring Performance

I'm particularly impressed by the way Mead has linked customer value metrics to internal process measurements, and tied their reward systems largely to the latter. Their success in doing so is, perhaps, a legacy of their quality background.

For example, one division found that they were consistently scoring low on questions relating to responsiveness to customer issues or complaints, and decided that this was a priority for improvement. They created a database that allowed them to log in every complaint or issue that came to them from a customer. An e-mail would automatically be sent from the log to the account manager or appropriate sales person letting them know there was an issue they needed to resolve. Through the database, the business unit tracked the interaction on the issue, so they would know both the amount of effort required to resolve the issue to the customer's satisfaction, and the amount of time it took. This gave them a hard measure of responsiveness they could use to track performance. John explains the impact:

The business unit that implemented this system saw considerable improvement in scores in the next survey. We didn't have to make a huge investment in training or process improvement to accomplish this. All we did was call attention to the issue of response time by letting people know that we were measuring it. Managers could go into the database at any time, see what kind of complaints had been logged and how long it was taking to resolve them. As soon as people recognized that someone was looking at response time, they got things done more quickly. The approach worked so well that other divisions soon picked up on this best practice and implemented similar systems.

I don't know any company that is really expert on internal measurement, and yet I think it's critical to get this right. Companies measure all sorts of things, but sometimes they end up with lots of numbers that don't really help them improve the business. The challenge is to always make sure you're measuring things that customers deem important, not just things that are convenient or easy to measure.

We've always had an annual process in which each division contracts with the corporation as to what results it's going to deliver in the next fiscal year. Customer satisfaction has been part of that contracting process for a long time. Traditionally, we've used survey scores as the goal: We contract to move overall satisfaction from x to y in a year.

I feel that this is an artificial method. We ought to hold people accountable for things that they can control, and it's not immediately obvious to people that they can control survey scores. So we select the three to five critical priorities that we believe will lead to improved scores – things that customers say are important to them or attributes on which we're trailing the competition – and then we set performance goals in these areas. We come up with an appropriate internal measure and track that.

This keeps the focus on learning. I keep coming back to the fact that the goal is to learn how to become a better business. We're not the in the business of generating survey scores. We're in the business of paper, packaging, consumer and office products, and we're ultimately measured on our profitability and shareholder value. The customer value scores give us insights into what we need to do to make our business more profitable.

- John Pelligrino

Remember the chart in Step 9 – *Reward Success* that showed an Attribute Tree starting from "worth what paid for" on the left and ending with internal measures on the right? I made the argument then that while it's appropriate to hold senior officers of the company responsible for overall CVA scores, process owners and their teams can make a greater contribution to improvements in CVA if the metrics they're focused on relate to what they do every day. That's what John's describing here: Link the attribute to an internal business process and find a performance measure that is truly monitoring what's important to customers. You heard another take on this challenge in the Vodafone case.

Delivering Results

The new approach is delivering results for the business units that have adopted it. For example, one Mead business unit in the Pacific Rim was losing money in 1997 when the work first started. The survey indicated that the unit was perceived to be worse than the competition on most variables, and was getting an overall value ratio against the competition of 0.90. The general manager put a stake in the ground and said, based on the survey, we need to focus on these key variables if we're going to be successful in the market. Two years later, the value ratio was still trailing, but had gone up to 0.94. The business had grown some and reached the break-even point. In a survey from early in 2002, the value ratio had risen to 1.10. The business has more than doubled and is now profitable.

Another business unit discovered through the research that it was trailing the competition on some key product quality measures, but doing reasonably well on service. It was clear from the surveys that product was an entry ticket item, meaning that differentiation on the product by itself was not going to be a key factor in beating the competition. But as with any entry ticket, if you trail your competition significantly, you're going to lose business because you've fallen behind the price of entry. As John put it, "They're not going to pay you a premium if you're significantly better, but they're going to kick you out if you don't measure up."

So this unit set out a strategy to achieve parity on product quality and superiority on service delivery. Within two years they had done that. They had also succeeded in gaining share in a market that was actually shrinking a couple of percentage points a year, by taking share away from the competition.

It's important to stress that customer value management is not applicable only to business units that are in trouble and in need of a turnaround. One of Mead's divisions has found that in 60% to 70% of their businesses, they're trailing on one significant factor. The leadership has said, "We need to grab this one and do something about it." They've let it be known that this is the number one issue to track worldwide, and they have begun to pull out verbatim comments from the survey to give them as much information as possible about the factor. While the business is doing well, they recognize that this one factor could put it in jeopardy over time, and they've decided to be proactive in addressing it and maintaining competitive advantage.

What Does it Take to Succeed?

When I share success stories like this in my sessions with clients, I know that the key issue on their mind is, "How much does all this cost? How many people does it take to make this happen?"

The direct cost is the cost of hiring an external vendor to do the interviews. In Mead's case, the business units pay these costs. Because all of the statistical modeling is done in house, John can make sure he's getting the best deal from vendors because they're all quoting for a specified number of interviews at a specified length.

In terms of the overhead cost and the people required to deliver a program like this, here's Wally's summary of their experience:

> *Once we'd decided that we would adopt a customer value management approach for our customer satisfaction program, we needed to sell it to opinion leaders across the corporation. That wasn't all that easy. We had developed credibility with the earlier success of our customer satisfaction program, so people were open to listening to us. But these concepts were new for Mead, and people were afraid that we were going to overcomplicate things and end up falling on our own swords.*

> *It became clear to me that we needed a full-time expert who understood the concepts well, could articulate the business case and sell it to the business unit leadership – what Ray calls a "change agent." This was a new position for the company, and as such had to have a solid justification. I knew it was critical, and the leadership agreed to fund it.*

> *John had been on the team representing the packaging division, and he had a deep passion for this work. He would argue that he's not a statistician, although his Ph.D. in Human Resources Development gave him a "handshake with statistics." But he's*

sufficiently knowledgeable about statistics and computers to make this whole program work. I didn't have enough technical depth (nor time!) to be able to cut the data in different ways and quickly respond to a division president's question. John can do that. The customer value management software that allows us to quickly create Value Maps, Slippery Slopes, Competitive Profiles and so on really helps here as well.

You need someone in this change agent role who is comfortable sitting down with the CEO once a quarter for a couple of hours to make sure he really understands what's going on: division by division, business unit by business unit. This is not about telling tales out of school – the businesses have seen and worked with the data long before the CEO does. It's about keeping the issues top of mind for the CEO. You need to have him out there talking about customer value and constantly reinforcing the importance of working on the identified priorities. The CEOs I've worked with in Mead have all been very active in spreading the word.

John is supported by a part-time administrator and the software administrator in the IT department who runs the data modeling. Our model has always been to designate people from within the businesses to lead the charge there. They're not part of the corporate team, but they work closely with corporate to make sure that data gets collected, packaged and acted upon in the business.

- Wally Nugent

So, for an $8 billion company, the corporate customer value management team is a change agent with a good knowledge of statistics, a part-time technical person who does the actual statistical modeling, and a part-time administrator. All the rest of the people who make it work are in the business units.

Wally doesn't mention it, but I believe it's largely due to his patience, perseverance, and understanding of how to make things happen that there's a program in place that has stood the test of time. He got all the elements of the process in place and put the right people in charge. Wally has been retired for two years now, and under John's leadership the program continues to thrive. The merger with Westvaco will no doubt lead to significant change in the coming months and years. Given Mead's history of being able to bring the best of their past forward with them into the future, I look forward to watching the next leg of their journey.

Part III:
Customer Value
Management Essentials

The Big Picture
chapter fifteen

A question I get all the time is, "So how does customer value management relate to customer loyalty, or customer satisfaction, or customer relationship management?" Some people ask because they have an either/or mindset and assume that the goal of the latest and greatest approach to business improvement must be to dismiss all earlier approaches. What they're really asking is, "Does this mean that we're wrong to worry about customer satisfaction?" Others are truly interested in understanding how all of these concepts fit together in a big picture view. They want to know how customer value management relates to the full range of business management practices like Six Sigma, Total Quality Management, Baldrige National Quality Program, balanced scorecards and so on.

The short answer is that in the most successful companies all of these concepts are integrated and together enable the company to deliver value to customers, shareholders and employees. The labels may not all be used, and some of the specific techniques prescribed by the proponents of these practices may not be evident, but the principles are understood and followed. In this chapter I'll describe what I see as the fundamental principles behind the labels and how they fit together.

Same Label; Different Meaning

The labels are useful shorthand, but it's important to be aware that they may mean different things in different contexts. Let's explore the term "customer loyalty" to illustrate the point. It seems to be the term with the most momentum at the moment, although "customer relationship management" is gaining ground and CRM has become a widely recognized acronym. Anything with an acronym must be important!

Some companies' customer loyalty programs are focused on measuring and managing the actual loyalty of customers. How long has the customer been with us? How much do they spend? Do they buy across our whole product offering? Have they brought in new business by recommending us to others?

They may be doing this as a performance measure, to assess how well they're doing at creating the type of value that makes customers want to come back. Or they may be using the information to help them decide where to focus time and attention.

I once picked up a newspaper in Australia and saw a headline that read something to the effect of "How Banks Measure Customer Loyalty." Great, I thought, this should give good insight into how banks go about creating value for customers and increasing their loyalty.

When I read the article, I discovered what they were actually doing was measuring the value of different customers to the bank. Simply having a checking account with the bank for 25 years didn't make you a loyal customer in the bank's eyes. Loyal customers were those who had all or most of their financial assets managed by the bank: mortgages, pensions, credit cards and so on. The purpose of measuring customer loyalty in this way was to decide which customers were going to get preferred treatment: a designated customer relationship manager, more time and attention from staff.

Now, knowing which customers are most valuable to you and going out of your way to keep them is a very good thing. My point here is the words "customer loyalty" in the headline had suggested an entirely different line of thought to me. I suspect it was also a surprise to those 25-year customers who suddenly learned that they weren't considered loyal and were therefore not going to be treated as well as others in the future. To my mind, any study of customer loyalty should include understanding how customers define loyalty.

Other companies are more interested in the predictive aspect of customer loyalty. They survey customers on questions such as, "How likely are you to recommend the company to others? How likely are you to buy again from the company? How likely are you to increase your spending with the company?" They use this information as a leading indicator of where the business is trending.

Other customer loyalty programs are actually aimed at building loyalty, not measuring it. The "frequent buyer" programs can be as simple as a free cup of coffee for every 20 cups purchased from a particular coffee house. Or they can be the more sophisticated programs offered by airlines that provide multiple options for both earning and redeeming reward points.

These are all good initiatives with different but complementary purposes. And they all share the label "customer loyalty program."

The "Latest and Greatest"

I'll come back in a minute to the relationship between loyalty programs and customer value management. But I want to stress first that I have no intention of promoting customer value management as the latest and greatest concept that makes all others obsolete. I'm continually disturbed by the tendency I see among businesses to greet each new business management technique that comes along as a great revelation that overturns all previous wisdom.

A book I read recently informed me that "customer satisfaction is worthless; customer loyalty is priceless." Why is there this need to believe that the new idea can be good only if an earlier idea can be proven to be bad?

What if we saw instead a continual evolution of management ideas and concepts that all build on one another? Some practices and techniques stick and are integrated into larger business improvement systems. Sometimes only one or two insights from a body of work prove to have lasting value. But all these ideas make a contribution to our understanding of how businesses work – even the ideas that turn out to be impractical or don't produce the intended results.

I frame my work as "customer value management" because I believe that label keeps me and the companies I work with grounded in the purpose of business. To be successful over the long term, they must be filling customer needs better than the competition. If they succeed in creating better value for customers, they're rewarded by better value for shareholders and for the people who work there.

So here's my view on how some of the other tools and techniques work together to contribute to this purpose.

Customer Satisfaction

No new theory that comes along will succeed in persuading me companies should not be interested in satisfying customers! I highlighted at the beginning of the book the dangers of counting the "percent favorable" scores on a customer satisfaction survey, concluding that customers are satisfied, and becoming complacent that all is well. But I've also stressed throughout the book the usefulness of transaction or recent event surveys that measure in detail customer satisfaction with a particular experience of the company.

Customer satisfaction surveys play an important role in helping determine how to fix processes that are negatively impacting customers' perception of the value you provide.

Customer Loyalty

Customer loyalty is the flip side of customer satisfaction. Customer satisfaction is about customers' assessments of what the company provides. It's about whether customers feel they're getting what they deserve. Customer loyalty is what the company gets in return. One book I read recently says that customer loyalty is about making customers love you and keep coming back and tell everyone they know about how wonderful you are.

The higher the satisfaction scores, the more likely customers are to be loyal. The Slippery Slope tool that we've used throughout this book shows how high you need to score on overall satisfaction with the company to achieve the kind of loyalty you're targeting.

Much has been written on the importance of focusing on building customer loyalty and I won't go on at length here. Loyal customers tend to be more profitable because it costs less to service an existing customer than to win a new one. Recommendations from loyal customers can play a big role in growing the business. That's why loyalty figures can often be a leading indicator of growth in revenue and market share.

They can be predictive of growth, but with two big caveats. One is that if you're focusing exclusively on the metric that tells you what percent of your customers are loyal, you could miss signs of deep trouble. If all your non-loyal customers are going to the competition, your "percent loyal" figure can be going up while actual numbers are going down and your competitor is winning market share.

The second is that your most loyal customers may not necessarily be your most profitable customers. That's what the bank in the story I told earlier was getting at in trying to measure the value that different customers represented for the bank. Customers who infrequently purchase very high margin items may be more important to you than "loyal" customers who routinely purchase very low margin items. Customers who frequently purchase the highest margin items are the most valuable of all. Airlines recognize this by giving frequent business travelers status designations carrying perks such as entrance to business class lounges, early boarding and priority reservation telephone lines.

Customer Value

You earn customer loyalty, attract higher revenues and grow market share by delivering better value than your competition. Customer value management is the art and science of measuring and managing customer perception of the value you deliver relative to the competition. While it may be labeled differently in different companies – customer value analysis and customer value added are frequently used terms – the focus is always on the question, "Is what you get worth what you pay?"

Customer value management looks at the whole set of experiences customers have with the company: what they get, how they get it, what and how they pay for it, the ongoing cost of ownership, their business relationship with the company, their perception of the company's brand image. It measures how customers rate these experiences in absolute terms, then puts the ratings in the competitive context and turns them into relative scores. It's about doing such a better job of satisfying customers in each of these experiences than anyone else does that when customers add everything up, they feel they've received better value than they could get from anyone else.

Customer Relationship Management

Customer relationship management or CRM is a new twist on a very old idea. In the days when a small general store met the needs of a small local population, it wasn't hard for the owners to learn the needs and preferences of their customer base and tailor what they stocked accordingly. As mass production and distribution models became the norm, the customer base both grew in size and grew more distant until it became just what the term "mass production" implies – an anonymous mass.

Mass production made it possible for more people to afford more items. Automobiles, for example, were once a highly specialized item for the very rich. Those who could afford to buy one probably dealt directly with the owner of the manufacturing shop and had one built to their specifications. With the advent of the production line, more and more people could have whatever car they wanted – as long as it was a Model T and as long as it was black.

Today's sophisticated information technology has made possible the phenomenon of "mass customization." Software programs capture details of each customer interaction with the company and package this information for use in tailoring future interactions to more precisely match customer needs and preferences.

Sometimes the information is used to segregate customers into broad categories, like the frequent business flyers I talked about earlier. They're your most valuable customers and they go through the set of experiences that influence their perception of value with great regularity. They therefore have higher expectations than people who may travel once a year on vacation at bargain rates. You want to put your focus on knowing everything you can about their needs and preferences as a group.

But it's also possible using the new databases to get even more specific. Don Peppers and Martha Rogers have written extensively about "one-to-one marketing," which is about knowing each customer as an individual and designing processes to meet individual needs – even when you're dealing with a very large customer base. A good example of this is the increasing popularity of "made-on-demand" clothing. Now shoppers can avoid the frustrating experience of trying on jeans in six different brands, searching for the pair that actually fits. They simply send their precise measurements via the Internet to an online clothing service – such as that run by US-based Land's End – and get a pair of jeans made just for them at a reasonable cost in about three to four weeks. Talk about delivering value and earning loyalty!

Quality Management Practices

So, we know what creates value for our customer base and earns their loyalty. We know in aggregate what influences their perception of what they get, how they get it, what they pay for it and the brand image. With the magic CRM databases, we even know the preferences of individual customers. Now, how can we be sure that we consistently deliver this value and build a profitable business?

This is where TQM, Six Sigma and other "quality" practices come into play. They're focused on ensuring that your processes consistently and efficiently deliver the quality the customer expects. If you think back to the Suncorp case study at the end of Part I, you'll recall that the Suncorp team used Six Sigma techniques to meet the service guarantees they had made to customers based on their analysis of what customers value.

Measurement Systems

Then the question becomes, "How do we measure the company's success in delivering value?" The customer value measurements I've described in this book look at only one piece of an integrated value chain: value to customers. To get the full picture of how the business is doing they need to be looked at in the context of the value that's being created for shareholders and for employees, perhaps also for communities and even for suppliers. This is the balanced scorecard concept.

While the actual measures on the scorecard vary from company to company, the principle is that these key measures are interdependent and should be analyzed and managed as an integrated system. In the final chapter of the book, I'll explore some of the opportunities I see opening up as we start to better understand how to measure value across the chain and the linkages among the measures.

Each business keeps its own internal scorecard. But it can also choose to measure itself against external standards such as Baldrige or the European Foundation for Management Development standard. Most countries or regions of the world have an annual quality award based on a third-party rating of companies. The best of these go beyond looking at the technical efficiency of processes and recognize that the customer is the ultimate judge of quality. They're integrated management models that assess the company's business approach, determine how successfully it's being deployed across the company, and measure the results achieved using a balanced scorecard approach. The focus is on how all the parts of the system work together to deliver results.

So you see why, in my mind, it's not a matter of choosing to "do customer satisfaction" or "do customer loyalty" or "do TQM" or to "do customer value management." The ideas, tools and techniques associated with these and other labels are all part of the ongoing evolution of the art and science of managing successful businesses that create lasting value. Instead of searching for the "latest," why not look for and apply the "best" from this body of work – the concepts and tools that connect best with your philosophy and are proven to work best in your context?

LEARNING FROM HISTORY

The Principles at Work: Behind the Arches at McDonald's

Some years ago I read John Love's book *McDonald's: Behind the Arches* and was intrigued to find many of the principles we've just discussed clearly reflected there. The 1995 edition includes an epilogue that tells the story of a turnaround engineered by CEO Mike Quinlan in the early 90s. Without ever mentioning Attribute Trees or CVA ratios or the other tools we've explored here, the account describes a typical customer value management initiative. It also talks about customer satisfaction with interactions with the company, customer care, customer loyalty, measurement systems, and the customer-focused process re-engineering usually associated with TQM.

The author sets the stage by quoting Quinlan's address to the company's world convention in 1994: "Together, we're changing our focus and looking at the business through the eyes of the customer. This is a one hundred and eighty degree change from where we were before."[1]   He goes on to cite an example of what that means:

> *We passed a major milestone when we sold our one hundred*
> *billionth hamburger a few weeks ago...But when it happened,*

[1] John F. Love, *McDonald's: Behind the Arches* (Bantam, 1995 rev. ed.), p. 449.

this milestone went practically unnoticed, and that's good. A few years ago, when we were focused on ourselves instead of the customer, we would have been running commercials and hanging banners and calling for a national holiday and breaking our arms patting ourselves on the back.

But you know what? The customer doesn't care. One hundred billion hamburgers doesn't mean a thing to the customer standing in line waiting to buy number one hundred billion and one. Today, we're focused on the customer – the next one, not the hundred billion that came before. The operation of our restaurants is the key to customer satisfaction and the key to our success. (p. 450)

They'd learned to measure success by what matters to the customer, not the company. The wake-up call for the company came when they discovered that while they were growing (from about 7,300 to 8,600 outlets in the US between 1986 and 1990), competitors such as Taco Bell and Pizza Hut were gaining market share at their expense. To cover the big investments McDonalds was making, they were increasing prices faster than the competition. When the recession hit in the 1990s, according to Quinlan, "It became abundantly clear that our US value perceptions were seriously out of alignment and we were paying the price of customer defections." (p. 452)

They'd also spent the past few years struggling to combat negative public perception on two issues: the environment and nutrition. They learned the hard way that customer perception is reality. McDonald's decision to use polystyrene foam for food packaging had been based on a Stanford Research Institute study that found it to be efficient, effective and environmentally sound. In the 1980s, when scientists determined that chlorofluorocarbons (CFCs) were destroying the ozone layer, McDonald's led the industry in eliminating CFCs from the manufacturing process. But foam packaging had become a symbol of environmental waste in the minds of some vocal public advocates, and company leadership eventually recognized that "being right was beginning to hurt sales." (p. 455) They switched to paper, entered a partnership with the Environmental Defense Fund, and launched 42 initiatives that would ultimately reduce as much as 80% of the waste they generated. "Virtually overnight," says Love, "McDonald's turned from one of the environmental bad guys to a nationally recognized green company." (p. 456)

A similar situation developed when a single citizen bought full-page ads in the 20 largest newspapers in the country with the headline: "The Poisoning of America: McDonald's – Your Hamburgers Have Too Much Fat." While the company could prove the statements inaccurate, a desire to counter this negative publicity stepped up ongoing efforts to improve and communicate the nutritional value of their menu.

While they won these two public battles, they eventually realized that they'd been distracted from the "front burner" issue for the majority of their customers. "If we had paid more attention to our research," said board member Bob Thurston, "we would have realized that our number one problem was value." (p. 457) The company had never had a national discounting strategy, preferring to leave pricing to individual franchises. But that had to change.

The first experiment, a national "Happy Meal" offer priced at $1.99, produced a 40% to 50% increase in transactions. This led to a full-fledged value strategy that included low-priced menu leaders and "Extra Value" combinations. Most importantly, for the first time McDonald's took the step of launching a national price advertising campaign to <u>communicate</u> the value to customers. While franchise owners could choose to opt out of the program, few did.

Love sums up the lesson in this way (I've highlighted an excerpt that I find particularly telling):

> *Value has become a key plank in McDonald's efforts to satisfy its customers...But the company also recognized that there is much more to value than simply price...**McDonald's believes that the total experience of what customers receive for what they pay is the true value equation.** And the one area where the company is confident it can differentiate itself from its competitors is through customer satisfaction – outstanding service enhancing the total McDonald's experience.* (pp. 458-9)

To do this, the company had to take a fresh look at work processes that had served them well for years. Since their quick-service concept was based on standardized operations, opening the door to special customer requests initially meant longer waiting times and less efficiency in the kitchen. The answer was to institute entirely new methods of preparing food, based on new technology that makes it possible to serve food hotter and faster while accommodating special orders. This is process reengineering for the right reason: to deliver better value to customers.

I've pulled four key points out from the remainder of the epilogue that tell me the focus on customer value has really taken hold:

- "The results showed impressive gains in service, particularly in the drive-thru, where the number of customers asked to 'pull ahead' and wait for their order declined significantly." (p. 460) (A good example of instituting internal measures that are predictive of customer satisfaction.)
- "There's been a significant change of emphasis from when McDonald's graded itself on how well it was doing, to asking the public how it was doing and making changes to deal with that." (p. 460) (The customer is the ultimate judge of quality!)
- "We have a vision of how to differentiate the customer experience at McDonald's, and we have the techniques to get us there." (p. 460) (Focusing on the Waterfall of customer interactions with the company.)
- "We're on a continuous improvement track and we will continue to pass those savings alone to our customers." (p. 461) (Creating shareholder value by delivering greater customer value.)

By 1994, CEO Quinlan was able to announce a turnaround from decline to growth. According to Love, "Quinlan sees the future in terms of executing the company's value and customer care strategies so well that the system opens a gap between itself and the competition that is impossible to overtake." (p. 470) A final quote from Quinlan:

> *If we can stand apart as the class act of the industry in satisfying our customers, we'll reach all our financial goals automatically.*
> (p. 471)

I've abbreviated the story considerably in this account, but I hope I've conveyed what struck me as important. As competition got tougher, McDonalds intensified their focus on customers, drew on the best of the full arsenal of business management techniques available to them (from transaction surveys to value analysis to internal performance metrics to TQM-style process re-engineering) and applied them in an integrated way to deliver better customer value and business results.

The Future of Customer Value Management

chapter sixteen

When I began this journey more than 20 years ago, I thought it was all about getting a better handle on customer satisfaction. Like most of my colleagues at the time, I was thinking about satisfaction in a way that I now understand to be quite narrow. We delivered something to the customer, then measured how happy customers were with what we delivered.

Over time, my perspective expanded. Yes, it's important to measure customer satisfaction, but satisfaction with what? Not just with our products or services, but satisfaction with the overall value we provide – with products and services and business relationships or brand images in the context of the price paid. Do our customers think what we delivered was worth what they paid for it? And more importantly, how do they rate our offering as being worth what paid for relative to our competitors' offerings?

As I worked further with the tools of customer value management, I realized that it isn't just about <u>delivering</u> value to customers, it's also about <u>choosing</u> the value to deliver. Customer value management is about learning what really drives value perceptions in your target market and making strategic decisions on what you will offer that market. And then, because customers' perceptions are customers' reality, it's about using this in-depth understanding to <u>communicate</u> the value to your target market.

I have no expectation that my learning will end here. I already see colleagues and business partners applying customer value management techniques in ways that continue to shape and expand our collective thinking about new possibilities. In this last chapter of the book, I want to highlight two innovative customer value management applications as examples of these new directions. The first is the work of two Americans who are exploring how companies can apply customer value management techniques for choosing value to major business decisions such as mergers, acquisitions, start-ups and spin-offs. The second innovator is an Australian who has adapted the principles of customer value management to other key stakeholder groups: shareholders, employees, suppliers/partners and communities.

Choosing the Value

Thus far, when we've talked about choosing the value we've tended to look at aspects like product features and service approaches. But the concepts and tools of customer value management are just as applicable to large-scale strategic activities such as mergers, acquisitions and spin-offs. Two people who are leading thinking and application in this area are Peter Donovan and Timothy Samler, founders of a Dallas-based company called eCustomerValue and co-authors of *Delighting Customers: How to Win and Retain Loyal Customers*.[1]

I first met Peter and Timothy at Nortel Networks, where they were leading the charge to implement customer value management within the Enterprise Solutions division. Enterprise Solutions' customer value team was recognized by the American Productivity and Quality Center with Best-Practice awards in 1999 and 2000.

Their current practice is focused on companies looking for dramatic and fast growth and a market leadership position. These may be small start-ups trying to meet big expectations from venture capitalists. They may be companies looking to leapfrog the competition by merging with or acquiring other companies. Or they may be large Fortune 1000 companies planning fundamental structural changes (merging internal divisions, launching a new division, exiting or spinning off a business) in a bid to boost productivity and catch the next wave of opportunity.

What these companies have in common is that they're all betting a lot of money on significant changes to their value proposition. Customer value management offers tools and techniques to help them choose the right changes to make and predict how customers will respond. Peter explains:

> *The companies we work with aren't just interested in incremental growth. If you've read Collins' book on market leaders, you know that market leaders on average grow revenues at twice the rate of their nearest competitor. Their share price also grows at twice the rate. When people join together to create a start-up – or companies decide to merge with or acquire another company – they're doing so in the belief that in their case one plus one equals a great deal more than two. Venture capital money is*

---

[1] London, Chapman & Hall, 1994 rpt. 1997.

expensive. So are acquisitions. People making this kind of investment want to hone in and get twice as good as the nearest competitor. They know they're leaving the highway and entering the race track.

We didn't go out looking for new areas to apply customer value management principles and tools. We were actively engaged in solving real-life business issues for these companies and we recognized that customer value management could really help them achieve their goals.

It's well known that about two out of every three mergers fail to live up to the expectations of shareholders, management and customers. The latter register their disappointment by voting with their feet. About 60% of customer relationship management projects also fail. I believe an important success factor for the initiatives that <u>do</u> achieve their goals is that they've got all the key players aligned around a really compelling value proposition – compelling to customers, that is.

That's hard to do when all you've got is historical financial data that tells you how much customers have spent with you in the past. But if you know what drives value for your target market, it's much easier to put together a forward-looking value proposition that leverages the strengths of the people or companies involved to create order-of-magnitude growth. If you've got a solid base of customer value data correlated to financials, you can also more accurately predict the impact on revenues and market share.

- Peter Donovan, Co-founder, eCustomerValue

When I first started talking with Peter and Timothy about their work, I was reminded of AT&T's purchase of NCR, which we had all agreed at the time was going to be a wonderful acquisition. After the purchase was made, our chairman Bob Allen asked me to work with the new unit – which had been renamed Global Information Solutions – to start capturing and managing customer value data. We were surprised to find that of the five major business units they had, only two had good CVA scores – well above parity – one was at parity and the other two were below parity. We tried hard to bring these disappointing CVA scores up to parity and never really did succeed.

In the midst of this struggle, I remember the leader who had masterminded the deal saying, "If only we had had this data before we bought them, we might have walked away from the deal." That made us all think about why we were finding out after the fact that two key divisions were perceived by customers to offer worse value than the competition. We looked at all the financial data we could get access to during the due diligence investigations. Why weren't we working harder to get customer value data?

Timothy describes what he sees as the importance of customer value data in each of the three major phases of merger and acquisition (M&A) activity:

> *In the first phase, the corporate development people are sniffing around to determine which companies it will be worth spending some serious time on. They might be looking at upwards of 100 companies a year if they work for a large company with a lot of M&A activity. During this qualification phase, any customer value data they can get their hands on will help them make intelligent comparisons among the various companies they're considering buying or merging with.*
>
> *In the second phase, they're serious about doing the merger or acquisition and going through the formal due diligence process. They should expect that any customer data already collected by the company will be made available to them, just as they expect to see key financial data. If the data isn't available, there are options to consider. If time and money permit, they could ask to collaborate on a formal survey. If time and money are tight, there's the option of what Ray calls "desktop research." This involves bringing together subject matter experts from within the company to brainstorm the drivers of value for their customer base and predict how their customers will rate them relative to the competition. This group can then create a straw model of a new value proposition that leverages the strengths of both companies and positions the new entity for significant growth.*
>
> *Customer value management also has a role to play in the third phase, when the deal is done and the focus is on integrating the two companies. Now you can start to get more rigorous and sophisticated in using the tools to get the value proposition right. The challenge here is to take two groups of people from two different organizational cultures and get them aligned around a common purpose. What better way to get people excited and*

motivated than to rally them around a compelling value proposition based on a solid understanding of what it will take to win in their target market? Our research and experience tell us that employees get inherent personal satisfaction from knowing they're delivering value to customers, in addition to the more tangible benefits of working for a highly successful company.

- Timothy Samler, Co-founder, eCustomerValue

In his comments about applying customer value management to the integration of the two companies, Timothy is reinforcing Peter's point about the high expectations people have of mergers and acquisitions. It's usually not just a matter of adding revenue stream A to revenue stream B. The purpose of bringing together two companies is normally to use the complementary strengths of both companies to create compelling new value propositions that would have been impossible for either one of the companies to deliver on its own. Picking the right value proposition is a critical success factor. The tools and techniques of customer value management can help ensure that companies get this right.

We've focused so far on what happens when companies set out to acquire or merge with another company, with the intention of integrating the two companies and creating a new value proposition. But the principles of customer value management apply equally to other types of major strategic decisions:

- Merger of two divisions within a company
- Start-up of a new product line or division within a company
- Exiting a product line or division
- Spin-off of a division
- Acquisition of a company, with a view to letting it continue as a separate arm's-length entity
- Start-up of a new enterprise
- Exiting a business.

In all cases, your chances of achieving your business goals improve if you have a clear understanding of how the move impacts your value proposition. Your customer value data can give you useful indicators, for example, of when spinning off a business will allow both entities to succeed and deliver better value. Another AT&T story illustrates the point: When the company was in both the service provider and equipment manufacturing/sales businesses, we ran into a problem. The network systems division (which was eventually spun off as Lucent) was selling equipment to the Regional Bell Operating Companies

(RBOCs). At the same time, the division that provided long distance services was competing with the RBOCs.

Early on, we were getting high relative value scores from the RBOCs, but then they started to drop. When we investigated the root cause, we found that it wasn't because of product quality, price or any of the basic services. The problem was rooted in the business relationship. "How can I buy from you," they were asking us, "when you're also my competitor?" This wasn't the only reason the senior team decided to spin off Lucent, but the dropping CVA score was a strong signal that something in the company's structure needed fixing.

Predicting Success

In our work we focus on the predictive capabilities of customer value management, and on those "touchstone" customers – the really profitable ones – whom you want to keep and find more of. If you're a start-up, you don't have a lot of time to develop business. You need to hit the ground running. We find that if you use customer value management techniques with a few lead customers, they'll help you paint the picture of how to win in that market.

- Timothy Samler

Consistently poor customer value ratings may also be telling you that you simply can't win in a particular market, and it's time to get out. NCR was spun off from AT&T at the same time as Lucent, but in that case Bob Allen also made the decision to shut down those two business units where we never had managed to get CVA scores up to parity.

For start-ups looking to be acquired by a larger company, knowing what the market values and how customers rate the value the company provides can ensure you get the best price for your business.

Meeting the Productivity Challenge

I was interested to learn that in the five years from 1995 to 2000, productivity in the US improved twice as much as it had in the previous ten years. And while technology certainly played a role in this increase, the more important role was played by the application of nontechnical innovations.

I see customer value management as one of these innovations that will help us get to the next level of productivity. And I'm particularly interested in helping start-ups apply the principles, because most new jobs in America are being created by companies with fewer than 100 people. The start-ups are funded by venture capitalists (VCs) and these VCs are always looking to catch the next cycle with a new product that completely outstrips the previous one. Customer value management helps them pick the right product – the one that will win with the target customers.

- Peter Donovan

Stakeholder Value Management

In Chapter One, I introduced the idea that companies have to win in three markets in order to succeed. They must attract and retain high value customers, shareholders and people to work in the company. Another interesting stream of work is focused on applying customer value management techniques to these and other stakeholders.

The importance of attracting top talent has been getting a lot of attention in recent years, as competition for highly-skilled knowledge workers has heated up in many parts of the world. Companies are putting a greater focus on creating a work environment in which employees will be motivated and productive.

I talked earlier about the work of my colleague Davis Steward, who has been introducing clients of his Customer Opinion Research firm to the concept of "People Value Added" or PVA. Dave produces Slippery Slopes that show the correlation between the extent to which employees feel they are treated as a valued employee and whether they feel they are performing to their best potential.

David Shieff, whom you met in the Roche Diagnostics case study, has also been applying the concepts and tools of customer value management to the value exchange between a company and its employees. The statement he uses to test overall value is, "I feel I have a worthwhile job." From there, he builds Attribute Trees that reflect how much importance employees place on the various aspects of what they give (the work they do for the company) and what they get (in terms of compensation and other rewards).

Which Levers Have More Impact?

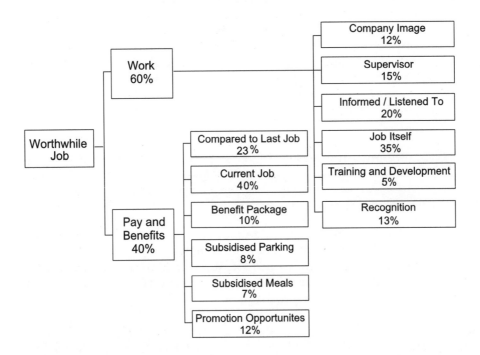

To get the equivalent of a relative-to-competition score, he asks employees to rate the last company they worked at as well as the company they're now with. With that information, he can create relative PVA scores and Competitive Profiles that allow the company's leaders to decide where to invest in creating value for employees, so that employees in turn will be motivated and able to create value for customers.

I focus on helping companies see that they need to win in three key markets – customers, shareholders, and employees – because we've been able to statistically demonstrate that these are linked and I think this is the right place to start. But as we think about how customer value management might evolve in the future, I'd like to highlight some work recently launched by my colleague Dr. Nick Fisher, founder of ValueMetrics Australia. I introduced Nick in Chapter Ten as an expert statistician and a former Chief Research Scientist in the Mathematical and Statistics Division of CSIRO. You've heard his voice throughout the book, commenting on some of the technical aspects of customer value management.

With ValueMetrics, Nick has adapted the concepts and tools of customer value management to explore how value gets created for four other stakeholder groups in a competitive environment – shareholders, employees, strategic partners/suppliers and the community:

- **The owners or shareholders of the company:** The focus is on developing an understanding of what drives business value and shareholder satisfaction – the return they receive for the risk they take with their investment, relative to what they could get by investing elsewhere.

- **Employees and potential employees:** This is about understanding how employees view the performance of your leadership and management teams (relative to alternative employers, if you wish) insofar as it impacts how employees feel about the work they do and the rewards and remuneration they receive.

- **Strategic partners and suppliers:** This is designed to help you develop and improve relationships with partners and suppliers who are key to your long-term success. It looks at partners' perception of what they invest in the relationship and what they get in return, relative to other companies they could choose to partner with.

- **The community:** "Community" can be defined as: 1. your peer community or the community of enterprises engaged in the same sort of activity; 2. the broader local, national and international communities. In either case, what you're investigating here is public perception of what your enterprise contributes to the community for the cost of your presence, relative to other enterprises.

Nick calls his approach Stakeholder Value Management© (SVM©). As with customer value management, the point of doing this research is to provide all levels of management with information that allows them to focus improvements on the areas likely to have the biggest impact on value perception among each of these stakeholder groups. Let's hear him describe in his own words how this work came together for him:

> *In the early 90s, some challenges I was facing at CSIRO got me interested in the whole area of performance measurement. I investigated what was available in terms of structured approaches to performance measurement, and was surprised to find very little. So I set about building a framework that evolved, with the help of a*

team of colleagues, into what is now called *Performance Measurement Framework© (PMF©).* The framework has three guiding principles:

- *Alignment – making sure that whatever performance measures you bring in help align people in their work with where the company wants to go*
- *Systems and process thinking*
- *Practicability.*

I recognized early on that the framework was a piece of the answer, but was not in itself a full performance management system. It was the carriage work, if you will, of the vehicle; but to make it run I needed an engine – a proper enabling process to move the business forward – that aligned with these three principles.

Ray's customer value management work formed the basis of the engine I needed.

I'd originally thought I was looking for key performance indicators. I eventually made the seemingly small – but crucial – leap to realizing that the right place to start was with the stakeholders, the people with a vested interest in the organisation. I needed to ask, "What does it mean to be successful with all of these stakeholder groups?" And the answer was, "You've got to be creating greater value for them than they can get elsewhere. They're all making an investment of some sort in your organisation, and they all have alternatives."

The next question I looked at was how to quantify this – how to measure success. And that's when I met Ray, and learned about his work, which provided precisely the answer I needed for quantifying "relative value added for customers."

Starting from there, you can determine what sort of lead indicators you might need to predict how successful you are going to be, and what type of information the leaders need to tell them they're headed in the right direction. The success measures are strategic measures that are difficult to manage because they take into account what customers think about your competitors as well as what customers think about you. The key performance indicators are tactical internal measures that you can influence and that in turn influence customer perception.

> *The great beauty of mastering customer value management is that once you've done that you can apply essentially the same approach to the other key stakeholder groups. You've got the skills and capability within your organisation to do so, and there's practically no additional learning required. It's just a matter of understanding how to create an appropriate Value Attribute Tree for the different stakeholder groups and then the whole machinery kicks into gear. You know how to administer the survey, how to analyse the data, how to interpret the data, how to act on the data. You can adapt tools such as the Slippery Slope. You know how to look at the value contributed by competitive alternatives.*
>
> *The ultimate goal, of course is to evolve beyond seeing the creation of value for each of the five stakeholder groups as five separate processes running in parallel, and to explore how they relate to one another. You want to know how customer value, employee value, strategic partner value and community value work together to drive business value – value to owners or shareholders. And then in turn to see how greater business value contributes to creating a better workplace for people, better value to customers, more prosperity for suppliers and the community – and so on. I see it as an ongoing upward spiral.*
>
> - Dr. Nick Fisher

I think these possibilities are exciting. In Chapter One we highlighted early work done at Nortel Networks to demonstrate that once you have a rich database of employee and customer data, you're able to perform statistical analysis that shows how employee and customer value are linked to each other and to shareholder value. You're able to identify the attributes that have the greatest potential to create value through the entire chain. Nick is pointing out how much more powerful it is if you can see the entire picture, including suppliers and the community. It's the balanced scorecard taken to the next level: a scorecard in which you understand how each measure is linked to the others and how they all work together as a system.

Nick and I have also talked about the possibilities of drawing on the customer value management work in areas where there is no price element *per se*, but there is an investment and a return. You could apply the same principles to the public health system, for example, or to not-for-profits. You could use the principles to analyze the value delivered by internal staff groups that provide service to other parts of the organization.

Turning the Tables

Nick's work in supplier value add looks at the value exchange from the perspective of the supplier. There's another way to look at the relationship with suppliers, and that's from <u>your</u> perspective as a customer of the supplier. I've sometimes heard people who are successfully applying customer value management to their own business say, "I wish my suppliers would do this, so that we could tell them what's important to us and what we feel about the value we're receiving from them."

Well, why wait for them to get the revelation that they should be doing this? In the Multibrás case study that ends the book, you'll read how this division of Whirlpool Corporation in Brazil actually took the initiative to do customer value research on themselves as customers of their suppliers. Why not get your team together to brainstorm in desktop-research style the Attribute Tree that best reflects the attributes that drive value for you as a customer for each type of supplier you deal with, and rate your suppliers' performance on these attributes? You can then take the initiative to sit down with them and say, "Here's what's important; here's how you're doing."

If you have supply contracts with several competitors in the same area, you can also tell them how they're doing against the competition. You could even show them where they sit relative to their competitors on a Value Map – with only their position actually labeled with a company name. Think how powerful it would be if you deal with four competitors and you let it be known that over time you plan to move most of your business to the two suppliers that rate highest on your value attributes. Now your suppliers know exactly what it will take to win and keep your business.

I see so many possibilities, and it's exciting for me to watch colleagues and friends around the world trying out innovative applications of customer value management. I hope that this book encourages others to start experimenting with the tools and concepts, and prompts customer value management practitioners whose voices have not been heard here to share their stories and learnings.

Multibrás S.A. Eletrodomésticos (Brazil)

case study

PIONEERING CUSTOMER VALUE MANAGEMENT IN BRAZIL:
A Multibrás Story

I've placed this story at the end of the book for two reasons. First, I think it provides a good summary of customer value management tools and techniques being applied to solve practical problems and deliver business results. Second, it looks at how Multibrás is breaking new ground and applying the concepts in interesting new ways. And so it fits in well with our consideration of where the work might go in the future.

In 1995 I had the privilege of meeting Luis Fernando Reyes at a conference in New York City. At the time, Luis Fernando was a visionary senior vice president at Multibrás, then a partially owned (now fully owned) division of Whirlpool Corporation. (He's now head of global product development in the cooking category, based in Italy.) He approached me after one of my presentations in New York, because he saw in the concepts and tools of customer value management a possible answer to a business problem that was worrying him.

For many decades, Multibrás had been leading the Latin American market, developing, manufacturing, marketing and selling home appliances under the Brastemp, Consul and Whirlpool brands. But in recent years, there'd been a trend in Latin America toward lower international trade barriers and increased competition. Multibrás was experiencing something quite new: declining market share in some important segments. Luis Fernando describes the situation.

The environment in Brazil was changing because local competition was becoming global competition. Local brands were being purchased by companies such as Bosch and Electrolux – GE came in a little later on. So we were now on a global playing field. Our Brastemp brand had a big market share, so we were an obvious target for the competition. We knew we had to defend our share or come out the loser.

I went to that conference in New York because I wanted to see what was going on in the world of marketing. At Multibrás, we'd done a lot of talking about how we could create better brand loyalty and more consumer loyalty, but we hadn't yet found the right model. When Ray introduced me to the concepts of Customer Value Add, I immediately saw an opportunity to build our strategies around it. I realized that the critical piece we were missing was that we weren't comparing ourselves to the competition. We certainly believed we were adding value to consumers – and consumers were telling us that they were satisfied – but we had no idea what consumers thought of the value of our offerings compared to that of many other competitors in the marketplace.

- Luis Fernando Reyes, Senior Vice President, Multibrás

This story relates how Multibrás applied the concepts and tools of customer value management to turn around declining market share. More importantly, it tells how the concepts of customer value management took hold and turned around the company's thinking about managing customer needs. It's also the story of how an innovation in the Latin American division of a US-based global company got the attention of headquarters and started to influence business practices throughout the company.

Three factors are particularly important in this success story:

- **Sponsorship of the leadership team:** The work was strongly and actively endorsed by the president and the entire leadership team.
- **Focus on priorities:** Resources were initially focused on one key market segment – the washing machine market. The success of this first initiative demonstrated the value of investing in customer value management.
- **Customer communication:** Multibrás understood that the investment in choosing the value and delivering the value would not pay off unless they could communicate the value to customers.

Sponsorship of the Leadership Team

The first meeting I had with Multibrás in Sao Paulo was with the president, all the general managers, and their direct reports. Luis Fernando knew that the best way to introduce these concepts into the company was to put the opportunity in front of the leadership team and let them make the decision whether or not to proceed. One attendee at that meeting, general manager Ronaldo Pinto Flor, would later become the executive in charge of our first project and an active implementer of customer value management in Multibrás. You'll hear Ronaldo's reflections on the experience throughout this case.

I described the opportunity. We gave people time to think and talk about it. By the end of the day we had the green light to go ahead. What impressed me was that the leadership team truly took ownership of what they christened the Consumer Value Add or CVA program. From the outset they were actively involved in making it work. Luis Fernando explains why:

> *So often things turn out to be a matter of timing: the right idea surfacing at the appropriate time. At Multibrás we were looking for answers that would help us build better brand loyalty in the marketplace. CVA really opened our eyes. All the leadership recognized that it was an important and appropriate methodology that would help us direct our efforts and create a winning proposition. We could clearly see the links to market share, to customer loyalty, to customer willingness to recommend, to going from good to better to best. Many of the things we were doing at the time were not so obviously connected to market share.*
>
> - Luis Fernando Reyes

As soon as we had the first set of customer value numbers, we brought the leadership team together again to ensure that they understood what the results really meant. It was a dynamic and participatory workshop. We started by having leaders estimate what they thought the impact weights and value ratings would be.

In many cases they were right on, but in some cases their answers were significantly different from customers' actual answers. The exercise highlighted differences of opinion across the team as to where Multibrás was strong and where it needed to improve. By the end of the day, the team was aligned around the need to get a better understanding of what consumers valued and how they perceived Multibrás.

This was the start of a process of cascading the learning throughout the organization. After the president and leadership team were confident that they understood how to interpret and use the data, they personally participated in learning events for their team and their team's teams. Luis Fernando himself would fly to far-flung company locations to kick off workshops and explain to employees why this work was being undertaken. Ronaldo reflects on the impact:

> *We didn't run into any emotional barriers with our people. Employees embraced the concept of CVA because they could see that all the leaders sponsored the work and were pushing the organization to use and understand the tools. Everybody from the CEO down was trained on what CVA was, how important it was, and how it would help us understand how consumers valued our offering. The total organization was very optimistic about the tools.*
>
> *Even the engineers – you know they're sometimes skeptical of new tools because they're afraid they're going to get boxed in and lose creative flexibility. But they soon understood the numbers and saw how this information would help them bet on the right technical solution.*
>
> *Everybody was willing to trust and use the results. It was a turnaround in the company mindset.*
>
> - Ronaldo Pinto Flor, GM in charge of the Da Vinci project

Focus on Priorities

The first application of CVA within Multibrás was in 1997 on a project code-named Da Vinci after the great inventor Leonardo, and led by Ronaldo Pinto Flor. The washing machine market was and is an important one for Multibrás. They had long held about 80% share of the Latin American market for clothes washers. But share had been shrinking and by 1995 it stood at just under 60%. There were many opinions about why this was happening and what should be done to reverse the trend. We decided to apply the CVA approach in this market and see what we could learn.

The story became clear when we looked at the numbers. The Brastemp washing machine was a high quality machine but it was also the most expensive on the market. While consumers gave it good quality ratings, the quality wasn't perceived to be significantly higher than the competition. And that fact combined with the higher price meant that overall consumers rated the machine at parity with the competition: a CVA ratio of 1.0.

The Problem with Parity

As I've pointed out before, while parity doesn't sound all that bad, it's bad news for the company with the largest market share. If there are four companies competing in a market and customers perceive all four offerings to be of equal value, over time the market leader will lose share and they'll each end up with about a quarter of the market. And that's what was happening to Multibrás. By the first half of 1998, market share was down to 44%. But in the background, the Da Vinci project was developing an entirely new machine, based on knowledge gained through the customer value data that by the end of 1998 would reverse the trend. Ronaldo explains how the data was used:

> *We've always said, "We need to understand what the consumer wants" but we didn't have a good tool to help us listen to the consumer. With CVA we did. Before, when we started to design a new product, we would look around internally and see what our best technical minds could come up with. Now we had a way to look through the window and see what we could learn from consumers.*
>
> *We could see that we weren't getting the best scores on quality and say, okay let's understand what the quality issue is. Ah, it's because the consumers don't think we're reliable. Well, why are we not reliable? Ah, because the product is noisy. So reliability issues in the consumers' minds have to do with noise. We might not have understood that on our own. We might have invested in fixing the wrong things.*
>
> - Ronaldo Pinto Flor

The mandate of the Da Vinci project was to design and build an entirely new washer that provided greater value to consumers. This wasn't about tweaking some functions; this was a completely new platform and one of the biggest investments the company had ever made.

Multibrás had long been committed to quality and used tools like the Quality Function Deployment matrix (linking a product requirement with the right technical specification) to build specifications on new products. Their technical people were indeed expert at linking the product requirement (clothes don't tangle) with the right technical specification (e.g. degree of pitch of the agitator).

Incorporating the Customer Perspective

What was different this time was that when the engineers, sales people, promoters, financial and marketing people came together to decide where to focus development efforts, they had more to go on than just the internal technical data. This time the decision matrices included the attributes that consumers said provide value, along with impact weights and competitive performance ratings (the ratio of the ratings Multibrás' customers gave Multibrás divided by ratings competitors' customers gave the competition) on each item.

Each item was broken down into sufficient detail to enable the engineers to determine the right technical specification for the new product. They knew it wasn't enough to know that customers think clothing care is important. They needed to know what customers mean by clothing care: removes stains, no clothing damage, no fading, no wrinkling, no lint left on clothing, and so on.

The data told them this, told them what impact each attribute had on the consumers' rating of the product and told them how the Brastemp was rated against the competition on each item. Armed with this information, they could decide where to focus. They knew exactly which features of the competition's machines they needed to study and match or beat with their new machine.

Communicate the Value

Another thing the Multibrás team did right was remembering that it wasn't enough to deliver greater value to customers. Having designed the best washing machine in the Brazilian market – one that incorporated all the best features of the competitors' offerings – they now had to communicate that message to customers.

The CVA data had told them where to focus in the development of the new washer. When it came time to develop the product launch and marketing materials, they went back to the data and built their advertising around what consumers had told them was important. They knew exactly which features to emphasize in the major marketing effort that supported the product launch.

Value Proposition

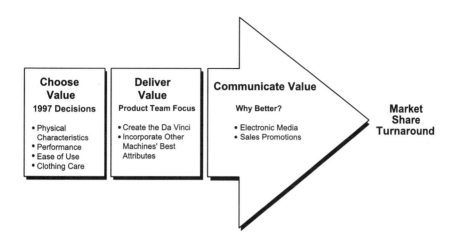

Market Share Turnaround

Da Vinci Turnaround

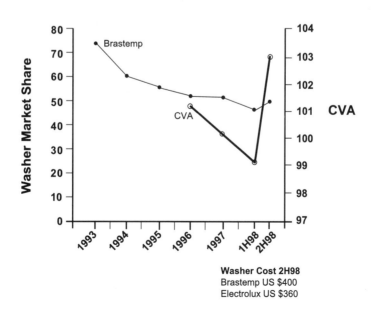

The Brastemp clothes washer developed by the Da Vinci project team was launched in the second quarter of 1998. CVA scores immediately shot up to well above parity, and the downward trend in market share quickly reversed. Even though the cost was about 10% higher than the cost of the top competitor's product (US $400 versus US $360), customers clearly perceived that the Brastemp offered better value. As important as the market share turnaround was the mindset turnaround that accompanied it:

> *According to leaders who worked on the project, this successful business turnaround story was the start of a turnaround in the company mindset. The initiative clearly demonstrated that the company's success depended on building and maintaining an in-depth understanding of what matters to customers, and of using that understanding to drive key business decisions.*
>
> *At first we thought that CVA was just a different way of looking at consumer satisfaction with Multibrás products. As soon as we started working with it, we realized how powerful the CVA tool could be. We understood that we could work with CVA to see the total solution – not only the product solution, but the whole offering and the whole process of adding value to the consumer and ultimately the company. It was a philosophical change in our thinking.*
>
> - Ronaldo Pinto Flor

The CVA measure was added to the company's balanced scorecard, and incorporated into the bonus program. Part of employees' pay is now attached to attaining target CVA scores.

Since the Da Vinci project, I've had the pleasure of helping nurture some pioneering customer value management work that is being driven by Ronaldo and others within Multibrás. They've been aided and abetted in this work by Marcelo Chanis, who became so convinced of the importance of customer value management during his time as part of the Multibrás CVA team that he is now devoting himself full time to helping other companies in Latin America make this journey. Luis Fernando talks about how they're embedding customer value management concepts:

> *The trick is to find an efficient and non-costly way of keeping data current. For a while we were collecting CVA data once a year. It could very well be that once a year is not enough, because things move fast and everybody's a target. If your data takes you something*

like three months to collect and you're still using it a year later, you might be picking the wrong things to work on. It could be that just after you finished the survey, the competition came in with a new product. So you might be correcting things that were important in the past, but aren't so important in the new market picture.

Today we really want to understand the consumer on all the "touching points": the point of sale/first purchase driver, the service driver, the first use driver, the communication driver, and so on. CVA's use is much wider than just the engineering world or the product development world. If you can get all these uses from one survey, it's both cheaper and more effective.

- Luis Fernando Reyes

Understanding Brand

One contribution that the Multibrás team has made to the field of customer value management is some in-depth work on the importance of brand image in their industry: Brand clearly isn't a "satisfaction" item – asking customers how satisfied they are with the brand doesn't make much sense. But it impacts the perceived value of a company's offering:

Brand is important. When you buy a refrigerator, you're not taking home just a refrigerator, you're taking home a brand. The brand gives an aura to the product. Because the brand means different things to different people, you have to include the brand perspective in your surveying.

Let's say you do a survey on Brastemp's service, and people give you low rankings. So you do a benchmark and you find that your service is just as good as the competition's. What's going on? Maybe what people are telling you is, "I'm well aware of the good reputation and strong image of your brand, and because of that I'm willing to pay more. But because of that, I expect more from your service than I do of your competitors' service." You see? You need to be able to read the hidden part of the equation. And that may very well be the more difficult thing.

- Luis Fernando Reyes

In the washing machine market Attribute Tree created by Multibrás and reproduced below, brand is so important that it appears twice – both as a main attribute of customer value and as a driver of quality perceptions.

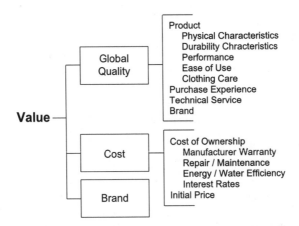

For Multibrás, brand is a key corporate asset to be carefully managed. When you're selling something like clothes washers that are designed to last for ten years or so, your opportunities for growth come from customers who've bought a Brastemp washer deciding to go with the same brand when it comes time to buy a different appliance, like a new refrigerator. Multibrás has analyzed what they call their "brand-building framework" and now use CVA to measure and manage every aspect of this framework:

- Product
- Communication
- Consumer relationship
- Purchase experience
- Services.

An Aside from Ray: "He's No Brastemp!"

What has struck me in my travels to Brazil is that Multibrás has had so much success in building brand image that "Brastemp" has entered people's vocabulary as a word associated with top quality. A friend told me he overheard a woman assessing the guy she'd just started dating by saying, "Fernando's great, but he's no Brastemp."

Understanding the Value Chain

Multibrás has found that the CVA concepts and tools can help them better understand and manage their relationship with trade partners. There are two main aspects to this relationship and they measure both.

First, because they depend on retail outlets to sell their products and on repair agents to service them, the Multibrás team has decided it's important to understand how these third parties create or destroy value for the customers during the purchase or repair experience. While Multibrás doesn't control these channels, they're well aware that a bad experience with an outlet or agent can have a negative impact on their brand name and the perceived value of their products. The customer value data they collect allows them to analyze whether some types of outlets have a more positive impact on perceived value than others.

Second, they understand that their trade partners are also customers in that they have the power to choose whether or not to carry or service Multibrás products. The tools of CVA help them measure how their trade partners perceive the value Multibrás provides as a supplier relative to the value provided by their competitors, and to better manage that relationship. Ronaldo elaborates:

> *By 1999 we'd added the concept of "Channel Value Add" to our thinking. We realized that just as CVA could help us develop products and communication, it could also help us understand and improve the relationship with our trade partners. We have multiple channels to the customer, everything from small stores to hypermarkets. We use CVA to measure all the different interactions with trade partners – negotiations, logistics, pricing, promotional approach, point-of-sales systems – and we compare our situation with that of our competitors.*

> - Ronaldo Pinto Flor

Lately, they've also started asking salespeople and repair agents how they would rate the value provided by Multibrás products relative to the competition. This brilliant move has brought them invaluable information. Who better than the salesperson who spends his or her working life helping customers choose among competing products to rate the relative value of these products? Who better than the repair agent with an intimate knowledge of product weaknesses to rate products on quality?

Understanding the Life Cycle

Another important learning from the Multibrás team is that the Attribute Tree changes significantly over the customer life cycle of a product. Because their customers typically own each appliance they buy for an average of ten years, lumping together value attributes and impact weights from everyone who has ever purchased a washing machine tells only part of the story. When they disaggregated data to get a clearer view of what consumers value, they found that the value drivers and impact weights were different at different points in the customer's experience of purchasing and owning the appliance. Some examples of points in the life cycle where value drivers change:

- When people are setting up a home for the first time, and having their first experience in choosing an appliance. In fact, if you really break down the data, you'll find that they have different value propositions before they walk in the door of the store for the first time, while they're in the process of choosing an appliance, and immediately after they've purchased the appliance.
- When customers are learning how to use the new appliance
- When owners are experiencing their first malfunction and need for repair
- After they've owned their appliance for years
- When they're thinking about purchasing a new machine to replace an old one nearing the end of its useful life.

With this level of understanding, Multibrás is well positioned to make development decisions and create market strategies that address the value propositions of their target segments:

> *You have to keep excelling. One of the key learnings for us is that good is not good enough. Customers of the Brastemp brand were saying, "We're very satisfied with your brand and we're willing to repurchase." But at the actual repurchase point, the number of people who said they were willing to repurchase didn't. What happened? Well, on a competitive basis, there was something out there in the market that was perhaps better. By not asking the relative-to-the-competition question, we missed out.*
>
> *We made the mistake of thinking we were great because our customers were satisfied with our brand. But if you don't then ask a Maytag or an Electrolux consumer how satisfied they are with these brands, you don't really know where you are.*
>
> - Luis Fernando Reyes

Exporting to Headquarters

It's a source of pride to the Multibrás team that they – who are so often on the receiving end of the latest best practice idea coming from North America or Europe – pioneered best practices in customer value management within Whirlpool. They have sustained this work over time and are contributing important understanding to the global body of knowledge on the topic.

For me there are two critical things that differentiate the Customer Value approach. It's different from other research because it's structured around what makes sense and matters for the consumer. You don't develop the survey on your own. You ask consumers what's important and how much weight they put on the different factors before you even format the survey.

The second is that all the measures are relative. It's important to know whether I'm stronger/weaker than or equal to my competition on the key drivers of value for consumers, because I live in a world where resources are scarce. I want to put the focus and the money exactly where I can change the equation in the marketplace. Why would I put my money in a given product if the market is telling me, "You're great in product development, but, you know what? Your service is terrible." Then I know I need to pick service, because somebody is beating me on service.

Once my colleagues in North America and Europe understood this, we were able to get CVA accepted as the company-wide measure of customer loyalty and brand value in our balanced scorecard.

- Luis Fernando Reyes

The Latin American successes have gradually convinced Whirlpool's North American operations of the value of this work, and word is spreading to the company's business units in Europe and Asia as well. CVA is now a key element of Whirlpool's global balanced scorecard, and the data is being used in many parts of the parent company to drive business decisions and results.

Since I attribute this success to the implementation skills of change agents like Ronaldo and to the vision of Luis Fernando as the executive champion, I'll leave the last words on the subject to them:

To summarize: We learned how to systematically measure how the consumer values our offer against the competitors. With that understanding, we could improve our internal processes on five key dimensions: products, communications, consumer relationship, purchase experience and services. We manage the business by managing these key drivers of how consumers perceive our brand and our offering.

- Ronaldo Pinto Flor

Change is the most difficult thing to make happen. Sometimes people resist without even knowing they're doing so. Many times, the problem is you've been successful in the past with the things you did. So people say, "You know, why should I change?"

But this is a fast-changing world. Competition is much more aggressive than it has been in the past. Consumers are more informed than they were in the past and they're more demanding. If we're not able to adjust to the pace and drop some of the things we did in the past, we won't get anywhere. There are orthodoxies that we just need to drop. They were good in the past. They're not good anymore.

- Luis Fernando Reyes

Customer Value
Management Essentials
conclusion

We've covered a lot of ground in these pages. I've shared my passion for valuing the customer and laid out my *Ten Steps to Mastery*. To demonstrate how these concepts and tools actually work, I've featured real-life success stories from small and large businesses in Australia, Brazil, Latin America, New Zealand and North America that have implemented customer value management, including a:

- small family hardware business
- white goods manufacturer
- maker of medical equipment
- global telecommunications company
- financial services institution
- public utility.

We've heard from CEOs, managers, change agents, and other champions of customer value management, as well as professional researchers and statisticians.

My goals have been to provide tools for implementing a customer value management initiative and to share the experience of clients and associates who have used them successfully. Throughout the book, my colleagues and I have suggested ways of turning this knowledge into practical action that will deliver results for your business.

While the principles of customer value are not new, there definitely is an art and science to applying them successfully. I hope the tools presented in the book and the accounts of people who are putting the principles into action have sparked insights and ideas for your own use.

To help you apply these principles, let me quickly summarize the essentials of mastering customer value management.

No matter what business you're in and no matter where in the world you operate, your challenge as a business is to win in three markets: financial, employment and customer.

You need to win in the <u>financial market</u>, attracting and retaining the investment required to keep your business alive and growing. And in the <u>employment market</u>, attracting and retaining the talented people on whom your ability to deliver value depends. But first and foremost you need to win in the <u>customer market</u>. If you're not doing that, over time you'll lose your ability to attract investors and employees – and ultimately everyone will lose.

To win in the customer market, you must first understand what customers truly value. Then you need to:

- **Choose your value:** Decide what value proposition you are best able to take to market
- **Deliver value:** Make sure your business processes are aligned with your value proposition and working together to deliver it effectively
- **Communicate value:** Educate the market on your value proposition.

The real key to success is doing all these better than the competition, because if customers perceive someone else to be offering better value, they'll vote with their dollars and take their business elsewhere.

One of the reasons why businesses find it difficult to master customer value management is that their focus is on the financial market. If you ask people, "What is the purpose of a business?" the answer you get most often is, "To create value for shareholders" or, "To make a profit."

I see profit and shareholder value as the reward rather than the purpose. To my mind, the purpose of a business is to create value for customers by providing products and services that improve the quality of life.

Businesses are not just legal entities with shareholders. They are functioning organizations in which people work together to accomplish what no one of them can achieve alone. After all, if it only took one person to satisfy customers, then most businesses would consist of an individual working solo without any partners or suppliers.

One of the most critical – and difficult – success factors for a business is to focus the company on the right priorities. There is only so much time, money and energy to go around.   If all the intelligence, skills and resources at a company's disposal are channeled toward accomplishing a few priority goals, they're highly likely to achieve these goals.

This is why collecting and understanding customer value data is so important. If people in your business really understand what customers value, agree on what needs to be accomplished, and are aligned around the single purpose of delivering better value than the competition, chances are high that your business will prosper. As they succeed they will attract the best people – people drawn by the opportunity to be part of a cohesive, high-performing team and to share in the rewards. Customers, employees and shareholders all win.

In my experience, this kind of alignment is powerful, but it is also rare. Most people accept that customer-facing processes such as sales, billing or technical support are key to the creation – or destruction – of customer satisfaction and loyalty.   But even here it's easy to let internal company concerns take the spotlight ("get the money," "keep the call short") instead of customer concerns (accuracy of the bill, resolution of problems in a single phone call).

As you get farther away from the customer, the idea that creating value for customers is everyone's responsibility gets more and more blurred. I created the image of the Kordupleski Cube to underscore how critical it is that all parts of the business are aligned.   People in back-office processes such as production, supply chain management and product management must understand clearly how they create value for customers. The same is true for people in support processes such as human resources, finance and legal.

The good news is that if everyone understands his or her individual contributions and the entire team shares an understanding of what they're trying to accomplish together, that's really powerful.   The tools of customer value management described in this book can help determine the right priorities for your business and build this understanding within your company:

- Building an **Attribute Tree** gives you a place to start in creating your value proposition – an accurate picture of what customers value about what you provide (products, services, relationship or image) and how they feel about what they pay (initial price, ongoing cost of ownership).

- Plotting your competitive position on a **Value Map** helps you focus strategic discussions on how to move into the better value zone and stake out the competitive high ground.

- Developing **Competitive Profiles** tells you how customers in your market perceive what you deliver on various attributes relative to the competition, and helps you decide where to focus investment in improvements for maximum return in customer loyalty and market share.

- Creating a **Waterfall of Needs** helps you connect this understanding to specific business processes that can be managed and improved.

- The **Slippery Slope** tells you what improvement in process performance is needed to gain the customer loyalty that will deliver the business results you want.

- Calculating your **Customer Value Added (CVA)** score – the ratio of the perceived value ("worth what paid for") of your offering in the eyes of your customers, divided by the perceived value of the competition's offering in the market – gives you a single overall metric to track progress against the competition.

These tools can be as simple or sophisticated as you need them to be. The minimum requirement is an opportunity for people within your business who know most about your market to pool their knowledge through a structured conversation. They can then use the tools to organize this knowledge into actionable data. At the other end of the spectrum, it's possible to do rigorous statistical analysis to get an in-depth understanding of how sub-attributes impact other attributes and overall customer perceptions of value, and make better decisions on where and how much to invest in process improvement.

These tools on their own cannot create competitive advantage. They're proven and successful methods to make sure you're collecting the right data, communicating what you've learned effectively, and applying this learning appropriately to business decision making. But they will have impact only if they're applied within a supportive organization.

What are the characteristics of a supportive organization?

- Leaders at all levels communicate through their words and actions that the **purpose of the business is to create value for customers**, and that the reward for doing so is shareholder value.

- They use the tools of customer value management to ensure that everyone in the business is **focused on the right action**. They set **specific and measurable targets**, and they tie rewards to these targets.

- All their "**people systems**" – selection, training, promotion, compensation, communication and engagement – **reflect the principles of customer value**.

- The local heroes are people who have devoted exceptional effort to understanding customer needs and filling them better than the competition. **Employees proudly tell stories about how their work improves the quality of life for customers.**

Whether you're a CEO or a small business owner striving to improve business performance, a market researcher or a statistician looking for ways to get actionable customer data used within your company, a change agent or line manager looking for practical methods for applying customer value management, I hope this book has given you answers, insight and new energy to forge ahead.

I also hope it's reinforced your personal convictions, taught you some tricks and techniques, and made you feel part of a worldwide community committed to mastering the art and science of customer value management.

In summary, you can do it! You can break new ground, increase value to your customers and your company, become wiser than your competition and be much better positioned for the future.

Good luck and best wishes for your success on your own journey. If I can be of assistance or answer any questions you may have, don't hesitate to contact me.

Ray Kordupleski
Customer Value Management, Inc.
Phone: 973-366-5206
E-mail: ray@cvminc.com

index